Me and The Monkey
Chronicles of the MonkeyGod Vol.1 by Andy Darby

This book is dedicated to The Monkey that lives in all of us, you know the one. No matter how bad an idea seems. No matter how much you know it's going to hurt... Here's to the little bastard inside who keeps shouting 'What could go wrong?'

You know you're far too serious, don't you? You are looking at me as if I knew the explosion would be that big. All judgmental and shit. It's not like it's something that won't grow back. Anyway, the ladies love a scar...

The Monkey

So it begins...

19 November

Okay, I'm writing this blog in an attempt to keep track of what is happening with my friend/companion, The Monkey. He has recently gone from being a totally id driven maniac to a more thoughtful maniac. I think there are changes happening to him and I can't think of a better way of cataloguing them. I will try to write daily updates (if anything interesting happens) and hopefully it will give me a better understanding, or at least something to take the piss out of him with.

At the moment The Monkey is sitting on the back of the sofa wearing a mask made of ham – he looks strangely like Justin Bieber...

20 November

Went in to wake up The Monkey this morning and found his teddy bear tied to the bed with black electrical tape and looking very much the worse for wear. The Monkey was still fast asleep with a very satisfied smile on his face. I knew it was a bad idea to let him download *50 Shades of Grey* onto his iPad. Cultural references he said... Just wanted to see what all of the fuss was about he said... My arse!

Me and The Monkey went to see *Skyfall*, the local cinema is running a load of Bond films over the next week. Nearly kicked off when the girl offered him Chunky Monkey ice cream – he doesn't like stereotypes (when it suits him...). Rescued it with Phish Food and a large box of butter popcorn but he kept giving the girl evils all the way to the screen...

22 November

The Monkey seems to be blaming me for the rain. I have tried explaining that I have no control over the weather, but he just wants me to, 'Switch it off.' Have to find something to amuse him. Is it too early for drink?...

To keep him happy I introduced The Monkey to the Xbox and Kinect. Great fun watching him playing *Rabbids Alive & Kicking*. Best bit was when he could see the Rabbid in the room with him on the TV then went mental trying to actually find it in the room. I nearly pissed myself! Although it did get less funny when he ran out and came back in with a hammer... Even though the Xbox is off now he keeps looking around the room suspiciously, and will lash out if I make a sudden movement.

I hope it stops raining soon...

23 November

There seems to be bad blood between The Monkey and next door's dog. I asked The Monkey what the problem was and he muttered something about being double crossed on a coke deal, and then told me to, 'Mind my own business, bitch.' Well at least he's not flinging shit about...

24 November

The Monkey has been on my eBay account and bid for a JCB. I really hope the bid doesn't win...

I'm sure The Monkey has been watching *Geordie Shore*... I heard drunken shouts of whey-aye coming from the living room but when I opened the door, he was watching *Family Guy*. Although he did have a guilty look on his face and the remote control was covered in monkey spit...

25 November

So, got to the bottom of the *Geordie Shore* thing. Apparently, The Monkey thought someone had shaved a bunch of Bonobo chimps and made a documentary about them. He couldn't watch it with me in the room because it embarrassed him so much (I think this may be a first for him). Since discovering that they are human he says he has gained new levels of contempt for our species...

Fook off Ryan

26 November

The Monkey has spent a lot of time on the internet this morning and he has concluded that we need a sacrifice to stop the rain. Worryingly, after seeing a picture of an Aztec temple, I don't think he is talking about giving up peanut M&Ms...

*

Found the beheaded corpse of The Monkey's teddy bear in the spare room. It was surrounded by a badly drawn chalk pentagram and arcane symbols – most of which looked like cocks – and on the wall was written *FOOK OFF RYAN* in Magic Marker (I'm pretty sure it's supposed to say FUCK OFF RAIN). That's going to need several coats of paint to cover...

*

The Monkey is having Nam flashbacks. I think it was those shrooms he ate, although he has always banged on about having fought in the jungles of Southeast Asia. He has daubed his face with Marmite *camo* and is clenching a butter knife between his teeth as he hides in the hedge... at least I think it's Marmite...

It wasn't Marmite...

27 November

The Monkey is well pissed off. It's still raining despite the *sacrifice* and he has been banging about the house with his own personal storm cloud over his tiny head. He is back on the internet now and some of the occult sites he is viewing are a little disturbing. I do hope this doesn't lead to an escalation...

*

Had to go out for a bit leaving The Monkey to his research, he had rounded up all the occult books from my bookcase and was partially buried in them. It stopped raining while I was out and, on the way back there were even patches of blue sky in the distance. When I got home I checked for booby traps and found The Monkey sitting waiting for me with a big smirk plastered across his face. He pointed out that the rain had stopped and therefore he was obviously awesome and all powerful. I pointed out that it was still grey and that there were still minor showers. He dismissed that and, rightly, said that it was no longer coming down like a biblical flood, and so this time he had won. That made me nervous – this time meant he had done something else.

My immediate concern was for the cat, so I ran upstairs but she is fast asleep under the bath. Then with growing trepidation I approached the spare room... Inside is a similar scene to yesterday except his teddy bear is lying spread eagled in the centre of a pentagram and has a pork chop gaffa taped to its chest out of which is sticking one of the kitchen knives. The wall now reads *I MEEN IT – FOOK OFF RYAN*.

I went back downstairs, pretty relieved to be honest, to find him sitting on the back of the sofa wearing the teddy bear's head like some trophy. Smug bastard. He's going to be unbearable for the rest of the day...

28 November

Well, the sky is blue again and The Monkey is very pleased with himself. He is currently sitting on the fence and tormenting next door's dog who is locked in the house – I can hear the barking from here. I sewed the teddy bear's head back on (at The Monkeys request) after stuffing it with old socks. And despite it smelling of pork chops I think he had his way with it again last night.

I spent the morning cleaning up the spare room and painting the wall. There is a black spot, about the size of a 50p, in the middle of where the pentagram was on the floor. I asked The Monkey about it and he was evasive telling me that it was a small rift in the space time continuum and that I should vacuum around it. I think he has burnt the carpet, although the spot is very very black...

29 November

Ordered The Monkey a little *Kill 'em all and let God sort 'em out!* T-shirt – the postman has just delivered it. He looks extremely cute. At the moment he is showing next door's dog – by showing I mean he is pointing to the T-shirt then to the dog and drawing his finger across his throat. He also seems to have got some mirrored aviator sunglasses from somewhere...

*

A large, aggressive looking youth stole The Monkey's pasty as we sat on the harbour wall. He had underestimated simian speed though. The Monkey grabbed him by the hoodie and as the youth frantically tried to hold onto the pasty and run off, The Monkey smashed his head repeatedly against a bin. He then sat on the unconscious would-be thief and finished the pasty while giving the youth's mates a murderous stare. I went to get a drink and was away for about fifteen minutes because there was a queue, and when I came back there were several crying children and distraught parents. The youth had gone, and The Monkey was lounging on the harbour wall smoking a cigar and swinging a pair of trainers around and around...

*

Heard The Monkey shrieking with laughter in the living room. He has drawn a shit moustache on a random reality show personality on the TV screen. Handlebar, I think...

30 November

Since the arrival of The Monkey the cat has taken to sleeping under the bath. I think The Monkey quite likes the cat, he doesn't try to grab her tail or force feed her with screws or any of his usual ice breakers. Although I do think he would try to have sex with her if she wasn't armed and dangerous...

*

Took The Monkey for an Indian. He demanded a vindaloo – I told him it was going to be too hot but he called me a pussy, so I gave in. Well, when the chilli hit, he went bat shit and started throwing samosas at the other diners and drinking everyone's yoghurt and mint dip. Then he emptied a water jug over his head, and we had to do a runner which he thought was hilarious. I've locked the bastard in the car boot to teach him a lesson, but I can still hear him laughing.

1 December

The repercussions from last night have been surprisingly mild. The Monkey didn't consume enough of the vindaloo to cause excessive toilet antics and he seems quite philosophical about the ride home in the car boot. I'm guessing he thinks it a good trade off against the mayhem he caused.

He has been very quiet this morning though, that always makes me nervous. I think he is up in the spare room – probably plotting something terrifying...

*

Walked in on The Monkey whacking off to *Tinga Tinga Tales* on CBeebies. He had it paused on the monkey character. I sneaked back out before he saw me – I didn't have the heart to tell him that the monkey character is male...

Maybe he knows...?

2 December

The Monkey has spent most of today on the Xbox again, this time playing *Call of Duty Black Ops*. He is scarily good at it. Although he has had most fun playing online co-op games. He waits until the game gets to a really crucial point and then goes totally spaz shooting anything and everything around him and blowing up all the explosives he has collected, killing everyone. This has resulted in strings of expletives from the other players that I never even imagined could go together. The Monkey just finds it all massively funny and rolls around on the floor laughing before logging back in under a different user name. There will be some angry young men not having sex with their imaginary girlfriends tonight...

The thing in the spare room

3 December

Gangnam dancing with The Monkey. Dead funny until I told him he had no rhythm. He's still hanging off the curtain rail but at least he has run out of shit...

4 December

The Monkey came home in the early hours this morning. He had been clubbing and was pretty smashed. I didn't hear him come in even though he let himself in with a brick. It was the smoke alarm that woke me up. Little bastard was trying to cook chips and he had passed out in the sink. Fortunately, I put out the fire before it got out of control then I turned the cold tap on him to teach him a lesson. He just crawled out onto the draining board, farted, and went back to sleep...

5 December

The Monkey has finally got over his hideous hangover, but it has left him in an evil mood. He just gave next door's dog a kicking. I think he has been watching too much *Dog the Bounty Hunter* – I'm sure I heard him scream, 'Go with Christ,' as he pepper-sprayed the poor beast.

6 December

I went into the spare room earlier and I am convinced that there were tentacles coming out of the black hole in the carpet – it's possible I could have imagined it as they disappeared almost instantly... I told The Monkey and he put down his copy of *Soldier of Fortune* magazine and went up to his room. After a couple of minutes of bumping about he reappeared with one of his machetes and what looked suspiciously like a spear. He said he was going up to the spare room for a bit and I could swear he also said something about calamari for dinner as he headed back upstairs...

*

Well I must say, that was the best calamari I have ever had – and the biggest! The Monkey is laying on the sofa with quite a bulging belly. He looks like he has swallowed a cricket ball, and as he downs his third glass of Chianti, he looks very pleased with himself. Fair play to him but I do hope those sucker marks are going to fade...

7 December

Ever since The Monkey came to stay with me, he has talked about having lived before, and I don't mean a sordid past as a pole dancer. I thought he was taking the piss but he seems really serious. I know he has some pretty wild dreams which he puts down to his past lives but lately he has been coming out with all sorts of stuff that I'm convinced he couldn't know about, even with his increasingly frenzied Google searches. I think I will take him to a hypnotist and see if they can do a regression on him and then maybe we can find out if this is just more of his crazy monkey *mess with my head* bull shit...

8 December

Nice day today so Me and The Monkey went to the zoo. Wasn't sure if seeing the other monkeys in cages would upset him but he just laughed at them and kept making L for loser signs with his little hand. For some reason the penguins got him angry and there was a lot of shit flinging, but I bought him an Almond Magnum and it was all cool again. Took me ages to find him when it was time to leave though – finally found him acting as the referee while the buffalo played conkers.

9 December

One of the neighbours has put up a whole load of Xmas decorations on the outside of his house. The Monkey is fascinated.

*

Fuck! I've just seen The Monkey run past the window with a machete in one hand and the severed head of an LED reindeer in the other...

Flashback!

10 December

Spent most of the day avoiding the neighbours while collecting the dismembered remains of various festive light up shite – and burying it in the garden... Couldn't find all the complete bits of anything. Don't know what The Monkey has done with all the other bits. I will need to check around the house...

*

And so it becomes clear. Now, on the roof of my house, is the nightmare abomination of The Monkey's fevered mind. Like some Frankenstein movie with tinsel, the hybrid creature that used to be the neighbours' Xmas decorations bestrides the ridge of the roof – reindeer head twisting from side to side on a fat Santa's body that convulses as the pistons of the Christmas train pump in and out of where its arms and legs used to be, and on its back two enormous wings from a Christmas angel flap feebly. Somehow, he has managed to wire the thing together so that it moves and lights up and shrieks what I can only imagine is supposed to be *God Rest Ye Merry Gentlemen*. Like some demon raised from hell to shit on Christmas it wails into the dying light while The Monkey sits in the living room watching *Man V Food*...

11 December

Finally managed to get the last of The Monkey's Christmas gift to the world off the roof this morning. Fortunately, he had used the Velux windows in the loft to get it onto the roof so at least I didn't have to get the ladders out, I could just lean out and drag Hells Christmas decoration away from its perch and let it crash into the garden below – seemed a fitting end. He seemed pretty chilled about the destruction of his project – I think he had proved a point of some sort.

Got an appointment with the hypnotist tomorrow, maybe we can get to the bottom of The Monkey's past lives... Or at least calm him down a bit.

12 December

Very interesting... While I sat in the waiting room the hypnotherapist (got told off for calling him a hypnotist) did the business on The Monkey and says he is convinced that The Monkey is telling the truth about having had previous lives, or at least he honestly believes that he has lived before. He described him as, 'The living embodiment of chaos,' (I could have told him that for nothing), and said therefore he is not going to behave any time soon and I am just going to have to get used to it – he looked a bit scared and said he really didn't want to repeat some of the things that The Monkey had said while he was in the hypnotic trance. But he did say that the most prominent *life* seemed to be related to the Vietnam war and a US soldier, so at least that confirms what The Monkey has been saying. He also said there is something else underlying the memories that kept coming to the surface in flashes – that was when he started to suggest we maybe ought to see an exorcist... Shame he doesn't record the sessions, something about client confidentiality, would have made an interesting listen... When he came out, The Monkey said the hypnotherapist had probably touched him up while he was under *the influence* as he called it, and wandered off muttering about, 'Fucking hippies.'

13 December

I always get people asking me how I have ended up living with The Monkey... Well here goes...

About eighteen months ago I split with my girlfriend – irreconcilable differences apparently – and I ended up in Amsterdam with a bunch of mates, partially to help me get over it and partially because I could. After a week the other guys headed home a bit broken and I stayed on feeling that I wasn't quite over it. Anyway, one night I was in a heavy metal bar along one of the canals in the red-light district and I spotted this dude with a monkey. The place was full of bikers and head cases, but everyone was giving the dude and his monkey a wide berth. I thought I was tripping a bit too much as they seemed to be talking, dude and monkey, and I got the feeling they were looking at me. So, paranoia won, and I left the bar.

I headed for a little Arabic looking coffee shop on one of the bridges back towards the main square and settled myself in for the evening. After about half an hour in walks dude and monkey and without a second glance they come and sit next to me. As you can imagine I am more than a little freaked out by this. The dude leans over and stares at me in a not too friendly manner and the monkey sticks a big old cigar in his mouth and lights it with a Zippo lighter he gets from a little bag slung around his shoulders. After what seemed like forever the dude asks me if I want to play a game. 'What sort of game,' I ask him – not really wanting to know the answer. 'Othello,' he says, and from a pocket of his long coat he produces the plastic board and a drawstring bag containing the black/white counters. I was always pretty good at Othello and I reckon that even toasted I can take him, so I say okay. 'Let's make it interesting,' he says and I'm thinking, 'I'm off my tits in a coffee shop in the Dam about to play Othello with a sinister looking dude who has a cigar smoking monkey with him. How much more interesting can it get?' So instead of saying that I just stupidly say, 'Okay.' At this he smiles the sort of smile I imagine sharks would smile if they found a sinking life raft full of puppies and kittens and says, 'Winner gets The Monkey.'

Well I'm a bit taken aback by this – I like monkeys but I wasn't expecting to get one, and what does he gain? So I ask him what I have to give him if I lose, 'Nothing, I will keep the monkey.' I am not at all sure what con trick is going on here, but my messed-up brain just keeps going, 'Yay, a monkey!' So we start to play.

It's a very intense game and he is very good and trying very hard which makes me even more convinced that I am being set up for some forfeit I have no idea about. But eventually I win and he sits back on his stool with a strange smile on his face and it's then that I notice the monkey hasn't moved during the whole game and his cigar has burnt right down almost to his lips. The dude packed away the Othello board and counters and put them back into his coat pocket then he stretched and said, 'I need a piss,' and got up and went into the bathroom at the back of the coffee shop. The monkey lit another cigar and clamped it between his teeth and was watching me with those little black eyes. An hour passed and the dude never came back – I checked the bathroom and there was no one there – he just never came back. I looked at the monkey and had a giggling fit. 'I will call you Kong,' I announced, feeling very pleased at the irony of the name, and then the monkey spoke to me for the first time, 'The fuck you will,' was all he said...

*

So, there I was in Amsterdam with a monkey and I'm thinking to myself, *How the hell am I going to get home with a monkey?* I had gone over on the ferry so I figured if I got The Monkey to hide in my bag, I could get him onto the ferry and if I upgraded to a cabin he could stay in there until we reached England... Well The Monkey told me in no uncertain terms that he wasn't getting in any fucking bag or staying in a cabin for the whole of the crossing. He said to just get him a ticket and everything would be fine. What about quarantine, I wanted to know? But he said he wasn't waiting around for me to get out of quarantine so I would just have to make an effort to not look like I had anything catching!

With great misgivings we got to the ferry terminal and I brought a ticket for The Monkey – no one batted an eyelid, much to my surprise and we boarded the ferry. During the crossing we sat in the bar and I had a few beers while The Monkey drank Jack Daniels and then went out on deck for a cigar. I watched him as he perched on the handrail and looked out to sea, and at that moment nothing seemed strange about the whole experience at all. When he came back in he was a bit wobbly from the Jack and headed off down the ship. I let him go because all of a sudden it seemed totally normal. A couple of minutes later he came bolting back up the ferry to tell me he had arranged me a fight with a truck driver...

*

When we got back to the UK we got to the train station, and following a couple of changes we ended up on the Paddington to Penzance train, me with a black eye and split lip from my brawl with the truck driver (although I did win following the impromptu use of a food tray as a guillotine – not my finest moment, but I did get approving looks from The Monkey and he didn't try to instigate violence for the rest of the trip). So in the five-hour journey I decided to ask The Monkey a few questions about his past.

Seems he had spent all his early years on a merchant sea vessel doing the rounds of Indonesia, the Philippines, Thailand etc. Apparently the dude in the long coat had been given The Monkey by a Buddhist monk when The Monkey was a baby and told to look after him, and being a merchant seaman, it was on board ship that The Monkey ended up. Strange things had started to happen on board. Crew members disappeared, strange lights appeared in the sea, a mixed box of Pot Noodles turned out to be all chicken flavour...

*

And then they had been attacked by pirates...

The waters around Indonesia are rife with them and they had attacked the ship at dawn in the Strait of Malacca. The Monkey said the ship had fallen quickly and he and the long coat dude had ended up cornered in one of the cargo holds. The pirates found them, and The Monkey told them to go fuck themselves while brandishing a knife he had taken to carrying. All of a sudden the atmosphere changed and the pirates had started to back away jabbering in their local dialect. Before long the pirate's cigar smoking shaman was down in the hold staring at The Monkey. The Monkey walked straight up to the shaman and took the cigar from between his lips and put it between his own. The shaman had, in the Monkey's words, gone all big eyed and twitchy and then said in Portuguese that The Monkey was *The Ever Changing One* (long coat dude had translated afterwards) and then he had gathered together all the pirates and they had left the ship at breakneck speed.

The next few years had been spent on various ships, but they were not able to settle anywhere as the strange goings on continued and eventually the long coat dude couldn't cope any more. At some point in the Java Sea, he wasn't quite sure when, The Monkey (like Skynet) had started to become self-aware and realised he needed to be somewhere else. When they had reached the next major port, they signed on to a ship heading for Amsterdam and that was where my part in the story began.

I asked The Monkey why they had chosen me, and he just said that I looked like I was up for anything and that I was so stoned I was an easy catch...

As I write this The Monkey is singing along to *Brixton Briefcase* at the top of his lungs. He hasn't got a bad voice...

14 December

Good news! The Monkey's bid for the JCB on eBay didn't win – phew! He seems a bit grumpy about it and I have just caught him checking out armoured cars. I'm slightly conflicted, I like military vehicles as much as the next man, but I think it is time to change my eBay password...

15 December

The Monkey is watching *Apocalypse Now* again. He has always claimed that he was in Nam, which I have always argued was completely unfeasible, but since his regression session the other day I am beginning to wonder. He does get a strange, faraway look in his eyes when he watches the film as well and can become quite agitated. One time after watching it he roared around Morrisons in a trolley, singing the *Ride of the Valkyries* and throwing frozen fish fingers at other shoppers... Why do I always get the blame?

A little introspection...

17 December

The Monkey has become a prolific reader. He has just finished *Beyond 2012*. I asked him if he believed in all of the end of the world stuff and he looked me straight in the eye and told me that when the world ends, he will be responsible for it but at the moment he is having too much fun... Well there you go...

18 December

There seems to be an uneasy truce between The Monkey and next door's dog. They are playing what looks like poker underneath the gazebo. The Monkey is smoking a cigar again although he promised me he had given up.

19 December

The Monkey is doing more rituals. He has locked himself away in the spare room and I can hear chanting and a weird howling noise. He had an envelope full of dog hair with him when he went up – makes sense of the poker game now – and he mentioned enslaving next door's dog to his bidding as he passed me on the stairs. I have asked him not to write on the walls again and if there is blood to clean it up...

20 December

The Monkey has reappeared with a strange, haunted look on his little face. I asked him what he had been up to but he just said, 'I don't want to talk about it, man.' I think the use of *man* was in the hippy vernacular as he has never called me man before, which is odd given his pathological dislike of hippies...

I checked the spare room – it smells of burnt dog hair and I found a small green steel helmet, with the words *Death From Above* written on it, in the corner. I don't remember ordering this for him or him sending off for it from one of his *special interest* magazines...

21 December

Been having a deep, metaphysical talk with The Monkey today. Still don't know what went on in the spare room but it was clearly weird even for him. He started by asking me a question, 'What if we are already dead? Or maybe we aren't born yet, and we are in some sort of ante room waiting to become manifest...' – I don't know which concept troubled him more. I said that if he knew he had had previous lives then how could he be dead or not yet born? 'Maybe it's just all a dream and we are just part of it...' was his reply, and then followed several hours of quite interesting but tortuous debate. He finally cheered up when I dug out a bottle of port and he sparked up a big cigar and we played several games of Pop Up Pirate. He really likes the game, I think it's the act of stabbing tiny swords into a captive pirate, and it always makes him laugh out loud when the pirate jumps up.

The Monkey is quite drunk now but in a better mood. He is ripping the piss out of the 2012ers on a variety of end of the world blogs.

22 December

Through a haze of cigar smoke I can see The Monkey playing with an early Christmas present. The throwing knives are smashing into the target with fanatical rapidity and accuracy. The target, by the way, is an old door with a variety of roadkill nailed onto it and each piece of roadkill has a picture of a cabinet minister taped to it. It's getting very messy and he doesn't miss...

23 December

Went out for a pre-Xmas drinky poo with The Monkey today. Managed to get through nine pubs and ended up on the beach doing handstands. We tried to make a festive sandman, but it didn't work out well – especially when I threw up on it. We couldn't stop laughing and I pushed him off a sandbar into the river mouth – that wasn't quite so funny as The Monkey doesn't swim well when pissed. I ended up wading after him and the pair of us splashed about like a pair of total twats as dog walkers stared on in disbelief. We managed to find a chip shop selling kebabs and fortunately one of the neighbours saw us and gave us a lift home in the back of his van.

The Monkey is passed out on the sofa, covered in kebab salad and wearing the pita bread as a hat. I am typing this while gripping the chair to stop the room spinning...

God rest Ye Merry Gentlemen...

24 December

Been a day of bad heads today... The Monkey eventually appeared around midday and has been huddled on the sofa ever since with his shades on. He is still picking kebab salad out of his fur. Think I will stick the *Elf* DVD on and suggest a hair of the dog. One of those things might perk him up...

Okay, bad choice of words... After that last ritual the mention of dog hair made The Monkey bolt to the top of the bookcase and he wouldn't come down until I had explained that what I was suggesting had nothing at all to do with hair or dogs. Not sure he still trusts me but it is Christmas Eve, so a Moscow Mule and Buddy the elf heading south have at least got him back on the sofa...

25 December

Merry Christmas! The Monkey has been very good about not ransacking the house for presents so we have some lovely surprises...

Someone suggested I buy The Monkey a fez, so with some trepidation I did. He took it quite well and has even worn it for most of the morning. His other presents from me consisted of a box of cigars (I have given up trying to get him to quit), the DVD box set of *Band of Brothers*, Hungry Hungry Hippos, a bottle of Jack Daniels, a vicious looking SOG combat knife, a new teddy bear, the collected works of the *Golden Dawn* and a night scope. He got me a load of things from Firebox I think – lollies with scorpions in them, tequila with scorpions in it, chocolate loaded with habanero chilli, a cool iPod speaker and what look like stun grenades (I don't think they came from Firebox – where the hell does he get this stuff from?).

Got the family arriving soon so better get on with the Xmas dinner...

*

The Monkey thought it would be funny to give my family a surprise for Xmas dinner. I bought a very large turkey, so I cooked it yesterday and let it cool overnight. The Monkey must have climbed inside it – I did wonder where he had gone. I placed it in the centre of the dinner table and just as I was about to carve The Monkey came bursting out through its chest like Alien. We are now spending the rest of Xmas day alone as terror induced by the spectacle caused all present to flee in panic, and Aunty Grace to lose control of her bowels... The Monkey doesn't seem to mind. He is drinking advocaat and eating handfuls of cranberry sauce off the walls.

26 December

Spent most of this morning on the phone apologising for yesterday's freak show while The Monkey spent the morning in bed having a threesome with his teddy bears. Still, yesterday wasn't a total disaster, we got to have a Hungry Hungry Hippos championship and drink scorpion tequila slammers – result!

28 December

The Monkey thinks we should go out tonight. He has found a club with a Goth night and is now hunting out black eye liner. Not quite sure where it is but I'm game!

29 December

Woke up in a Travelodge with The Monkey and two girls who looked like Monster High dolls – or at least their older sisters. The Monkey was already awake and going through their handbags. I stopped him and we quickly got our stuff and made a very ungentlemanly retreat from the trashed room – giggling...

Last night's club was the usual dark, sticky-floored affair, and the usual selection of children of the night were in attendance. Emo kids who looked like they had just fallen off the pages of a *Manga* comic, pretend vampires looking down their pale noses contemptuously at those not in their clique, random industrial, techno and fetish Goths wearing rubber, leather and UV armour, the odd *Fields of the Nephilim* cowboy, and a surprising amount of fat Goths – Robert Smith look-a-likes to a man. We hit the bar with a vengeance although we had already downed a half bottle of Jack on the walk up to the club, and very soon the dry ice, swirly gobos and throbbing drum machines got us up on the floor. In fact we cleared the floor at one point as we Gangnam danced to Sisters of Mercy – got some hate for that one. I also remember an epic pogoing session to some thrashy industrial track.

All a bit of a blur after that. Piecing together our memories it appears we managed to offend many people and even have a minor scuffle with some chavs on the way back from the club. Seems they were giving the Monster Highs a hard time and we rescued them only to then lure them back to the Travelodge with promises of more booze and 50 shades of Me and The Monkey.

Having a big fry up at a roadside café at the moment. I have just told The Monkey what black pudding is made from and he is now staring at it as if it has committed a war crime...

*

Going through the pile of clothes on the floor to throw into the washing machine and in the pocket of The Monkey's black leather trench coat there are loads of IDs – student union cards, driving licences and citizen cards. By the looks of the photos they are all Goth/Emo types, so I am guessing that they have come from the people we shared the club with last night.

Asked The Monkey to explain his new found love of collecting IDs and he just said that it is always good to have other forms of identification, especially when shopping on line for some of the more legally dubious stuff that he seems to procure. 'A bit like having someone else's fingerprints on your knife,' was, I believe, how he phrased it.

Left him shopping on the dark web while I try to get this black nail polish off...

Fireworks

31 December

Plans for tonight – invite everyone we like and drink and dance outrageously until broken. The Monkey has got a surprise for midnight as well. He has managed to get hold of a big bunch of Chinese fireworks (I have a feeling some of them might actually be classified as WMD) and he is determined to give London a run for its money – at least in terms of close-up violent explosions! I have asked The Monkey several times now whether he plans to stay marginally sober in order to operate this extravaganza, but he just gives me that look and continues to twist together fuses and sip vodka...

Happy New Year in advance.

1 January

Well, it could have been worse... At least no one died...

The drinking and dancing reached a crescendo about 10.30pm and then just got even more insane. We started making human pyramids around 11.00pm and managed to get to the ceiling so we decided to take it into the garden so we could go higher. In all the falling bodies I didn't see The Monkey disappear (I must admit that everything was a bit fuzzy anyway) but I think he took the chance to go and make his last-minute firework preparations. Anyway, as we counted down to midnight The Monkey gave me the thumbs up from the end of the garden and I watched as he lit the first fuse with his cigar. A salvo of rockets roared skywards and lit up the night with an explosion of silver and gold. Everyone dutifully went ooh and aah, and to be fair it was pretty impressive. Several more volleys of rockets went up and it looked really cool. Then he lit a row of short pipes and one after another glowing balls of light popped from the tops of them and floated lazily upwards. That's when it all went a bit wrong. As the shiny fairy glow balls reached about twelve feet in altitude they detonated – and I mean detonated. Like mortar bombs going off in aerial bursts they went off with a blinding flash and the sound of multiple car bombs. I was temporarily blinded and disorientated and staggered into the pond along with several others. As the fuzzy glowing balls of terror continued their explosions everyone started hitting the ground and covering their heads. As my vision returned, I looked up from the pond to see The Monkey cavorting with glee and lighting another fuse. This one turned out to be more rockets and gave us a chance to recover a little and scramble out of the water. People were getting to their feet and laughing nervously as they pointed to the show up in the sky. I glanced down and saw The Monkey lighting a short fat cylinder in the centre of the garden. Then I saw his eyebrows raise and him scamper up to the back of the garden and dive behind the shed. *Fuck*, I thought as the thing gave out a massive white flash and did a summersault, landing on its side totally in flames. I guess this was a misfire because then it began to shoot tiny exploding stars out of what had been its top and was now facing towards the house. Panic followed as everyone dived for cover or tried to get back indoors. Then, while this was still raining fire on our guests, the mother of all rockets blasted off from the top of the shed. This was the one I would have classified as a WMD. Whether it was another faulty firework or The Monkey's tampering I don't know but it didn't get much higher than the roof of the house before it went boom. I went back in the pond and every car alarm in the area went off. Eventually the smoke and blindness cleared, and I could see dazed and sobbing party goers comforting each other as they patted out smoking patches on their hair and clothes. The Monkey sat on the edge of the pond with an almost ecstatic look on his face as his singed fur gently smoked. Somehow he still had his cigar clenched in his teeth. There was another sound in the background and then I realised it was ragged applause from some of the guests (mostly those who had made it back into the house) and it gradually grew until more or less everyone had joined in and there were even some cheers. It's amazing the response of people when they realise that they are still alive...

I have spent a good part of today explaining to the police through a hangover that it was all a big misunderstanding with some faulty fireworks and that we are not a terrorist cell...

2 January

Quieter day today. The Monkey has spent the day with his head buried in his new *Golden Dawn* books in a quest for more esoteric knowledge and some sort of idea as to what is going on in the spare room. The black hole has grown a little bigger and if you go in there it can be hours before you come out, even if you think it has only been minutes. A couple of Thursday night's party goers went in there for a quickie and didn't reappear until yesterday evening – much to everyone's surprise.

I have been trying to get some work done, with Soundgarden as my backing track, mixed with The Monkey's attempts at pronouncing occult phrases in weird languages...

3 January

I pointed out to The Monkey that there has been a van parked across the road since yesterday morning. He said he had noticed it and it had been around for a few weeks now, parking in various places along the street. That made me feel better – I thought we had picked up surveillance after the firework blitzkrieg – but The Monkey stoked my fears again by telling me he is sure he has seen some sort of scanning equipment poking out of the side. As there are only trees and fields over the road, they could easily get away with quite a bit without being spotted. I asked The Monkey what he thought they were after as, except for New Year's Eve, we had kept off the radar. He just looked upwards in the direction of the spare room. I think we need to take action...

*

Not quite what I had in mind by taking action. I caught The Monkey constructing an IED from some leftover fireworks and stuff from the shed which he was going to attach to the van. He begrudgingly agreed that this probably wasn't the best course of action but said he was keeping the IED, 'Just in case.' So now we are scouring through books on esoteric law, quantum physics, mythology, the Maplin catalogue and for some reason *The Cat in the Hat*. Think it's going to be a long evening and that I am going to have to keep an eye on The Monkey just in case something goes boom...

4 January

It was a long night apparently... It was about 1am when we had enough information together to head up to the spare room. Turns out what I really needed to do was ask The Monkey what he had done in his rituals that had caused the black hole in the first place. Seems the first unsuccessful one had included the invoking of Tlaloc the Aztec rain god – probably why it kept raining. The second more successful one had involved the invoking of Tezcatlipoca – The Smoking Mirror – one of the Aztec gods associated with the sun. Although this bad boy was also god of the night and I think had some issues... The Monkey had mixed this with some ritual magic, peyote, blood sacrifice and chanting passages from Stephen Hawking's *A Brief History of Time*. So, we came to the conclusion that if we sort of repeated the ritual but in reverse, we might be able to close the black hole.

Well, we had no peyote left so we elected for a combination of dope and Red Bull – yes, we were just winging it. I got a chicken out of the fridge and we taped it to the teddy bear, and with all our books and accoutrements in tow we headed into the spare room.

It was 10.00am when we finally got out. It had only seemed like an hour but like I said time does seem to distort in the spare room – although we think we now have that under control. It was all a bit fraught and everything warped and twisted into fractal plains. At one point a child with no arms and eight spider legs appeared from the black hole and proceeded to scream with the voices of ten thousand tortured souls. It really pissed The Monkey off and he smashed it in the face and forced it back into the hole. We haven't managed to close the hole but at least it seems a little more stable...

Checked on the van when we came out and there was definitely a whole bunch of antenna and dishes poking out of its roof all pointing in our direction. I bet they weren't expecting that much action...

5 January

A second van has turned up. I think they will be a bit disappointed though as the spare room has gone quite quiet. Went up there earlier and was in and out in minutes so it looks like the time distortion has calmed down.

Just found The Monkey in the living room engrossed in the *Tibetan Book of the Dead*, a large Jack in his little hand. I glanced at his open notebook (his spelling is improving) and was fascinated by the little sketch he had drawn of himself, then I realised that in the sketch he was sitting on a throne of human skulls. I asked him about it and he just laughed and said that it must be, 'Contact Goth,' from our outing a few days ago.

I might need to keep an eye on The Monkey tonight. He wasn't impressed by the arrival of the second van and I spotted he was charging up his night vision goggles in the kitchen...

Van

8 January

Bugger... Couldn't keep The Monkey away from the van for ever I suppose. We are back to one van as the spare room has gone very quiet, but I should have guessed that The Monkey wasn't going to let it lie. I can see him up on the roof of the van, perched over a small hatch from which they poke their scanning equipment, and he is taking one hell of a crap. Explains the three helpings of chilli and beans he had lunchtime. He did keep his promise about the IED though but I'm not sure if this doesn't constitute a biological weapon attack...

9 January

Seems that they are not sleeping in the van overnight, so it wasn't until they let themselves in this morning that they found The Monkey's gift. I could hear the swearing and retching from here. 'Most gratifying,' said The Monkey. Took them all morning to clean it out and many cans of air freshener.

I went out to get some more printer ink this afternoon leaving The Monkey reading a book on Max Planck. His reading is getting more and more sophisticated. Don't get me wrong, he will still pick up a *2000AD* comic or pulp fiction paperback at the drop of a hat, but his literary tastes have moved outwards yet again as has his understanding. I noticed that next in line in the pile of books by the sofa is one on Tesla followed by a history of the Mongol invasions.

When I got back, I parked the car and as I walked towards the house I glanced at the van. Spray painted in black on its pale blue side is now a four-foot cock and balls plus spiky pubes and schoolboy spunk trail – it's like being 14 again. But next to that, and obviously written in marker pen, is this – *All matter originates and exists only by virtue of a force which brings the particle of an atom to vibration and holds this most minute solar system of the atom together. We must assume behind this force the existence of a conscious and intelligent mind. This mind is the matrix of all matter.* Signed – Max Planck. No prizes for where that came from then...

10 January

Drunken game of Twister with The Monkey. I fell on him. Him not happy. Big monkey lip and shit flinging because I laughed so hard. I didn't see the plant pot coming though. Little yellow cartoon birds flying round my head. Cheered The Monkey up no end – he spent ages chasing them and pulling the wings off until they finally disappeared. Both nursing injuries now, The Monkey bruised ribs and me a cut on the back of my head. Still, nothing a couple of rounds of shooters can't fix...

11 January

Seems a road trip is in the offing. The Monster High lookalikes from our Goth night phoned up. Apparently, The Monkey wrote our phone number on both their arses with a Sharpie. They want us to go to some Goth get together in Nottingham with them.

As The Monkey is fond of shouting – 'Adventure!'

12 January

The van disappeared yesterday evening but it was back bright and early this morning with The Monkey's artwork removed. I'm guessing a heavy weight T-Cut session was enjoyed by someone.

The Monkey had some strange dreams last night. He was making really odd sounds and after deciding that they weren't sex noises I went in to check on him and found him sitting bolt upright in bed with his eyes wide open but still fast asleep. Spooky. I asked him this morning what he had been dreaming about and he went quiet for a bit and then said, 'The jungle – the jungle and death.' Took him a while longer to elaborate but it seems the Vietnam past life stuff is flooding in again. He believes that he was a member of a covert group called Project Phoenix that was embedded with the locals way behind enemy lines. With the aid of these friendly locals they operated kidnap and assassination missions amongst the VC to gather intelligence and just generally put the fear of god into them. The Monkey is such a prolific reader that I can't tell whether he is genuine or making it up but he does seem to know lots of detail and he gets a look about him that I don't think he could act.

We went to the cinema and have just got back from an early showing of *Seven Psychopaths*. Very entertaining, The Monkey laughed all the way through...

13 January

Ah the simple joys of a monkey knife fight, at least that's what he claims it would be. I have refused to get involved...

*

We are watching reality TV simply because neither of us can be bothered to reach the remote which is on the shelf by the DVDs, and The Monkey is getting more and more exasperated by the wannabes who are humiliating themselves for the entertainment of the masses. He can't grasp why anyone would willingly do this – and I am afraid that I can't give him an answer. We both agree that it is far better to not be in the spotlight as you can get away with far more shit if no one is looking at you...

Hostage

15 January

I came back this afternoon to find that The Monkey had taken a hostage. One of the van men had strayed away from the vehicle and The Monkey had spotted him immediately and ambushed him. We now had a young black guy tied up in the spare room and sedated. To be honest I panicked a bit, but The Monkey assured me that his victim had no idea what had happened as he had been unconscious before he hit the floor. Next door's dog had helped to drag him into the house. After a fair bit of shouting I managed to convince The Monkey that we risked drawing too much attention to ourselves and that we should drag him back outside and hope that when he came round, he would think he had had a seizure or something. Besides, he hardly looked like a bad ass spec ops agent, with his boyish face and old school Atari T-shirt he looked like he would have been more at home in the student union bar. Begrudgingly The Monkey agreed and we sneaked the van man back out and left him propped against a garden wall around the corner. He will never know how close he came to being dumped into the black hole...

16 January

Think we got away with the kidnapping. Me and The Monkey are very drunk – shhh, don't tell anyone...

18 January

Shit, The Monkey's lunchtime mushroom omelette had a little bit too much of the magic in it. Apparently, we have spent the last 11 hours in the woods. We both look like extras from *Lord of the Flies*...

*

It's looking increasingly likely that our road trip with the Monster Highs this weekend will be cancelled because of the snow. Although The Monkey is talking about high jacking a gritting lorry...

19 January

Right, sat in Ye Olde Trip to Jerusalem. We have hidden the stolen gritting lorry up the road for the return journey tomorrow. Picked up the hugely inappropriately dressed Monster Highs en route (I suspect they may already be dead, it's the only way I can explain them not freezing) and spent the day driving north and spreading grit. I should have known The Monkey wasn't joking about the high jacking. It was easier than I thought it would be, just walked in and took it from a council depot in Exeter. At least we had plenty of time to chat to the girls and find out a bit more about them other than just their sexual preferences. It seems that they had spotted us early on at the Goth club and were attracted to our auras. The Monkey gave me a sideways look and I half expected an outburst regarding hippy new age shite but he held it in and that was when I knew that he liked them. They then told us they had caused the confrontation with the chavs outside the club in order to get to meet us. I was quite adamant that they could have just come up and said hello as neither of us would have been offended by scantily clad, beautiful twins wanting to get to know us, but they just smiled their mysterious little smiles and changed the subject to favourite movies and, of course we got sucked into the debate.

No one is sure whether the Goth do is on or not but there is talk of a party at someone's house so it shouldn't be a total wasted journey...

20 January

On a train somewhere near Bristol. We had to abandon the gritter where we had left it because of the police checking it out. So, the four of us jumped a train to Birmingham and now we are on the second leg of the journey to get back to the car in Exeter.

The party was amusing. It was hosted by a local pagan group and there were a variety of alternative belief systems on show all vying to be the baddest/most outrageous/scariest. Mostly total wankers with the exception of one or two who didn't take themselves too seriously. They were all over us (I think being new blood) but soon started to give us a wide birth. The Monkey has more genuine chaos in his middle finger than that whole bunch put together and the Monster Highs are actually quite scary if they don't like you. I am more and more convinced that they have been dead for quite some time but don't want to lay down. I asked The Monkey what he thought, and he grinned and said, 'Fine by me,' and strangely it seems to be fine by me as well. So we took over one end of the living room and had our own little party. It's funny how all these radical *Do what thou wilt* types get all precious when you start getting nasty on their turf and not giving them the attention they think they deserve. We left in the end and found a Premier Inn and continued our party there but not until The Monkey had threatened someone with a taser and the Monster Highs had bitten three people.

Going to be a long journey home, I think. The drugs are wearing off, we have run out of Jack and the coffee is shite...

Most Haunted

21 January

Spent the day sleeping off the weekend. It was two in the morning by the time we got home, and The Monkey insisted on a night cap s9o it was nearer four by the time we got to bed. But not before I had held the torch for The Monkey while he super glued tin foil all over the van's windscreen. That's going to be a bastard to get off.

Don't feel so bad about vandalising the van now as we have found signs this evening that someone has been in the house – showing particular interest in the spare room. It's a good thing The Monkey asked me to put a lock on the door, a key code one as well so I don't think they got into the room, at least not on this occasion... The Monkey doesn't take kindly to anyone encroaching on his territory. I am going to have to be on the lookout for booby traps again...

22 January

Managed to get some work done today while The Monkey laughed at the efforts of the van men as they tried to pick the constantly tearing tin foil off their windscreen.

I walked past the spare room earlier and there is something up. There is a low-level hum or maybe a vibration coming from the room. I think our efforts at controlling the black hole may have failed. I have set The Monkey to try to work out what is going on, he needs to be kept occupied or I fear for the safety of the van men. Oh, and The Monkey has started wearing false Groucho Marx style nose and glasses – your guess is as good as mine...

23 January

The Monkey reckons that the vibration was coming from something on the other side of the hole. It has stopped now and having had a look in the room there doesn't seem to be anything out of the ordinary – well any more out of the ordinary for this house!

The Monkey is reading at an incredible rate. Books on political thought have appeared in his reading pile and he has already waded through Hobbs *Leviathan*, Mill's *On Liberty* and Marx and Engel's *The Communist Manifesto*. Seems the false nose and glasses were to get him in the right frame of mind. I had to explain – I knew I shouldn't. Still cleaning up shit...

24 January

Watching *Most Haunted* with The Monkey. He is crying with laughter which is making me cry with laughter. Says it's the funniest thing he has ever seen and keeps gasping, 'Wankers!' when he can catch his breath...

25 January

This could prove awkward. The Monkey has a plan to invite the *Most Haunted* crew to our house. He reckons that if they are going to shit their pants on TV then they might as well have something real to shit their pants about. He is talking about stirring up the black hole and just locking them in the spare room with it. He has told me that he has sent several emails to various websites today but hasn't had a response yet. I am trying to convince him of what a genuinely bad idea this is given the fact that we have a van of undisclosed origin monitoring us from across the road, we know someone has been in the house, and we have a genuine rift in time and space in one of our bedrooms.

The Monkey seems to think that putting the paranormal explorers into a fear induced coma on national telly would be great sport. I have a feeling that the show isn't running any more – at least I hope the show isn't running any more – if The Monkey doesn't get any responses to his messages it can only be a good thing, much as I would enjoy the spectacle...

26 January

The Monkey hasn't had a response and I did a bit of research and it seems that there is no current *Most Haunted* – phew!

I mentioned to The Monkey, half-jokingly, that he could make his own TV show featuring the black hole and things coming through it. He quite likes the idea of a predator coming into the house to try and kill him. I have no doubt that it would be a slaughter with him coming out on top. He has now gone off to find out who he should pitch that sort of programme idea to. I suggested Richard and Judy, so he did some searching and reappeared briefly to call me a, 'Fuckwit,' before disappearing into the internet again...

*

It seems The Monkey has been chatting to someone calling themselves Snakebite on a dark web site. The sort of things he looks at and buys online are bound to attract a fair bit of interest from the fringes. This Snakebite has all the hallmarks of being some extreme right-wing recruiter trying to groom The Monkey, but he thinks it is hilarious as usual and is having great fun leading Snakebite on a merry dance. I told him that under no circumstances is he to invite Snakebite round for dinner – he just laughed and called me a spoilsport...

27 January

Noooo! The Monkey has found *Apocalypse Now* on ITV4. It's going to be a long, long night...

Death of a delivery man

28 January

Have you any idea how freaky it is to see The Monkey rising out of the garden pond in the style of Martin Sheen's Captain Willard? I lost him for a while last night and it was on the third pass of the garden that I shone the torch across the pond and saw him. I've seen some shit with The Monkey but that made even me go cold. He went up onto the top of the garden shed for quite a while after that, despite my best attempts at talking him down. I left him to it in the end, mainly because it started to rain.

This morning the extent of The Monkey's night-time excursion became apparent. The tires of the van were shot out and there was a dead sheep hanging down the windscreen, a bullet through its face. I questioned him about the lack of gun shots and therefore the lack of police cars. He just said, 'Home-made silencer,' as if that was the end of it, and then asked me if I wanted some pancakes. I did...

29 January

Well, the van is gone. Got towed away this morning. I am surprised there haven't been any police considering the obvious bullet holes but then again perhaps that goes some way to showing the clandestine nature of the surveillance we have been under. As I stood watching through the living room window The Monkey hopped up onto the window ledge and lit up a cigar. After a while he blew out a big cloud of smoke and said, 'Smells like victory,' then he laughed and said, 'Until the next lot.' I am sure he is right. We haven't seen the end of the van men and next time they probably won't be so obvious.

The Monkey is back on the occult books. He thinks we should have a look through the black hole and is searching for references to anything similar. We have quite a library in the house as I inherited rather a lot of old books from a slightly strange uncle, among the Victorian erotica these included a few esoteric titles to which The Monkey has been adding.

I'm not sure if I am losing the plot. I find myself agreeing with The Monkey's crazy ideas and not knowing why. For some reason this seems normal, and if I'm honest, quite exciting...

31 January

The Monkey knocked out a delivery man today.

The guy came to the door to ask if we could take a parcel for the neighbours who were out. Anyway, The Monkey answered the door and the delivery man asked him to sign one of those electronic pads they have but the Monkey had never seen one before so he wanted a better look and the guy got funny because he was in a rush and called The Monkey, 'A stupid ape.' Well, being a monkey, The Monkey has very fast hands, combined with past life military training (it would seem) and he grabbed the brass knuckles that are hidden by the front door and put the delivery man down with a couple of vicious blows. I got there as the delivery man bounced down the step and landed like a sack of shit. It took a bit of effort but we dragged him back to his van, put him in the driver's seat and, after tipping whisky down his throat and onto his clothes, took off the handbrake and set the van rolling down the steep hill and into a tree in the hedgerow. Then we ran like fuck back to the house. The Monkey held up the neighbour's parcel and rolled his eyes before running back out again and lobbing it into the passenger seat of the van and sprinting back. He reckons that no one saw us and to be honest it was quite a while before anyone went out to the van. An ambulance turned up after a bit with a police car in tow and they carted off the driver and then dealt with the van.

We have had no visits so far, but I am guessing that when the driver comes round and tells them his version of what happened we will get a visit from Plod...

1 February

The expected visit materialised around midday, but it went a lot better than I had thought it might. Seems the driver started telling the police how he had dropped the parcel off with us and then got right hooked by The Monkey. But the police had checked his van and found the parcel and of course he hadn't managed to write a card and stick it through next door's letter box so that blew his story apart. Plus the fact that we had managed to get at least a couple of doubles down his unconscious throat and soak him in whisky all just pointed to the fact that he was pissed and had lost control of his vehicle. The police visit just turned out to be a formality and the officer had quite a laugh with The Monkey.

Seems we didn't get away totally unobserved though. Next door's dog told The Monkey that he had seen everything but that, 'The bastard had asked for it,' and that he had been going mental barking at him and would definitely have bitten his face off. He said that we had nothing to worry about – he wasn't going to tell anyone. The Monkey told me that the dog is all talk and would have pissed himself if he had been face to face with the driver, plus he said the dog knows that he would end up as a hat if he blabbed...

2 February

Lovely day today so me and The Monkey drove up to Tintagel and had a walk along the cliffs to Boscastle. Plenty of new age pagan sorts about – the nice weather brings them out you know. We stopped off in a pub (well it would have been rude not to) and were treated to an overweight, middle aged woman in multi coloured velvet talking loudly about how enlightened she was and how she knew all of the *real* masters either in person or on the astral plain. We did our best to ignore her but after a couple of Rattlers she seemed to be the only thing we could hear. Then she expounded upon the concept of *twin flames* and how your perfect matched soul was out there, even if they didn't know it. This developed into something quite weird and stalkerish as she advocated basically just being there all the time, even if the other person had no idea who you were, as eventually they would see the light and realise they love you – or something like that! The docile chumps she was surrounded by all nodded knowingly and made little appreciative noises as she pontificated about golden auras, purple children, pyramid power and the usual Lady Bird book of the New Age tripe that passes for law amongst these sorts. The Monkey was remarkably calm during all of this. I really was expecting him to jump onto a table and shout abuse or perhaps punch her in the tits. Instead as we got up to leave, he made a detour around the back of her chair and did a massive shit in her cavernous shoulder bag. Sometimes you have got to love the fact that The Monkey doesn't wear trousers and seems to be able to crap on demand.

Anyway, we left the pub and went into the occult/new age shop by the bridge and had a look around. Mostly fairies and buddhas and Wiccan stuff but then The Monkey stopped dead in front of a little glass case by the window and pointed at something right at the back. There was a moldavite pendant, a deep grassy green, and it was carved with a monkey's face – The Monkey's face. He paid for it (rather a lot) and as the woman wrapped it in tissue paper, he asked her where it was from. She said that it had come from a private collection that the shop's owner had picked up at auction a few years ago but that most of it had come originally from the Far East – Thailand, Vietnam, Cambodia etc – and that the monkey piece was quite unusual because moldavite wasn't usually carved, which is why it was so expensive. I asked why, if it was so unusual, no one had bought it before now? She said that no matter where they put it no one seemed to notice it and if they did, they passed over it very quickly. It made people feel uneasy.

We walked back via the road as a couple of Rattlers doesn't make for safe cliff path walking (at least for me) and all the way back The Monkey held the pendant in his hand and every now and then he would stare at it and make little, quiet, monkey noises...

3 February

The Monkey was pretty quiet and thoughtful last night. We drank a fair bit of Jack and he smoked a few cigars but mostly he just stared at the pendant. I have learned to leave him to it when he is like that and he normally comes out of it on his own soon enough.

This morning he was mostly back to normal. I asked him if he wanted a chain or something so that he could wear the pendant, but he said that he had used a length of string and hung it on a nail by his bed. Then he made a massive pot of coffee and bitched about the sudden turn in the weather again while we guzzled mug after mug. He wondered if the Priestess of the New Age enjoyed her bag of poo and we laughed until we were blowing coffee out of our noses.

The Monkey had a chat with next door's dog this afternoon. The dog spends most of his time looking out of the window and barking at anything and everything that it sees – The Monkey blames the cocaine – but it seems that the house down the street that has been up for rent had some potential new tenants come to look around yesterday while we were out, and the dog recognised one of the van men amongst them. We knew they would be back, but this looks more serious...

Breaking and entering

4 February

The Monkey wants to know why they buried Richard III in a car park. He thinks it may be because he didn't return his supermarket trolley but just left it in one of the bays, so they killed him and buried him there as a warning to others. Ah, drugs...

5 February

I watched The Monkey today launching himself on what can only be described as a homemade hang glider into the gale force winds that have been shrieking around us all day. With his little steel *Death from Above* helmet strapped to his head and some swimming goggles he looked like the craziest Wright brother ever! Over and over again he threw himself into the maelstrom, sometimes getting smashed to the ground or into the bamboo growing by the shed, other times getting swirled away over several garden fences before, like Icarus, crashing to earth. Each time he would scramble back over the fences dragging the adapted power kite with him, make a few running repairs and then back onto the shed roof for another kamikaze flight. I didn't notice for a while that my face was aching and when I did it took me a few moments to realise that it was because I was smiling so much. Watching The Monkey's blissful intensity was amazing and suddenly made me aware of how much we miss when we don't just do what gives us pleasure.

Took me a while to stitch up the gash on The Monkey's shoulder, mainly because I had to shave the fur off first. He hit a satellite dish on a house about eight doors away. Proper comedy crash, and it was difficult to tell who came off worse – the neighbours' TV viewing or The Monkey. It had been his last flight anyway (so he says) and I helped him clean up the evidence and got him into the house for first aid. He was still grinning like an idiot. It was during the shaving and stitching process that I realised that under his fur The Monkey has a tattoo – an anchor surrounded by an octopus. I asked him when he had got that and he said that when he had been on the ship they had stopped in Jakarta and during their shore leave they had found an ex-US marine who had set up as a tattooist. They had already had much drink and it didn't take much persuading to get The Monkey into the chair. I suggested that I should shave him completely just in case there were more surprises. He called me a pervert and we had a couple of Jacks as I finished blanket stitching the wound.

Sky engineer turned up this evening. Guess The Monkey came off best...

6 February

The Monkey was a bit sore this morning. I asked him if he regretted pushing it so far yesterday and he gave me a look like I was stupid. 'Why would I do that?' he asked. I said that in hindsight it might have been better to stop before he had injured himself. Still, I got the idiot child look. He made himself some breakfast and I could see him thinking as he sat and ate it. When he had finished, he looked at me and said, 'I see the problem,' then followed it up with 'You're being a dickhead. Just because you struggle to live in the now doesn't mean we all have to worry about everything we do.'

I got a bit annoyed about that – probably because it is true – and said that it was okay for him as he is the incarnation of chaos. He just laughed at me and told me that was bollocks, why should that make a difference? I said that he was quite happy with uncontrolled change but that humans liked some order. This got a whole series of face pulling and laughter. 'Change is eternal!' he said. 'Nothing, and I mean nothing stays the same.' He then made some point about not waiting for perceived perfection but enjoying the true perfection of now. I pointed out that just sounded like an excuse to do whatever you want and damn the consequences and he said that sometimes that was the case but more often it was a case of doing what needed to be done at that moment, and if what needed to be done was to leap off the shed roof with a makeshift glider in a gale then that was fine. But what about the gash on his shoulder? 'So what? It will heal,' he replied.

I sat and thought about how much I had smiled yesterday watching him have fun and I knew he was right. When he hurt himself all the what ifs came crashing in and I realise now that they are only really part of the human mind and nothing to do with what is actually happening. I have resolved to try to live without worrying about the future and I think it is just in time as The Monkey has informed me that the men from the van have started to move into the house down the street. In The Monkey's words 'This means war.'

7 February

Been discussing with The Monkey what our tactics should be. I asked if we were going to break into the house, but The Monkey says it will only be a recon to try and gauge who they are. He wants them to come to us as he says that having them on our turf will be easier. Not sure about that but I think he has something in mind and he's holding off giving me the details at the moment.

I found my old copy of *The Dice Man* and gave it to The Monkey to read. Be interesting to see what he thinks of it after our conversation yesterday...

8 February

Went into the house last night. Well, The Monkey went into the house, I stayed outside and kept watch on the escape route. He said that I would make too much noise and not be much use. I objected to that, but he said that the only place I was a ninja was in my head. So, I crouched outside the back door while he slipped in through a kitchen window that was open just a couple of inches. Comes in handy having small hands, long arms, and a massively powerful grip if you are breaking and entering – apparently. Then he opened the backdoor a little so that he would have a clear exit if it all went tits up and I stayed there to make sure it didn't close.

The Monkey was in there for nearly fifteen minutes and I was starting to get anxious, and cold. Then he came slinking back through the shadows of the kitchen and indicated that he was going to lock the kitchen door again and get back out through the window. It all went smoothly, and we were back in our house a few minutes later. I cracked open the Jack while The Monkey lit up a cigar and told me what he had found. Seems they have very little stuff downstairs other than a couple of chairs and a TV. Upstairs is where the good stuff is. They had a bedroom each (The Monkey had sneaked a look and found them snoring on camp beds) and the third, biggest bedroom was filled with computer equipment and oscilloscope type displays. There was also a video camera on a tripod which The Monkey guessed they would use for recording reports if anything major happened. He followed a thick bundle of leads that led out through the bedroom door and then up through the loft hatch into the roof. He easily jumped up to the edge of the loft hatch using the doorframe for purchase and crouched there for a short while to make sure he hadn't been heard. Then he turned on the little Maglite he was carrying and had a good look at the new contents of the loft. He said that it was like a satellite TV convention – loads of dishes all pointing towards our house. He had seen enough then, so he lowered himself down from the loft and made his way downstairs. It was then that he noticed the boxes on the floor by one of the kitchen cabinets. It was an alarm system, brand new, and waiting to be installed. We were lucky to get in when we did, a day or two later and we would have triggered it off. Although The Monkey says there is no such thing as luck, just like there are no such things as coincidences, or free lunches. I asked him if there was any indication of who they were, but he said it was all rather sterile and looked a bit shiny to be the authorities.

Today The Monkey has been formulating a plan – which he still won't tell me. I'm sure he does it just to wind me up. So I just got on with some work and left him to it. Guess it's going to happen whether I know the details now or not...

9 February

The Monkey has stirred up the black hole. He threw a box into it that was full of meat and decorated on the outside with sigils and runes and occult diagrams (also some Mr Men stickers?). This while chanting some stuff he had discovered in one of his books. The hole has got a lot noisier, not back to the levels of New Year but it should attract some attention. All part of the plan apparently.

He has been thinking about the stuff in the van men's (must think of another name for them) loft. He says that having gone over what he saw he remembers that one of the dishes was pointing straight up rather than in the direction of our house. He wonders whether they have access to a satellite that can pick up activity from the black hole. It's quite possible although they would need some serious clout to get that. Once again – who are these people?

10 February

Went out for lunch at a pub by the beach and The Monkey explained his plan. We are going to lure them into our house when they believe we have gone away for a couple of days. The spare room door will be left unlocked and when they go in, we will have them trapped. The Monkey is a little fuzzy on the next part, but he says we will *persuade* them to leave us alone. I asked him if we would question them to find out who they are, and he said that might happen. This is set for the end of the week to give us time to let it circulate that we will be going on a trip and also to let the energy from the black hole build up enough to get the van men excited.

The Monkey told me he had finished *The Dice Man*. And? 'The guy is a pussy,' was the response. 'Why exactly is that,' I asked. 'Because he hands over responsibility to the dice. If he wanted to do something, then he should just do it? If it's going to happen it will and if not then so be it.' I told him that that was the point. It gave him freedom to act without worrying about the consequences. 'Yeah, he's a pussy. Should have just done it without the dice,' was his answer to that. I told him that he wasn't like humans – we generally don't work like that unless we are sociopaths or psychos. Then he wanted to know why it always had to be so extreme with humans, why we can't just do what we want without hurting others or getting so uptight? Over another pint we both agreed that people are pretty stupid. Then we went for a walk on the beach and built a sand mermaid with massive tits.

I asked The Monkey again what he meant by *persuading* the van men and he just said 'Whatever is necessary.'

Occasional rain — moderate or poor

11 February

Well, had a brief chat with the divorced woman a few doors up and happened to mention that we would be going away for the weekend. I know she likes to gossip so that should do the rounds nicely amongst the neighbours. The Monkey has been *feeding* the black hole as well – just throwing random objects into it really. Seems to be working though as it has started a sort of low-level throbbing that you can just about feel if you go into the room. He thinks that by the weekend the van men won't be able to contain themselves...

*

Came in to find The Monkey staring at the radio. He was listening to the shipping forecast on Radio 4 and he is convinced that they are giving out secret massages. I did my best to explain that it was just a weather and sea conditions forecast for fishermen but he looked at me as if I were some naïve fool and said that he would be listening carefully from now on, and taking notes. Why me?

13 February

The Monkey says that next door's dog overheard his owners talking to the divorced woman and she told them that we were going away for the weekend. She also said that she had been chatting with one of, 'The new men in the rented house,' which is great because she could easily have let slip that we are off somewhere. Oh, and apparently she thinks they are a pair of *poofs* based on the fact that they are two men living together. I have no idea what she must think of us then!

Spent a good part of today being taught capture and restraint techniques by The Monkey. He may not be very big, but he is very strong. I will have some bruises from that. He also took me through the use of night vision goggles this evening. We ended up running around the house pretending to be in *Silence of the Lambs*. Very funny...

14 February

Went to a military surplus store called The Bunker today because The Monkey didn't think I had enough black combat gear. He was right – I didn't have any! Now I am the proud (?) owner of black combat trousers, a black combat smock, a black tactical vest with more pockets than anything has got the right to possess and some combat boots. I asked The Monkey if all this was strictly necessary and he said that it was going to be dark and it was going to get a bit fighty – so yes, it was necessary. He gave a knowing look to the bloke behind the counter who nodded in agreement and mumbled something about, 'Getting some,' and then he and The Monkey shared a look that said they had been there, wherever *there* was.

Because it was so sunny we spent the afternoon in the back garden sharpening knives. Fortunately, we aren't overlooked by anyone other than our direct neighbours, and they were at work. After a while I asked The Monkey if the knives were going to be necessary and he gave me a despairing look and without a word took out his Glock 17 and started cleaning that. I am not a coward and I certainly don't mind a punch up but fucking hell this is going to get messy...

*

There is now a notebook and frantic scribbling involved in the midday shipping forecast. I get shushed at if I try to say anything as The Monkey frantically writes down every Biscay, Cromarty, Dogger and occasional rain – moderate or poor. I have even shown him a map of the fishing areas but to no avail, so I am leaving him to it as he compares his daily notes and highlights sections with a knowing look on his little furry chops...

15 February

So it's started then. We have left the house with bags packed and as much noise as possible and have driven about ten miles away to a caravan site owned by a friend. We will hang around here until it gets dark and then drive back in a borrowed car and sneak back into the house. Then the waiting begins...

16 February

Long boring night. We got back about eleven and left the car a couple of roads away from the house. We then sneaked in via the passage at the back of the houses and through the garden. Next door's dog was waiting by the fence and The Monkey had a quick word as I opened the back door. The dog said that no one had been round and that he would do his best to bark a warning if they showed up.

We settled in to wait in The Monkey's room which is at the back of the house. The Monkey thinks they will come in through the garden and back door rather than the front of the house, but we took turns to check on the front every now and then. At some point I fell asleep and woke up as the grey light of dawn was filtering in through the window to find the cat curled up on my lap and The Monkey still sitting by the window – he wasn't impressed with my inability to stay awake...

*

Little bastard! I have just seen myself in the mirror. While I was asleep The Monkey drew a monocle and a cock on my face with a sharpie and my combat blacks are covered in white cat hair. He thinks it's hilarious but says I need to stay awake tonight. Fucker...

17 February

Couldn't wash my face as The Monkey doesn't want us to run the taps as someone might notice the water going down the drain. Sharpie doesn't come off with wet wipes... Got most of the cat fur off with the sticky side of the gaffa tape – I know you don't get extra points for looking smart as you beat people but somehow it takes the edge off my inner warrior to be covered in fluff!

We spent the day avoiding going near the windows and eating the *rations* that didn't need cooking. Then we got some sleep to be ready for tonight.

It's a cloudless night out with a crescent moon and we are sat by the window again. Wait, next door's dog just barked – this could be it...

17 February

Holy crap! That wasn't at all what I was expecting...

The Monkey hid in the spare room and left the door slightly open while I hid in my bedroom opposite. I was straining to listen for sounds and wasn't sure if I could hear anything or whether it was just the blood thumping in my head. Then I heard footsteps on the stairs, and I gripped the extendable baton The Monkey had given me and got ready. Three figures came into view on the landing, the night vision goggles turning everything green. I wasn't expecting three and I had no way of warning The Monkey so just decided to go in as hard as possible. The figures stopped at the spare room door and looked at each other briefly before pushing it slowly open. As they filed in, I could see that they were armed – bollocks. Suddenly The Monkey dropped down from above the door and I saw a bright flash as he used the taser on the first man. I leapt out to get the last one going through the door but he span around with amazing speed and punched me in the face sending me back against my bedroom door frame. My night vision goggles flew off and I was left dazed and blind as a kick hit me across my right arm. I think what saved me was the drawings on my face. My attacker switched on a torch and pointed it in my face. I heard a grunt of surprise – he obviously wasn't expecting to see a badly drawn monocle and cock – and in that split second, I reflexively kicked him in the balls. He sagged down and I swung my numb right arm at him and connected across his face with the baton. He fell backwards onto his arse and I heard a dull phut sound and the middle of the three fell backwards onto the one I had just put down.

The Monkey turned on a torch and I could see that the one who had just fallen out of the spare room had a neat hole in his head just above his left eye. I looked at The Monkey and couldn't say anything. He just gave me a, 'Well what did you think was going to happen?' look and told me to help him pull the body into the spare room. When I was inside, I looked around for the first guy but he was nowhere to be seen. I looked at The Monkey and he nodded at the black hole that was pulsing rapidly. I guess a look of horror must have crossed my face then and The Monkey just told me to help him throw this body into it and not to be a pussy. I was acting on autopilot and did as he asked, watching with fascination as the vortex sucked the body into oblivion. Then The Monkey turned his attention to the third man who was beginning to come round. We dragged him into the room and shut the door then The Monkey slapped him across the face and told him to get to his knees. As the man got up it was clear that, like the second man, he was oriental possibly Japanese. The Monkey stood in front of him in the shadows and pointed the gun at his face then asked him who he worked for and why they were so interested in the black hole. The man just spat on the floor and glared at the gun. I shone my torch across them both and for the first time the man really saw The Monkey. He recoiled as if he had been hit again and pointed a trembling finger before screaming something in a language I didn't understand and pitching himself sideways into the vortex of the black hole. I stood in stunned silence as The Monkey lowered his gun. I asked what the man had screamed, and The Monkey looked into the black hole and said, 'He called me the Monkey God.'

*

Had a debrief with The Monkey. We don't think any of those three were the van men which means the van men must still be in their house. The fact that our intruders were carrying weapons (even though they didn't get a chance to use them) and the fact that one of them willingly threw himself into the black hole points to a more hard-core intent than we have seen from the van men. And what the hell was that *Monkey God* business?

We have to go into the van men's house. The Monkey wanted to go straight away but the adrenalin dump fucked me up and I persuaded him to wait until tonight. There might be more armed men in there and apart from that The Monkey was incredibly angry, and I think it would have just been a blood bath. So now we are sitting in our loft room watching their house through the Velux window and I am trying to reconcile the fact that three men died with the fact that they might have killed us. The Monkey is eating peperami...

Nerds!

18 February

We broke into the house at about 2am. I had asked The Monkey about the alarm system but when we got to the back door, he shone his torch through the window and we could see that the boxes were still on the floor. The window was shut this time but not latched and The Monkey slipped the blade of his combat knife into the gap and popped the window open and was quickly inside and opening the door for me. We checked the living room, but it was empty apart from beer cans and a pizza box so, with The Monkey taking the lead, we slowly climbed the stairs. At the top he signalled me to stop and pointed to one of the bedrooms. I could hear people talking and see a glow coming from under the door. The Monkey quickly checked the other bedrooms and the bathroom and indicated that they were all in the one room. The door opened and a man began to come through, half turning as he continued his conversation with whoever else was in the room, he didn't see us until it was way too late. The Monkey tasered him and he dropped like a sack of shit and then we were in the room and The Monkey had his Glock pointed at the second man, as I knelt on the chest of the first to keep him down, while pointing the Sig Sauer P320, that one of the home invaders last night had dropped, at his face.

The second guy went about as white as it is possible to go without turning into a snowman and started gibbering. The Monkey told him to shut the fuck up and to get on his knees on the floor. Then I dragged the first one over to the wall and cable tied his hands and feet and then did the same to the other one. As we stood waiting for number one to come round, I looked around the room at the computer equipment and monitors. Something didn't quite seem right. Although there was a fair bit of kit none of it seemed massively high end and a couple of the laptops had game stickers on them. Now both were conscious The Monkey started to question them. He asked who they worked for and if there were any more armed men who might come to the house. Both bound men looked at him in total confusion and abject fear. He took out his knife again and was advancing on them when I stopped him and asked if I could have a go at questioning them. He shrugged and sat on a swivel chair and picked his nails with the knife point, glaring at the two men. I squatted down beside them and asked what their names were. Kev and Tony came the answer. I asked why they had broken into our house and sent armed men in there. They both looked horrified and frantically denied doing anything of the sort. So, I asked them why they were monitoring our house and then the story came out.

It seems that they were three mates who were into ghost hunting and the paranormal. They had come to the village because of news reports about a big black cat that had been spotted in the fields opposite our house. When they had finished their fruitless search of the fields they had gone back to their van and found that their electromagnetic field detector had been left switched on and was going bonkers. They identified that the disturbance was coming from our house and decided to do some investigating. So, they went off and kitted out their van with whatever they could (mainly brought at an electrical wholesaler and cobbled together) and then parked over the road and began to monitor the disturbance. I asked them where the third member of the group was and they said that he had had some sort of fit and woken up around the corner in a pool of his own vomit. After that he had been really freaked out and had gone home to his parents (I glanced at The Monkey and wondered exactly what he had sedated the man with). After their van had been vandalised, they decided to rent the house so that they could stay there. I asked them who employed them and they said that they were all computer programmers who did freelance work writing apps and game stuff and that paid for them to be able to follow their all-consuming interest in the paranormal.

Nerds! We were being stalked by Nerds! What about the stuff in the loft? They said that the dishes were to amplify the EMF detectors' range and were for a bunch of other experimental measuring devices they had invented. So, what about the one pointed upwards? They both looked guilty and said that they had been stealing satellite TV –

mainly football and European porn it seemed. I sat back a bit stunned, then I took The Monkey downstairs for a chat. It was obvious that he had misinterpreted the technical equipment and he begrudgingly accepted that. I suggested that we could use the Nerds to do some research on the black hole for us and it might be to our advantage to have someone watching the house as we still had no idea who the armed men were. We argued for quite a while – The Monkey still wanted to execute them both, I think because he felt a bit silly for misreading their equipment. Eventually I calmed him down and we went back upstairs.

The Nerds looked pathetic. They had obviously overheard some of our argument and were shitting themselves in case the Monkey really decided to kill them. We cut them loose and told them that we would like them to research the black hole for us, as long as they said nothing to anyone else. The Monkey went to great lengths to explain to them that he would find them and kill them in horrible ways if they crossed us and they nodded until I thought their heads would fall off. Then they were pathetically grateful to us for the chance to study the black hole and only stopped short of hugging us when The Monkey drew his Glock again.

So, we have adopted some Nerds. They are coming over tomorrow to begin their research but right now we are back at the caravan site and after some shut eye, we will drive back home this evening to complete our alibi. We still don't know who the men that broke in were. I think I need to ask The Monkey some more questions when we get home…

19 February

Kev and Tony – the Nerds – came round this afternoon. Now we have seen them in daylight, not with torches shone in their eyes and begging for their lives, it is obvious that they are not threatening at all. Kev has shoulder length mousey brown hair and is quite rangy like someone who cycles or runs a lot, although I suspect it may be genetic as he doesn't look that coordinated. Tony, on the other hand is shorter, with dark curly hair, a straggly goatee, glasses, and is a bit chubby. They couldn't wait to see the black hole. In fact, they are still here. They have been more or less orgasmic about it and I think they are as grateful for being allowed access to it as they are at not being brutally murdered by The Monkey. No accounting for people's priorities really, are there…

They reckon that it is not a black hole as such but a portal to a different dimension and a massive argument developed between them which involved references to *Star Trek*, *Stargate*, *Quantum Leap*, *Adventure Time* and several other TV shows. It got very heated and The Monkey threatened to tase them or worse if they didn't stop. They then said that there had been a massive surge of activity on Saturday night and we explained that had been the three bodies going into it. They were surprisingly okay with it and me and The Monkey think that they are living this whole thing like it's one of their TV shows – whatever gets 'em through the night.

On the subject of our armed attackers the only real clue that we have is that the one who called The Monkey, Monkey God had used a Cambodian term. The Monkey is convinced that they were looking for something but not the black hole. He thinks that if it was them who broke in before, they must have thought that whatever it was they were searching for was in the spare room because it was securely locked. The Monkey is going to have a think.

In the meantime we have got a take away curry and some beers and when The Monkey has finished cross referencing his latest shipping forecast notes we are going to pry the Nerds away from the black hole/portal thingy and make sure everything is cool between us. I know The Monkey has reservations but even he can see the sense in having some dedicated dweebs doing the science for us...

20 February

The Monkey has been going through the few possessions he had when he came to me. They were all in a little leather satchel-type bag and consisted mainly of trinkets he had picked up in various ports and a knife. The only other thing was a small bundle wrapped in oil cloth and tied with a red, braided cord. The Monkey said that he had owned the bundle as long as he could remember and thinks he opened it a long time ago but wasn't interested in the contents. We laid the bundle on the table and after much fiddling undid the cord. Inside the oil cloth were fourteen narrow sticks, a bit like ice lolly sticks, honey brown in colour and marked with tiny writing and symbols and at each end of each stick was a symbol. No two sticks carried the same symbol at each end although the symbol at one end of a stick was repeated on the end of a different stick. I said that they looked a bit like I Ching sticks used for divination but that they would be impossible to read without knowing what the writing and symbols meant. We checked the inside/outside and strap of the bag and there was nothing there, so we went back over the contents of the bag again and the sticks were still the only things of any interest.

We are now drinking Jack and The Monkey is smoking a cigar as we look through a couple of heavy books on occult symbols and scour the web for anything that might resemble the writing. He had a few messages from Snakebite which had stacked up while we had been otherwise engaged and he scowled a bit as he was reading them. I asked if everything was okay and he said that he didn't like how much probing his internet chat buddy was doing, so he just made a few off-colour remarks and quit out of the message board.

The Nerds, wearing what I can only describe as Ghost Buster boiler suits, are trying to construct a measuring device that they could lower into the black hole. So far they have had a massive electric shock and attracted the attention of some sort of flying tentacle thing that tried to drag them through the hole. They are game I will say that for them, and it is giving us a good laugh...

21 February

Relaxed day today after all the stress of the last few days. The Monkey decided that he was going to teach me to shoot so we went up to the woods with his Glock and my Sig and shot some stuff. A lot easier than I thought it would be, except for the first couple of times when I didn't pull the slide back properly to chamber a round and managed to cause a jam. After that (and the general abuse that came with it) I was hitting targets all the time. I think The Monkey was impressed but of course wasn't going to show it.

After a morning of killing beer cans we found a pub and killed some more beer as well as some pasties. The Monkey had the pendant with him and thinks that it, or at least the image of him on it, has something to do with what is going on. Obviously, the armed men who broke in were not after the pendant because the first time they did so we didn't even have it. He wants to go back to the occult shop where we got it and ask the owner exactly who he brought it from, he also thinks we should show the owner the fourteen lolly sticks in case he has seen anything like them before.

22 February

Back to Boscastle today and the occult shop. We got there early, and the owner wasn't there so we had to go and find something to do while we waited. So, the Museum of Witchcraft beckoned, and we killed an hour in there. Some interesting stuff and certainly not twee and New Age. In fact some of it was totally full on. We even thought we might find something that looked like the lolly sticks but that would have been too good to be true. Had to stop The Monkey from stealing a few choice items though. He was quite prepared to smash the display cases to get at them and then make a break for it but I told him that if he did that we would have to do a runner from Boscastle before we had talked to the occult shop owner. Sense prevailed and we left the museum but I am sure there were some muttered promises to return under his breath.

Back in the occult shop, the owner was standing by the counter and we introduced ourselves and enquired if we could ask him about a few things. He led us into a back room, and we sat at a small table while The Monkey fired off questions. As we were told before, the pendant was part of a private collection brought at auction in Tiverton. The collection had come from a large country house on the edge of Dartmoor and apparently was sold by the widow of the collector. The shop's owner didn't know much more, and he kept eyeing The Monkey with something approaching awe. He gave us a business card with the address of the auction house and said that they should be able to supply us with more information about the seller even though it had been some time ago. Then we asked him if he had ever seen anything like the lolly sticks before. He unwrapped them and had a good look, but he too was at a loss as to their purpose. Like me he thought they might be some sort of divination tool but said he had never seen the symbols before or, in fact, anything quite like them. We thanked him and as we left the shop, he asked The Monkey if that really was his face on the pendant. The Monkey just jammed a cigar between his teeth and left the shop, I shrugged and thanked the owner again before following The Monkey.

The Monkey wanted to head straight off to the auction house but the opening times were on the back of the card and it wouldn't be open again until Tuesday so we made do with a trip to the pub...

23 February

The Monster Highs turned up this morning. Seems The Monkey had given them our address in case they fancied partying. Fair enough. The Nerds were here as usual, and I more or less had to pick their jaws up off the floor. I know the girls wear skimpy clothes, but I thought the Nerds might faint as all the blood seemed to go straight to their dicks.

*

Spent most of the day in bed, although I did get to ask The Monkey how his shipping forecast conspiracy theory was going and he said that it was bloody stupid and he didn't want to talk about it. I think one of the girls had asked him about it and pointed out the logical inconsistencies in his theory. He didn't smash anything up in a tantrum – it's nice to have females around...

*

The Nerds have come back with their electromagnetic testing thingy. Apparently, it is going mental and most of the paranormal action seems to be centred around the Monster Highs. I think it is time to explain that they are not strictly alive in the conventional sense of the word...

24 February

Didn't go completely to plan...

We were trying to explain to the Nerds what the Monster Highs were when we realised that we actually didn't know. So, we asked them to explain. Turns out they are ghouls which means they are somewhere between living and dead, and they feast upon the flesh of the newly dead. Yum. They can also see things in the living world and the spirit world. That little explanation completely freaked out the Nerds (too much *Walking Dead* I think) and they had to go home. Still think the girls are hot, although obviously not in the warm to the touch sense. I think that all this time with The Monkey has somewhat warped my idea of normal.

The girls said they had a confession to make and admitted they knew we would be at the club that first night we met. How? Something about a glitch in the Matrix or ripple in the Force or some such other weirdness. Anyhow, they knew we would be there and wanted to get reacquainted. Yep, the use of the word *reacquainted* made us both sit up and take notice. They explained that we have known them before – a very long time ago – and that they have been waiting for us to reappear. I told them that, to be honest, if I had ever seen them before it would have been branded into my brain for no other reason than they are so damn sexy, but The Monkey just looked at me and said, 'They mean another life.' I tried to get more details out of them but there was an increase in the hum coming from the spare room and the girls asked if they could go and have a look. So that's where they are while me and The Monkey sit drinking JD and try to make sense of this latest bit of information...

*

The girls went home this morning, but they spent a couple of hours sitting and staring into the black hole last night. I asked them what they saw and they both said at exactly the same time, 'Infinity.' We asked them about the lolly sticks as well in case they had ever seen their like before, but they said they hadn't although they said that they had an interesting glow that extended into the spirit world. I also tried again to get further details about this *known them before in a previous life* bombshell but I just got cryptic smiles and French kisses then I watched them drive off in their red Lancia Delta with the very heavily tinted windows.

The Nerds came back round this afternoon and apologised for being rude, but it really was the first time they had come face to face with any overtly supernatural beings. We told them it was cool and that the Monster Highs hadn't taken offence – they would have known if they had – then they went back up to the spare room with their latest monitoring device and tried to get some readings while not killing themselves...

Going, going, gone!

25 February

Quiet day today. The Monkey has been pacing about with impatience. He wants to go to the auction house, but we have to wait until tomorrow and it's driving him nuts. I have been trying to do some work and he has been vindictively sabotaging the Nerds to pass the time. I feared one or both of them might die as he set up trip wires, balanced heavy things on the top of doors and generally made a nuisance of himself. The Nerds laughed good humouredly and did their best to avoid the booby traps with the minimum of blood loss – to be honest they are more than a little scared of The Monkey and I think they fell over a couple of times just to keep him happy.

He is now in front of the TV with a bottle of Jack and a cigar watching *Allo, Allo*. He hasn't got a clue what's going on but keeps making little grunty amused noises and I don't think he has lowered his eyebrows for the last half hour...

26 February

The Monkey couldn't wait to get to the auction house today so consequently we were there 45 minutes early and then I had to sit in the car with him while he fidgeted. Eventually they opened up and we went inside and found someone who looked like they might be able to help. After explaining what we wanted, they said they didn't normally give out client's details but because we were after background on a specific piece we had brought they were willing to help. There then followed a half hour wait as they hunted through records and finally they came up with the goods – but they said that they would phone the client first to make sure that she was okay with us being given her info. So, another wait while they went off and did that. I could tell that The Monkey wasn't going to take it lying down if we were told no, and I asked him if he wanted me to go and start the car for a quick getaway. He called me an idiot and then was just in the middle of telling me that actually it might be a good idea when the man came back and said that the lady had agreed to see us and then he gave us a post-it note with the address written on it. So, we pointed the car in the direction of Totnes and set off.

After getting lost several times and reversing down a very narrow farm track for about a mile we finally found the house; a big, rambling place that had seen better days. Having rung the bell I was waiting for a warty old butler to answer the door but instead a mousey middle-aged woman appeared and said that her aunt was waiting for us in the drawing room. She led us to the door and then left us to go in. The Monkey stared around the room suspiciously and asked me where the *drawings* were, I said I would tell him later. Waiting for us was the seller of the collection. She greeted us with a degree of suspicion and when we asked her if she had any information on the pendant she stared at The Monkey for a long while and then slowly nodded her head.

She was an old lady and in need of the money that the collection fetched in order to help with the upkeep of the house. Apparently, her husband had taken himself off to remote corners of the world in search of occult artefacts and any slight rumour had been enough to set him off, leaving his long-suffering wife to raise two children and manage the house. In the early 1970s he had heard tales of occult treasures in Cambodia and despite the war going on in Vietnam he managed to get himself smuggled into the country and come out again with a small collection of esoteric objects. One of these was the monkey pendant. Many of the other pieces were far more valuable and complex but the pendant had fascinated him. One of the reasons, his wife said, was because it was carved from moldavite, a substance like green molten glass that is believed by some to be the result of an impact between a meteorite and the earth. But moldavite is only found in one place in the Czech Republic and is almost never carved, so the pendant's presence in Cambodia and its decoration had thrown her husband into a frenzy of research. The link with moldavite to all manner of mystical powers and a belief by some that it was the material of the Holy Grail had resulted in almost thirty years of obsession.

In his later years her husband had become reclusive and after his children left home, spent most of his time in one or two rooms in a wing of the house. One morning as they sat having breakfast (one of the few times in the day she saw him) he suddenly fell face first into his porridge and was pronounced dead of a brain haemorrhage by the coroner. She had no love for his occult obsessions and had quickly sold off the books and manuscripts that had filled his rooms. When she realised that there were ready buyers for this type of stuff she moved on to the charms and other paraphernalia which included a large collection of crystals and the pendant. The Monkey asked her if she had any idea where in Cambodia he had obtained the pendant but she just shook her head. 'Had he left any journals?' The Monkey asked. Oh yes, she replied but she had burnt them in a fit of pique, blaming her husband's obsession on the loneliness of her marriage and his subsequent death. At this point I thought The Monkey might be about to kill or at the very least fling shit about, so I thanked her very much for her time and we headed for the door.

The Monkey sat and fumed on the way back and when we got home he disappeared into the back garden and threw knives and axes at a tree stump for an hour before coming back in and punching one of the Nerds in the balls. He has now gone up onto the roof to smoke and glare at the world...

27 February

Amazing! Found Kev playing with the lolly sticks on the kitchen table. He was putting the symbols that matched on the end of the sticks together and after doing that for a short while he began to cross the sticks so that the symbols still touched but he could join them up with other symbols. He looked a bit confused for a moment and then began to make a second pile of crossed symbols until he had two seven-pointed star shapes. At this point Tony came in carrying a laptop and something on the end of a long coil of cable. He stopped by Kev and watched over his shoulder. 'Can you weave them together then the ends would still touch and they wouldn't fall apart?' he volunteered. Kev nodded enthusiastically and began to dismantle his creations and remake them by overlapping the sticks. Then The Monkey came in and gave me a look that said, 'And why are they touching those?' but I held up my hand and signalled him to watch. After a few minutes Kev had constructed two seven pointed stars that didn't fall to bits when he held them up. But the really odd thing was that when he brought them close together, they repelled each other like the same poles of two magnets and the omnipresent electromagnetic field detector on Tony's bat utility belt went ape shit...

*

I have been having some curious black windows pop up on the laptop for the past week. I hadn't worried about them because they appeared and disappeared so rapidly, I thought it was just some background processes kicking off when the laptop was booted up, and there is very good anti-virus software loaded so I figured it was not an issue. But this morning I asked Tony to switch it on as he was walking past, and he stopped dead and said, 'Ah fuck. You have been hacked.'

Tony and Kev spent the rest of the day recovering as much as they could from the laptop, but they say that we either need to bin it or reformat it completely as whoever has gained access has been using the camera and microphone to spy on us and has been cloning what is on the screen. The Monkey asked how that is possible as we run decent security software, but the Nerds just shrugged and said that it if someone really wants in and you give them a way then etc etc... I told them that I had only noticed it about a week ago and The Monkey looked at me and grabbed the laptop and said, 'Mutha fucker!' He opened up a folder he had created for stuff he had saved from his chats online and then showed us a jpeg that had been sent to him by Snakebite. It was an advert for a gun range in Vegas and featured a well-endowed blonde in a bikini holding two machine guns at a jaunty angle. There was a QR code in the bottom right corner for you to scan for extra information. Kev pointed his phone camera at it and suddenly we were on the laptop screen in all our confused glory...

Kev has run the jpeg through some software, and it seems that the image contains a shit load of hidden code that basically provided a backdoor into our computer. The Monkey wants to keep up the pretence of not being aware of it but the Nerds reckon that we have already given the game away and the best course of action is to bin the laptop – just in case. Great, now we need to worry about who the fuck Snakebite is and what we might have given away...

28 February

A long cardboard tube turned up in the post today for The Monkey. I handed it over to him and after popping the cap on one end he produced several rolled-up maps. I looked over his shoulder as he unravelled them – Thailand, Cambodia, and Vietnam. The pendant has raised questions that The Monkey is going to want answers to...

1 March

Working on one of the Nerds' spare laptops we did research on seven pointed stars today or septagrams/ heptagrams as they are called. Loads of stuff about alchemy, occult groups, druids, Knights Templar, sheriff's badges and flags but nothing about two wooden stars made of lolly sticks that repulse each other and cause the black hole in our spare room to flare and pulse alarmingly if brought anywhere near it.

We are currently sitting in the living room drinking 1979 Colheita port and eating cheese and onion crisps because we have no Stilton and have run out of cheese of any sort. The Monkey says it could have been worse, we could have only had Dairylea Dunkers. I suppose he has a point...

2 March

Beautiful weather today so we had a day off from research and went for a walk on the cliffs. Kev and Tony came with us and we bought them ice creams. The Monkey has warmed to them slightly after they managed to assemble the stars and identify that we had been hacked, and I felt confident that he would not try and *accidentally* push one over the edge. They are not bad lads and their constant chatter about *Star Trek*, *Star Wars*, *Dr Who*, *Buffy the Vampire Slayer*, etc is actually quite amusing. They are both obviously highly intelligent, they just have underdeveloped social skills from mixing within the same social group since they were teenagers. Even The Monkey has begun to find their conversations and arguments funny and will often drop something contentious into the mix to set them off. He says he wants to get then really really drunk or stoned or both and see what happens. Actually, I would like to see that as well.

The Nerds have said that the other member of their troop is feeling well enough to return so we could soon have a third nerd working for us. Have to hope that he doesn't get flashbacks...

*

Odd news report on the internet today. Seems that some pagan goth sorts up in Nottingham have been arrested for the cannibalism of newly buried bodies which they have been digging up. The photos of the three looked familiar and I showed them to The Monkey which made him laugh outrageously. He thinks it's the losers that the Monster Highs bit when we were up at the party in Nottingham. I think he may be right in which case the Monster Highs are contagious. Have to make sure they don't bite during sex or we could end up snacking on *mortuary takeaway* as The Monkey put it. Have to add that to the list of things to ask them about that next time we see them...

3 March

Woaw! Just seen one of the neighbours and he asked me if I had noticed any dodgy looking Orientals hanging around. At first I thought he was talking about our visitors of the other week but he said there had been a car with three or four oriental men in it spotted around here over the last few days. I said that he was probably being a bit racist and that I hadn't seen anything, and it was probably nothing. He reluctantly agreed but said that another neighbour had notified the police just in case. Fuck!

The Monkey says he is not too surprised, there was always a very strong chance they would come looking for their buddies, plus whatever is going on is doubtless bigger than three people. Guess I hadn't considered that, I just wanted it to go away. The Monkey has fetched out his weapons and is talking about giving the Nerds a crash course in combat principles. They look quite excited by the prospect but I think that is the enthusiasm of men who watch too many action movies, played too much COD, have run through too many heroic what if scenarios in their heads, and have no experience of real fights. Anyway, I have asked Kev to dismantle the stars, they are going to be easier to hide if they are not bouncing away from each other, and we are convinced now that whoever these people are, they want the stars...

Do you want to buy a second hand caravan?

4 March

We have shuffled the lolly sticks and split them into two groups, The Monkey is keeping one and I have the other (there's not many occasions you can say that in a sentence!). We figure it is the best way to keep them safe.

The Monkey took us all for basic combat training this morning and it quickly became obvious that although the Nerds knew lots of martial arts terms and the names of different guns and knives, they had never ever hit anyone in anger. If they are to join in this carnival of violence they had better get it straight, and quick. They say they want to help but I am not sure they really understand.

This afternoon they are back to what they do best – risking their health in the name of science by hurling homemade monitoring devices into the black hole. The Monkey has stationed himself by the loft window to keep an eye out for the car full of Orientals and I am checking out the cost of flights to Cambodia on the newly acquired laptop...

5 March

Pretty uneventful today. Tried to do some work while The Monkey intermittently studied his maps and spent time watching from the loft window. He hasn't got a great deal of patience.

Think we will go to the pub in a bit to break the boredom. Just have to hope The Monkey doesn't pick a fight...

6 March

The Monkey had a pretty bad hangover this morning. We didn't go to our local last night but instead ended up in town. There were a few stag parties around and we managed to join in with a group of lads for a while. I had already decided that I was going to attempt to stay relatively sober just in case The Monkey did decide to kick off. In the end we managed to have a good night without any damage other than to The Monkey's liver.

The third nerd has arrived, still wearing the Atari T-shirt, although it had been washed. His name is Dave and I felt slightly guilty meeting him after having been partially responsible for him believing he'd had a seizure. The other two got him up to speed pretty quickly and his face was a mixture of raw terror and childish excitement as they showed him the black hole and explained about the lolly stick stars, the Orientals and the Monster Highs. I thought he was going to shit himself when The Monkey, cigar between teeth, came strolling in and just looked at him before heading to the kitchen.

I have found some cheap flights to Cambodia and now we just need to decide when to go. The Monkey would leave tomorrow but we need to sort a few things out first – not least our oriental friends. I don't really want them wrecking the house while we are away, and it would be unfair to leave the Nerds to face them given that the last lot were armed. The Monkey wants me to ask the neighbours if they have spotted them again and also what sort of car they were in. I will go and do that in a bit. He is cooking something up, he has that look, and he is impatient to go to Cambodia...

7 March

Neighbours told me that the Orientals had been spotted two days ago driving a beat-up silver BMW. The Monkey is pleased with this intel and is heading off to scout the area...

*

I can hear sirens and there is smoke in the distance in the direction of the woods. One of the Nerds says they heard a noise like a distant explosion a while ago. I don't know where The Monkey is, and I have a bad feeling...

*

I found The Monkey lying in some undergrowth at the side of the road. If he hadn't feebly managed to wave at me, I would have missed him.

It seems he spotted the Orientals and followed them to a clearing in the woods where a caravan was parked. He watched and waited for a while and then decided *fuck it* and lobbed one of his IEDs through a window. The caravan went boom, far more than The Monkey had anticipated (he thinks there was a Calor Gas bottle in there along with munitions) and he got caught in the blast. Mainly concussion and a few burns, I think. He refuses to go to the hospital as he says there would be too many questions. The suggestion of going to the vet, which I made from a safe distance with a large grin on my face, was met with a torrent of abuse, and fortunately there was nothing at hand to throw, not even shit on this occasion. Anyway, the Orientals are toast.

I have patched him up as best I can, and given his awesome recuperative powers I think he should be okay in a few days. Close one though – didn't realise how much the thought of losing him would affect me...

8 March

The Monkey is singed and sore today. His head seems okay although he has a pounding headache but like he says, 'That's what happens when you get blown up!'

Probably unfair of me to ask while he has a bad head but as he isn't about to run off, I thought I would ask him a question that hasn't really occurred to me before. I asked him why his previous companion had given him to me? Couldn't he take the stress and lunacy anymore, and was I at some point going to have to do the same thing for the sake of my own sanity? The Monkey thought for a little while and when he answered he looked genuinely sad. He said that his previous companion had contracted an illness and they both knew he was going to die before too long; this had been about the time when The Monkey had realised that he had to be somewhere other than on board a ship for the rest of his days. The other man hadn't wanted to give him up but he knew that The Monkey needed someone else and so at The Monkey's suggestion they had found someone (me) and we had played Othello to determine whether I was a worthy companion. It struck me that I had never asked why Othello? The Monkey said that there was something about the game that he could not explain but that the way I had played had told them all they needed to know.

I have left The Monkey to sleep but I do keep wondering, one day will I be playing against someone else for him and hoping they win...

9 March

The Monkey is feeling a bit better today – I've had to keep him away from the Jack.

We have been watching local news reports and it seems that the police think that the caravan was being used by a terrorist cell who accidently blew themselves to bits. Fair enough. It keeps the authorities away from us and might just dissuade any others from coming if they think the police are on the lookout for them. The Monkey is quite pleased with himself...

10 March

Forced the Nerds to watch the three hours of UFC with us and drink a lot. We dragged them out lunchtime as well and rounded off a nice carvery with several pints. Kev is doing quite well, and Dave is giggling at everything but Tony has passed out in the corner after throwing up in the garden. We have propped him up so that he doesn't choke, and The Monkey has drawn a massive wang across his face – I sympathise. I wasn't sure The Monkey should be drinking but he told me to fuck off and proceeded to down several pints of Guinness. He got a few odd stares in the pub as he has a couple of sizeable scorch marks on his fur but apart from that he seems pretty much none the worse for wear. He has just fetched the Jack, and Kev has suddenly got a worried look on his drunken face. Must admit that I feel fairly pissed and The Monkey is wobbling quite a bit. Have to hope I don't pass out before him – need to visit my accountant in the morning and I would rather not do it with genitals and swear words daubed all over my face...

Yellow fever

11 March

Very messy yesterday.

I survived without getting graffiti all over my face, mainly because The Monkey was so busy persecuting the Nerds even before they passed out. Kev actually looked like Papa Lazarou by the time The Monkey had finished – that is going to take some serious scrubbing to remove and I think quite a lot of skin will come with it. Ouch! Dave got off very lightly, being black The Monkey could not use Sharpies on him, so he contented himself with shaving his eyebrows off. I think he has a pass at the moment after being so heavily drugged by The Monkey on their first encounter. Anyway, we managed to avoid loads of vomit in the house although the garden looked a proper mess especially as it was very cold last night, and the puke all froze. Nice treat for the birds...

Saw my accountant (had to wear shades though as my head was banging, think he may have thought it was some random fashion statement) and worked out that I can disappear for an unspecified number of weeks to South East Asia and put most of it through my business. Result! When I got back, I told The Monkey the good news and he managed a grin even though he is in a pitiful state. I still think he is suffering from the concussion of the explosion and having a massive hangover is not the best thing. There has been a lot of lying down in the dark done by all concerned today...

12 March

Went to the Bunker again today. The Monkey said it would be the best place to get *gear* for our trip. The dude behind the counter looked at him and said, 'Get caught in a blast?' The Monkey nodded, and they just shared another one of those been there, done that looks and the guy tapped his leg which made a hollow, metallic sound. Where do these fucking people come from? We bought several items including small camo day sacks, a couple of new machetes, various bits of webbing, new boots for me, lightweight combat trousers and smocks and a couple of bottles of 100% Deet for the mozzies. The Monkey says he will order some more stuff online and some other kit we will pick up *in country* – this I am guessing is the sort of stuff that would get us arrested if we carried it across borders.

I have booked open tickets for our flights as we have no idea how long we will be out there but we are flying from Heathrow to Kuala Lumpur and then to Phnom Penh on April 1st (seemed fitting), and then we will see what happens...

*

The Monkey is outraged that we have to pay for travel insurance. I don't think he can separate it from the on-line adverts and phone calls we get stating *You may have been in an accident...* and then attempt to convince you that for the good of all concerned you need to litigate and give them 60% for the privilege.

Then he stomped into the kitchen, aiming a swing at a frantically dodging Tony as he passed, and marched back into the living room and slammed a bottle of tequila onto the table. A little pain relief perhaps?

14 March

So, the Nerds have assembled a ring of monitoring devices around the edge of the black hole. They are sure that there is something on the other side that is moving and testing the boundaries of the opening. They don't think that it can get through at the moment, but it is definitely looking. Oh, and Kev's face is still quite Sharpie stained.

Meanwhile The Monkey has found the Pogues on my iPod and is ripping the living room up to *The Sick Bed of Cuchulainn*. He does a mean jig especially when he is powered by Jack. If you can't beat 'em join 'em. He is singing loudly – something about devils with bottles and dreaming of foreign lands. That seems strangely prophetic...

15 March

Booked in with the practice nurse at the docs to get a whole raft of vaccinations. The Monkey laughed at me until I told him he would need a Yellow Fever vaccination certificate or they wouldn't let him across borders in the region – not so cocky now, is he.

*

The Nerds have had a lovely day measuring electrical field disturbances emanating from the black hole. There has been much heated debate amongst them as to the possibility that it is a form of corridor between different locations in space, I heard the word *Stargate* used on several occasions with absolutely no irony. The other current contender is the possibility that it is a door between different dimensions. Much babbling about string theory and quantum foam along with references to film and TV programmes. Me and The Monkey hung in there for as long as possible then we came down to the living room to look at maps and watch *Total Wipeout*...

16 March

Oh England, what have you done... The Monkey had money on you winning the rugby and the ensuing drunken carnage was terrible to behold. He has no bias as far as nationalities are concerned but he doesn't take losing very well and several gloating South Africans in the pub couldn't take a hint and will be very sore tomorrow. Managed to get him out of town before the police turned up, and I let him have a proper simian fit on the beach in the rain until he was calm enough to get on a bus. Fortunately, one look at The Monkey was enough to keep the Nerds from saying anything stupid and getting themselves savaged. I wouldn't mind but The Monkey couldn't care less about rugby – he likes the inherent violence but apart from that he doesn't give a fuck.

He appears to have passed out now so I think I will shave some swear words on his back...

17 March

Had a sudden horrible thought today – The Monkey hasn't got a passport! He got to Amsterdam on a merchant ship, he got back to the UK with me on the ferry and no one asked for anything then, but if we are going to get on an airplane at Heathrow, he is going to need paperwork – and it's only two weeks away! Ah! Blind panic! (The fact that he is a monkey doesn't really enter into it – no one seems to care about that.)

So I looked on the internet to see how quickly we could get him a passport and it seems if we drove to the nearest passport office and paid extra we could get him one in time but, and it's a big but, he is not a British national so that causes all sorts of problems. I grabbed The Monkey and explained, or rather shouted the situation at him. The Monkey just gave me a look and went to his room and after a few minutes came back with four passports, one UK, one Thai, and two Canadian. Seems a *friend* has a useful line in fake documents and The Monkey has had these for a while *just in case*. I asked him why two Canadian passports and he handed one to me with my face in it. 'Just in case,' he said. And why Canadian, I asked? No one bothers with Canadians was the answer...

The glowing eyes

18 March

The Monkey is so bored! He really can't wait to go, and the thought of two more weeks is driving him insane. I told him to go and do some more research on the internet to give us some info on where we are going but he says he doesn't want to read anymore, he just wants to get in amongst it. I have been trying to do some work but it's hard to concentrate when you keep getting shot by paint balls or air soft pellets and the bruises were beginning to mount up. In the end I suggested that The Monkey show me how to throw a knife and he warmed to that idea pretty quickly. I didn't realise how dangerous rebounds can be and after getting one in the top of my foot I wished I had stuck to the paint balls but The Monkey thought it was great fun and told me I would try harder next time.

Well, I'm not sure I tried harder, but it turned into a game of lethal hopscotch and eventually I started to get them to stick in the target more or less where I was aiming.

That killed a few hours and now, cigar in mouth and Jack in hand, The Monkey has gone upstairs to persecute the Nerds. Maybe I can finish this work...

19 March

Today we reassembled the stars. The Nerds wanted to do an experiment with them and the black hole. Holy fuck...

One star on either side of the black hole caused it to bulge outwards as if it was prolapsing. Lightning crackled around its event horizon and we began to see things within the darkness as if looking at a black mirror that was reflecting something that wasn't there. Impossibly tall mountains and clouds of fire and gigantic spikes of what looked like stained glass and things that I can't even put a name to. The Monkey sat fascinated, staring into the void until eventually something massive and formless came rushing towards us. At that point the Nerds' bottle finally went and they ran out of the room taking the stars with them. The black hole collapsed back in on itself with a sound like a massive crack of thunder and a blast wave propelled me and The Monkey into the far wall. It must have been a few minutes before we came round and found ourselves out on the landing where the Nerds had dragged us. They had dismantled the stars again and were gibbering about screaming coming from the Monkey's room. We went in and there was no noise but immediately we all saw that the eyes on the monkey pendant, which hangs above his bed, were glowing like miniature suns.

We are all sitting in the living room now having a debrief to try and make sense of what we saw. It seems we all saw similar things but depending on where we were in the room, we each saw something slightly different as if we were looking through a series of prisms. The Jack is out and there are some frayed nerves that need calming. The Monkey is rolling a massive spliff *to take the edge off things*. Ah well...

20 March

Bad dreams last night... Dark, dark jungle. Overwhelming insect buzz. The burning eyes of the monkey pendant. A strange, plastic-faced (that is the only way I can describe him), grinning figure in a grey suit. And lots of explosions. The Monkey had similar dreams except his were full of blood.

When we spoke to the Nerds their dreams featured visions of the black hole and something trying to get out of it, but they all saw the grinning, grey suited figure. They have decided to take the day off from research and get their heads straight – they look pretty spooked.

The monkey pendant is still blazing away like a bastard and I have no idea where this is going to lead now so I am going to get drunk with The Monkey and hope that I don't dream tonight...

21 March

The Monkey is back into his books today. Possibly a bit of a backlash from the last couple of days but he has been calmer and more thoughtful. On his reading list today has been the *Lonely Planet Guide to Cambodia*, several books on Cambodian temple sites, *Knife Fighting and Knife Throwing for Combat*. He also appears to be trying to grow a moustache! Is that even possible? I am not sure...

We talked about the possibility of tracing this Snakebite dickhead who hacked us but Dave reckons that it would be almost impossible as The Monkey was talking to him via a Tor browser that routes through different locations all over the globe. Almost impossible, unless you are part of the military-industrial complex apparently. Dave quoted cases proving that the CIA, NSA, GCHQ, et al is indeed watching the dark web and is using it for its own covert purposes. So, the Nerds are back at work in the spare room, but more cautious and subdued. They are talking about working out a way of locking the black hole so that nothing can get through – some sort of trans dimensional kids stair gate. Not sure how that's going to pan out, but it should keep them occupied and at least they aren't so freaked that they didn't want to come back. They still had bad dreams last night although me and The Monkey drank ourselves into oblivion and if I dreamt, I don't remember it...

24 March

Still another week to go before we fly, and The Monkey has had us in the woods again shooting at stuff. This time the stuff was army style human targets like you see on all the best cop shows and military shooting ranges. He had set them up at different locations throughout the woods and the object was to make our way through the area shooting the targets as we went. Great fun! But there was a twist. The Monkey had hidden flash bangs on the ground and when I asked him why, he said that as we were going off the beaten track, we would also have to look out for mines left over from the wars. This was news to me. So, we sat on a tree stump and had a long conversation about landmines and booby traps as much as forty years old that could be lying in wait for us as we go temple hunting. The Monkey's mentality is that as long as you look where you're walking you will be okay. Okay... In the first twenty minutes of our stroll through the woods I detonated seven flash bangs. 'You'll get better,' he said – I'd fucking better...

Euler's identity

25 March

Did a little better this morning and only set off two flash bangs the whole time we were out – The Monkey says I would probably have just lost part of a leg and my balls. Yay me...

*

We have just had a call from the old lady who auctioned the monkey pendant (I forgot I had given her a business card). Seems that last week some strange shit happened in her mansion – stuff flew off shelves, ornaments exploded, and there was a lot of weird screaming. While they were cleaning up the mess, they found a document case stuck to the wall at about head height. When the old lady opened it, she realised it contained one of her husband's journals, and she spent the next few days debating whether to burn it or to give us a call. In the end she decided to call, so we are going to see her tomorrow to pick up the journal. The Monkey is most pleased and excited and consequently we are having a celebratory drink – again...

26 March

Back to the mansion we went. Once again, the mousy niece answered the door and led us without comment to the drawing room where the old lady waited for us. When we entered, she was standing with her back to us gazing out of the French doors at the sweep of garden beyond. It has been a cold day and she had a thick shawl pulled tight around her thin shoulders; the room was not very warm at all despite the fire blazing away in the huge fireplace. She continued to stare out at the garden and after a couple of minutes The Monkey, with his customary impatience, coughed loudly. The old lady jumped slightly as if she really had been unaware of our presence and as she turned towards us, we saw that she was hugging a rather worn leather document case to her chest along with the shawl. I felt The Monkey start to move forward and I put my hand on his shoulder to keep him calm. The old lady stared at him and I am sure that she shivered, then very slowly she held the case out for him to take. He shrugged my hand off his shoulder and moved forward to take it. The old lady drew her hand back quickly to avoid touching him and pulled her shawl tighter around her shoulders. The Monkey began to open the ties on the case immediately and it was left to me to say thank you. I asked why she had decided to give us the journal rather than burn it as she had the others, and she said that she had really wanted to but for some reason she couldn't and her dreams had become full of The Monkey's face with burning eyes. I thanked her but she said that she didn't want our thanks; just to never see us again. The Monkey gave her a sidelong look and we made our exit, and as we drove away, I could see the two women in the rear-view mirror as they watched us from a window until we turned along the drive and the house was obscured by trees.

We stopped at a pub to get some lunch and over a pint had a look at the journal. Lots of hand drawn maps and sketches along with copious notes but as we got further into the journal the writing became an unintelligible foreign script. I glanced at The Monkey and it was obvious that he was capable of making some sense of it. He looked back at me and said that it would take some time, but he thought he could work out what it said. As the food arrived, he unfolded a larger map that had been glued in to the book and we looked at it as we ate. The map seemed to be an area of the border between Cambodia and Vietnam and was marked with various symbols and more foreign script in the same small, neat hand as the rest of the journal. As he traced his finger along the lines of the map, I looked through the leather case, and in a pocket I found an old, tatty manila envelope, there was a small wad of photographs inside. They were dog eared and faded but I could make out various shots of a group of men, obviously in South East Asia. A few were relaxed, almost touristy type pictures, but most were in jungle clearings with overgrown temple buildings and featured a few local bearers. On the back of each photo was a date and note as to where it was taken along with the initials – obviously of those in the photo – in the same neat hand as the notebook. In one group photo a tall man in military gear, a cigar in the corner of his mouth, stood at the back gazing off into the trees, while at the other end of the row was a figure with a smooth, out of focus face, except for the weird grin that seemed to split his lower face in two. I felt my stomach lurch as if I had just gone over the edge on a roller coaster. I put the photo on the table and quickly went through the others. The same man was in several of them and in each shot he was slightly out of focus as if he was moving quickly. Then I got to the last photo. This one was larger and had been folded down the middle. I couldn't make sense of it at first because I was no longer looking at jungle photos, this one was quite obviously of the American Civil War. A group of men who looked like cavalry officers, sat on folding chairs in front of a tent, a Confederate flag flying in the background. Someone had drawn a circle in ink, now almost invisible, around one of the heads – a smooth, slightly out of focus head, split by an insane grin. I turned the photo over and in a different hand was written *Shiloh, April 6th, 1862* but beneath that in the neat writing of the notebook *AW?* I looked back through the photos and AW's initials appeared on the back of every photo with the out of focus man. I suddenly became aware that The Monkey was staring at me and I pushed the photos over to him with a shaking hand and told him that the man in the photos looks like the man from my bad dreams. What the absolute fuck?

I showed the Nerds the photos when we got back, and they all agreed that AW looks like the dude in their bad dreams. Like Tony said, 'It's not as if he did anything – he was just creepy and somehow menacing with that fucked up face,' we all agreed with that. None of us can explain the Civil War picture, maybe it's one of his ancestors? Then Kev ran off and came back a few minutes later, clutching a sheet of paper. He had printed out the Vegas gun range jpeg that had caused the hacking of our laptop, and now he put it on top of the collection of photos and pointed to the row of grinning men in the background. And there he was, his face somehow out of focus but grinning even harder than the others, AW. We went through all the other photos again and agreed that, ignoring the Civil War picture, he would be in his 90s if it was the same man in the jungle shots. A relative maybe? And is he The Monkey's dark web chat buddy Snakebite? Tony said that it felt like we were being forced along a path that we couldn't see. The Monkey grunted some obscenity I didn't quite catch but ended with something about skull fucking him if he ever caught up with him. Dave was staring at the photos and I could clearly see goose bumps raised on his arms. He looked up as if coming out of a dream and said, 'Maybe it's hitsuzen.' We all looked at him and when he didn't explain The Monkey said, 'It means inevitable, a state in which all other outcomes are impossible,' he was reading from a Google search on my phone, and then he said, 'Well, it's more likely than coincidence...'

The Monkey disappeared up to his room for a couple of hours and he has just come down to the living room very excited. There is a double page of the journal that was stuck together, and he has managed to separate it. Drawn across the pages is a sketch of a jungle temple with an enormous carved monkey head and either side of it are what look like seven pointed stars. The cigar is lit, and the Jack is out, and the Nerds have just come in with a

Chinese takeaway – happy days...

27 March

Well, looks like our temple of choice is in the region depicted in the map that is stuck in the book. The Monkey has been working hard to translate the markings and text around the map. I asked him if it wouldn't be better to start at the beginning of the journal and find out what all the other stuff is about, including the geometric symbols that have been carefully drawn on some of the pages, but all I got was a, 'Yeah, yeah, I'll get round to that.' Seems that some of the markings on the map represent mine fields and there are a lot of them around the temple – good thing I've been practising getting blown up, wouldn't want to look like a complete beginner when I get vaporised...

*

The Nerds are making some progress with their gate for the black hole. They have stationed loads of little metal balls around the perimeter of the hole and connected them all together with tight coils of copper wire. I believe the idea is to fire them up and have them form a sort of crisscrossing net of energy over the hole and thus prevent anything unwanted coming through. There has been much discussion of Tesla coils and shifting things out of phase – have to admit I glazed over – and there was I believe some concern over possibly melting a large portion of the South West of England if things went badly wrong, but there seemed to be a consensus that that probably wouldn't happen...

Tony has also offered to do some digging into this AW character. He is going to use some facial recognition software and some AI that is one of their pet projects to trawl the web for anything that might be of interest. He does love his research.

28 March

The Monkey is a bit perplexed. There are lots of mathematical references in the journal and he doesn't really do maths. He came and stopped me working so that I could help him out, but I don't really do maths either. I suggested that he try the Nerds, but they are out for the day, they have gone to Maplin's with a vast shopping list and they were also talking about hunting out some new video games. Guess they need a bit of R'n'R as well. It was obvious that I wasn't going to get anything done with The Monkey fidgeting, so I suggested that we go to the beach for a walk as the sun was shining – even if it was cold.

Ended up with The Monkey throwing stones at my feet as I tried to dodge them for an hour. He says it will make me faster and lighter on my feet, although I suspect any benefit to me was outweighed by the malicious pleasure he derived from trying to break my toes. Then we went to the pub and The Monkey filled me in on some of the stuff in the journal that he had been able to work out plus some of the stuff that was written in English. The collector (never did find out his name) had crossed into Cambodia by way of Thailand and then Laos in the company of a couple of other rabid occult explorers, what he describes as a strange American who had joined the expedition in Thailand, and led by a US Airborne Ranger who had stumbled upon the temple when he had become separated from his unit during heavy fighting on the border. With the aid of well-paid locals, they had managed to travel along secret routes and avoid the patrols that constantly scoured the jungle. It was at this point in the story that the text changed to the foreign script and The Monkey's understanding became scrappier. There were passages where they lost the locals after some sort of massacre and then they were hunted along a river by someone or something which The Monkey couldn't translate. As they approached the region of the temple the journal began to fill up with geometric designs and this is where the maths came in. We sat in silence for a bit having a few more drinks, and I was lost in daydreams of benighted jungle, frantic explorers, shattered ruins, and a man with a plastic face.

The Nerds still haven't come back – they may just have gone straight back to their house, especially if they got some new games – so The Monkey hasn't been able to question them. To stop him having a massive sulk I have got out Pop-Up Pirate and we are having a drunken best of a hundred games. It's 28:36 to The Monkey but I feel like my luck's changing...

29 March

The Nerds got a bit moist today. The Monkey grabbed them as soon as they arrived and showed them what he had translated from the journal. After staring at the Monkey's scribbles and then at each other they went into raptures and eventually told us that what The Monkey had translated was Euler's Identity. None the wiser we asked them to elucidate and then got a full-on lecture about this dude called Euler who lived in the eighteenth century and was a brilliant mathematician. They kept rambling on about it being a most beautiful equation and I kept on asking them what it did. Apparently, it has something to do with circles. They wanted to see what else The Monkey had but he said that he hadn't translated much more of the maths stuff but he showed them the geometric drawings in the book, some of which look like they have been drawn with a Spirograph. Once more the Nerds went into an excited huddle and then asked if they could copy the drawings to study. The Monkey grudgingly allowed them to photograph the pages with their phones and they scampered off like kids on Christmas day.

With only a couple of days to go before we leave, we spent the afternoon laying out clothes and kit and then gradually packing it into the large backpacks we are taking. Then we decided that we needed food, so we are now at the Mexican restaurant in town eating chimichangas and drinking tequila. There are loads of people about – had forgotten that it was Easter! All these holiday makers desperately trying to have a good time, bless 'em. Anyway, there is another round of Jose Cuervo on the table and The Monkey has just sprayed lime juice in his eye and is having a screaming fit, not helped by the fact that he has wiped his eye with the back of his hand which is covered in salt. I am trying not to laugh but we could end up having to leave...

30 March

Managed to stay until the end last night. Fortunately, the restaurant know us quite well and cut us a little slack, plus we spend a whole lot on Mr Cuervo. Think we frightened some of the holiday makers though (sorry if it was you who got involved in the naked arm-wrestling contest – you're just lucky that The Monkey couldn't find any scorpions).

The Nerds stayed up all night working on the diagrams and this morning (late this morning over a fry up and some paracetamol) they told us what they had found. The diagrams represent the orbits of the planets in our solar system, and the order and way that they are laid out has a specific meaning. The Nerds put the orbit layout into one of their astronomy programs and it produced an alignment of planets that only happens once every five thousand years – give or take a couple. 'Okay, so it's going to be a race to the temple in time for the alignment,' I said. 'No,' came the response. The alignment happened in December 2005 it seems – how rude, and here was I thinking I was going to be all Indiana Jones and shit. But the alignment must have been important for it to feature in a journal written three decades earlier? The Nerds had done some research around that too and it seemed to be the harbinger of a terrible new age for many cults, esoteric societies and occult groups around the world. So, something must have happened, it just hadn't made the local news. The Monkey has promised to send the Nerds any more info that he translates from the journal while we are away. I have got hold of a sat phone so I can keep the Nerds updated even without internet access (jungle WiFi is probably shit) and we can keep everyone in the loop.

Tony likes to be thorough, so he started his search for the mysterious AW back in the 180's and has found a possible match. Arno Whitaker, Alabama snake handling preacher, died 14 June 1859 after his rattle snakes bit him in the face multiple times. Risen from the dead 16 June, caused a minor stir amongst the locals who thought it was a miracle although the doctor quoted in The Independent Observer newspaper stated that he thought it was just the effects of the snake venom and that Mr Whitaker had been very lucky although he would always be disfigured. Tony is going to try the Confederate military records next to see if he can get a match on the Shiloh photograph.

Going to have a quiet night tonight as we will be driving to Heathrow tomorrow ready for our flight early on Monday. Well, quiet – Universal Soldier is on the TV and the Jack has just come out. 'Hair of the dog,' says The Monkey – hmmm...

31 March

Said our goodbyes to the Nerds earlier and The Monkey gave them the keys to the cupboard where he keeps his guns – just in case there are any unwanted visitors from either the black hole or outside the house. I have also left them instructions to feed the cat. Suddenly occurred to me that we hadn't said goodbye to the Monster Highs, or in fact talked to them at all for a couple of weeks, so I sent them a text.

Driving to Heathrow now, just stopped at Gordano Services to fill up on crap before we hit the M4. We will be stopping in a hotel tonight, it was going to be the Travelodge to save money but The Monkey found a last-minute deal and we are now stopping at the Hilton T4 and as we are flying from T4 it does seem easier, and nicer...

*

Ahhh! Drunken session in the bar – pretty sure we have managed to offend many guests. Good job the flights not until midday tomorrow. Fuck – The Monkey's in the mini bar...

Snake eaters!

1 April

Ohhh, headache... Ended up in the ornamental pool outside the hotel at 3 am. Very surprised we didn't get arrested. We are now at the gate waiting to board the plane and armed with sleeping pills for our 19+ hour flight. Got through check in and security without any problems – the hangovers probably helped as The Monkey is too fragile to play up – his passport was accepted without a second glance although they did look long and hard at mine. Gate is opening now after a slight delay so I will update when we get to Kuala Lumpur tomorrow. Ha! The Monkey looks pitiful. Wonder if I look like that...

2 April

At Kuala Lumpur airport we had an eight hour wait before the flight to Phnom Penh. It's a nice airport but eight hours...

I slept really well on the plane but woke up twisted into a pretzel and was very pleased to get up for a walk to the toilet. The Monkey didn't take his sleeping pills, so he woke up a few hours before me and got back into the journal. He has translated a passage relating to the planetary alignment that states it is the harbinger of the return of a god – a monkey god. He was genuinely concerned and asked me to shave a small area of fur off the back of his left ear. I know it sounds strange – let me explain... He remembers when he was very young, having something done to his ear and seeing markings on the ears of other young monkeys. He wanted me to shave the fur off between flights. I told him that we had no razor and he showed me a combat blade made of razor-sharp plastic that he had hidden in his carry-on bag. I feel slightly sick. I didn't know he had carried a blade onto the plane. He just gives me that look. So, it was off to the toilets for some barber work...

*

Damn! There's a barcode tattooed at the base of The Monkeys left ear! I downloaded a barcode scanner onto my iPhone but it couldn't make sense of it, so I took a photo and emailed it to the Nerds and asked them to try and decode it ASAP. I the meantime I put a plaster over the barcode to keep it away from prying eyes and we went to find somewhere to chill for the next few hours...

*

We are now in a hotel in Phnom Penh, in the bar, and it is 2.00 am. We still haven't heard back from the Nerds and The Monkey is getting twitchy; drunk and twitchy...

*

Bloody hell! The barcode contains info about The Monkey – stuff that even The Monkey didn't know. His date of birth is 21/12/2005, he comes from a breeding centre in Thailand and was part of a US Army testing programme, and he was scheduled to be given a psychotropic compound. How he ended up with a Buddhist monk and being given away to a merchant seaman is anyone's guess, and did he ever receive the psychotropic?

2005... That puts The Monkey's birth right in the planetary alignment. Harbinger of a god – a monkey god...

The Nerds are trying to hack some US military sites to find out what the hell was going on in that testing programme – Project Fire Serpent...

3 April

Shopping today. The Monkey's idea of shopping that is. We went to see a man in an office in a street at the back of the Central Market who it seems The Monkey has been in contact with since we decided to come. He sold us a lovely bag of toys – two Glock 9mm pistols with silencers, a Remington 870 shotgun, a H&K 416 assault rifle, half a dozen grenades, night vision goggles (we decided that bringing ours would arouse suspicion), and a shed load of ammo. The Monkey paid him in gold coins and I was a little worried that this dude in his little office might have some henchmen waiting for us outside, but he treated us with enormous respect and his bodyguards stationed in the corridor didn't make eye contact and opened the door for us before showing us to our taxi.

Still waiting for the Nerds to get back to us with anything they might have discovered about Fire Serpent and we are hoping they will come up with the goods before we head out into the country in a couple of days. In the meantime, The Monkey has found us a local magic man to talk to tomorrow and we have guns to clean and zero in (don't I sound the bad ass!) but before that we are off to dinner with our friendly local gun dealer at a club he part owns...

4 April

Last night we became snake eaters. I think I had better qualify that before everyone thinks we have found a new sexual pastime...

Our host for the evening served us up a little treat which he told us was for warriors. It began with a salad containing fried cobra skin. Next came a plate of roasted cobra meat along with crispy noodles, shredded ginger, and chillies. Then came cobra eggs – I looked at The Monkey and without hesitation he just chopped off the tops and wolfed them down so I followed suit (I could hear my mum's voice in my head going, 'If The Monkey jumped off a cliff would you?' and I got the giggles, also I thought that I probably would). Then a tray of glasses arrived – brandy in one lot and dark stuff in the other. 'Cobra blood,' our host announced, and we proceeded to knock back the shots followed by the brandy. Blaghhh! I looked around at our fellow dinners and I realised that this wasn't a test. They all tucked in as well and had no expectation that we would not devour whatever was put in front of us. So, when the last course rolled out, I knew that there was no going back. Large brandy glasses appeared with a good double measure in each and floating in the brandy was a deep purple blob. I looked enquiringly at our host and before he could answer The Monkey said, 'The poison sac of the cobra,' and raised the glass to his lips and necked it. Our host smiled and nodded and raised his own glass, and as I lifted mine I could see the others around the table doing the same. I swallowed, a massive swallow, almost gagged and then it was down. Boom – my skin went ice cold while my insides burnt like fire. Sweat sprang from every pore on my body and I shivered as if I had the flu. Everything swirled and it looked like it does when you push your knuckles into the corners of your eyes – yellow and black spiralling squares that flooded my vision and threatened to make me pass out. Then suddenly it was gone, and I looked around the table at all of the faces grinning back at me and then at The Monkey who was looking at his glass and muttering, 'Fucking snakes.'

This morning I woke without a hangover despite the abuse of last night and the fact that I could remember very little of what happened after the meal. I asked The Monkey why I had woken up singing a Fields of the Nephilim song and he said that our host had asked what sort of music we liked and I had told him to play the Nephilim obviously expecting him to be stumped. But The Monkey said that he had got really excited and shouted over to the club DJ and the next thing a full-on Goth night was in session! Turns out our friendly gun runner is a closet Goth and any excuse to play them is fine by him. Flashes began to come back to me, and I asked him if I was correct in thinking that there had been girls involved – 'Several,' came the response.

After breakfast we went to see the local witch doctor/shaman dude who The Monkey had got lined up. This guy was skinny, and his long hair was in dreadlocks with beads, bits of metal and bones woven into it. Around his neck hung a bunch of talismans and charms that looked heavy enough to weigh him down. Apart from that he was wearing a red Tupac t-shirt and brand-new Levi's which sort of ruined the whole mystic thing. We sat down on the floor in the back room of his riverside shack and he and The Monkey went at it in Cambodian. Every now and then I caught a word of French that I understood but most of it just went in one ear and out of the other. I gazed out of the doorway at the passing river and nodded off. I jerked awake and The Monkey was showing him the pendant. He was fascinated but had actually backed away until he was against the wall. I asked The Monkey what was going on and he explained that the shaman had confirmed the story of the planetary alignment and that the pendant only proved the rumours that had been circulating that the monkey god was finally coming to claim what was his. The Monkey showed him the journal and asked him if he could read it, but he said that it was in an ancient Khmer dialect that he could not translate. With The Monkey interpreting I managed to follow the conversation at last and ask a few questions. We got some info on where to look for the temple and it corresponded pretty much with the map in the journal. When we had finished, I shook hands with the shaman, he gripped my hand tightly with both of his and in broken English he said to me, 'You are The Monkey's companion. It is an honour and a heavy burden.' Then he gave me a look of respect and something I suspect was pity and we left and headed to the shooting range.

Spent the rest of the day blowing holes in targets until The Monkey was happy with the way the guns were shooting. He has given me the shotgun. He says it doesn't take so much skill to kill things with and also when he fires it, he ends up on his back – a little too much recoil and far too much amusement.

Back at the hotel now and food and drink. Still nothing from the Nerds. They are digging through several classified websites but keep running into dead ends. They have asked if they can get a friend of theirs involved who is apparently the best they have ever met at getting into cyber places they shouldn't. I am a little concerned about getting anyone else involved but they have concerns of their own. It seems that someone may be onto their digging and is trying to chase them back through cyber space to their location. They have assured me that they have been taking a very circuitous route that should not be traceable but whoever is onto them it seems is pretty good, and given what I now know about the not so secure dark web I'm just a little dubious. They think that the best way for them to get the info and avoid getting tracked is to bring in their friend and let them do their magic. After talking it over with The Monkey I have given them the go ahead. Tony also had some more news on the AW thing. Looks like it is Arno Whitaker in the Shiloh, photo as a search of the Confederate army records shows him as a captain in the Alabama Cavalry Regiment. What's more, the initial AI facial recognition search produced a couple of possible matches, but they are stretching credibility a bit too much. One is a hit on a photo of a group of westerners in Iraq in 1915, and the other is a photo of Soviet *advisors* in Vietnam in 1959. He reckons that there could be more as the program sorts the images into stacks of unlikely, maybe, definitely, and then runs back through them several times and learns every time you agree with one of its definites, so we will have to wait and see. We don't want to delay leaving much longer, in fact The Monkey wants to head out tomorrow afternoon on a boat owned by the gun runner that is heading upriver to Kampong Cham City. Would be nice to have answers before we leave but at least we will still be in easy communication for a while yet. Anyway, the Jack is calling...

5 April

On a slow cargo vessel crawling up the Mekong River. Sitting on an open area next to the wheelhouse and drinking Angkor Beer with the captain and a couple of other members of the crew. Plus, we are eating some very tasty noodle soup and beef skewers – I get the feeling that the crew don't normally eat this well and it is probably another reason they are being so nice to us. The captain is letting us use his WiFi, suppose I shouldn't be surprised that they have it on board – got to get ya porn somewhere!

The Nerds came up with the goods this morning. Their friend had worked through the night and managed to finally get into a classified US army site via god knows what back doors. Project Fire Serpent – delivering huge doses of N,N-Dimethyltryptamine (DMT) to soldiers in order to trigger latent psychic and possibly super normal powers. First stage: give monkeys heroic doses until they break and watch what happens to them. Second stage: extrapolate the data back to human testing and then work out safe doses on some willing jar heads. Third stage: take soldiers already trained and groomed and showing possible psychic potential and give them the upper limit doses while pushing their training to the limit. Result: super soldiers capable of exploding an enemy's head through the power of thought or some such shit. Having played with DMT while in Amsterdam I know exactly what low doses can do. The thought of ODing monkeys on the stuff makes me squirm.

Seems the programme got derailed after a bunch of Buddhist monks peacefully highjacked the breeding centre and freed the monkeys creating a bit of an incident and causing quite a lot of embarrassment to the US army.

Questions got asked in congress and the testing of LSD on troops during the Vietnam War got dragged up again, causing the whole project to disappear into the shadows. There are hints in the classified files that the testing had reached human stage and that there could even be *super soldiers* out there.

Well at least we now know how The Monkey ended up with the monk. He seems to think that makes sense as well and says it sort of fits with the fragments of memories he has from when he was very young. The Monkey looks very at ease here on the deck of a boat drifting past jungle in the night, cigar clamped in teeth and beer in hand. Today is the first day he has had Nam flashbacks for a while but instead of sending him off on a violent spree he just seems to have merged with his surroundings and become part of this ancient country...

6 April

Woke this morning to find The Monkey playing dice with the crew. Much shouting and swearing from all concerned as The Monkey took their money by the furry fist full. At first I thought they were letting him win but it soon became apparent that his luck was as good as ever and that they really didn't stand a chance. I managed to separate them before things got nasty although The Monkey did say that there was a possible fight on the cards – winner takes all. I just knew he meant me, and I got flashbacks of the ferry journey back from Amsterdam and the truck driver punch up, although these guys looked a lot meaner.

We eventually docked in Kampong Cham City around midday without me having to take part in a remake of Kickboxer – I think I have the captain to thank for that. The Monkey looked disappointed and told me, 'A bit of broken glass never hurt anyone,' yeah, well fuck you very much...

Our arms dealer buddy had given us the address of a good hotel owned by his cousin and we are supposed to be on *mate's* rates which is nice considering The Monkey gave back all the money he won before we disembarked. I asked him why the sudden generosity and he said that you can only spend so much money before you die – cheery thought! The hotel is an old French colonial building and is basic but okay and we have air con in our room and a restaurant/bar next door. Our friendly arms dealer has also given us the number of a helicopter pilot who he says would be able to take us closer to our goal. I had asked Mr Guns R Us why he was being so helpful, and he had rolled back his shirt sleeve to show me a tattoo of a monkey carrying a sword and surrounded by a ring of fire. 'It is destiny,' he had said as if that explained everything and I just accepted it – I have accepted much stranger things.

We phoned the pilot from the bar and a dude with a gravely Texas drawl answered. I explained what we needed and after a few moments of silence he laughed and said he would meet us for breakfast in the restaurant. So now we are sitting and drinking again as The Monkey talks to the bar man about a nearby massage parlour...

7 April

Our chopper pilot is called Hambone and he is mental. Sort of a cross between Murdock from the A Team and Ted Nugent except this dude is in his mid-70s, built like a wrestler, and has a massive moustache and sideburns in the style of Lemmy. He and The Monkey hit it off immediately and he didn't think it at all strange that The Monkey should have a previous life as a Nam veteran. Seems he has seen some weird shit in his time... He told how he flew combat missions in the war and that after the war he went back to the US of A but got treated like shit by all and sundry. A little private soldiering came his way and he ended up in Africa flying missions in Angola. Then he gradually made his way east again until he found himself back in Indochina and flying drug runs across the Golden Triangle and ferrying the still operational CIA backed black ops boys in and out of sensitive areas. As a thank you he got an army surplus Huey at a discount price and has been flying it ever since. Once again, we explained where we wanted to go and once again he laughed and called us crazy fuckers but said he would take us as close as he could. Seems the area we want to go to is massively forested and he may have to drop us quite a few kilometres out just so he can land. That means my land mine dodging practice is going to come in handy and, to be honest, it's better than walking from here!

We have checked out of the hotel and gone to Hambone's for the night. He has an old colonial place a couple of kilometres upriver and a lot of twenty something Cambodian female housekeepers. He says that he can fly us out tomorrow and therefore tonight we need to party. Neither I nor The Monkey have any problems with that. Jimi Hendrix is playing very loudly through the stereo and there are Cambodian language versions of *Family Guy* on the 60-inch plasma TV hanging on the wall. The Monkey has just got extremely excited as he has spotted a giant Jenga game out on the veranda. I will have to keep an eye on him, this one is large enough to crush him if it falls on him.

From tomorrow the updates will be via the Nerds back at home. I will try my best to pass reports on to them through the satellite phone.

So tomorrow we go into the heart of darkness and tonight we go into what is starting to look like an episode of the Banana Splits...

I love the smell of Napalm

8 April

Hello, this is Tony – the Nerd. Here is the update we got texted from the satellite phone earlier. Crazy shit!

Woke up in a pile of naked bodies in a room smelling of opium and hash. Apparently, it was a good night...

On the flight out me and The Monkey sat in the open door of the Huey. I hung on to the gun mount for support, but The Monkey just lolled against the frame as if it was the most natural thing in the world and smoked cigars. I noticed Hambone glancing back at him every now and then, a frown visible even with the aviator sunglasses. We flew north along the Mekong for a while before banking towards the north east and flying through mountain valleys. The Monkey had pulled me to one side before we boarded the chopper and said that he thought there was something wrong. He was suspicious of Hambone's reluctance to take us into the deep jungle. He said that all of the Huey pilots he had known had been capable putting their birds down just about anywhere. I said that maybe Hambone was a bit crap, but The Monkey just shook his head and told me to keep one in the chamber just in case.

We left the mountains and headed out across sparse jungle crossed by the occasional road. Hambone shouted over his shoulder that we would be landing soon, and The Monkey looked at me and patted his sidearm. We descended into a wide clearing and it was immediately obvious that we were not alone. The Monkey was in Hambone's face straight away, gun drawn, but Hambone just held up his hands and said, 'Sorry guys but we can't go any further without this meeting. I hope you are doing this stuff for the right reasons – for all our sakes...' I thought for a second that The Monkey might shoot him, but he flipped on the safety and made his way back to me as Hambone killed the engine.

Those waiting for us were a mix of Orientals, men and women, but my attention was drawn to the seven tall, thin Chinese men in long black robes. I almost laughed out loud at the long white moustaches, beards and eyebrows. It was like a Shaw Brothers kung fu movie. I glanced at The Monkey but he wasn't laughing and I swallowed it down and kept my hand by my Glock (that's not a spelling mistake). One of the tall Chinese began to speak in exceptionally good English, 'Welcome Monkey Lord,' he said with a little bow of his head. The Monkey stared back through a cloud of cigar smoke. 'We could let you get no closer to the temple without discovering your true intent. When you made your journey to the West, we thought that you had been seduced by the Illuminated Ones, that your previous life had biased you towards them.' The Monkey took the cigar from his mouth and said, 'What the fuck are you talking about?'

Over the next two hours he got his explanation. The Orientals are the heads of a Chinese based secret organisation called The Green and Red Society. They have been around for hundreds of years and stretch across the whole of South East Asia and count their members in the millions. Their mission is to oppose the Western Illuminati. When they heard, seven years ago, of the monkey who could speak, they saw the myth of the monkey god becoming reality. Then The Monkey disappeared and they were thrown into a state of flux. The Shaw Brothers rejects are Mao Shan sorcerers who, from what was hinted, have been alive for a very long time. They used their arcane arts to determine the possible location of The Monkey but it wasn't until he became self-aware that they could finally locate him and at this point, to their horror, he headed to Europe. They knew of his previous life as a US soldier, this it seems was an unexpected twist in the plot and they believed that because he was aware of that life and heading into the West that he would be attracted by the Illuminati who would eventually become aware of his presence. They then located the Buddhist monk who had rescued The Monkey. When asked why he had given The Monkey to a merchant seaman instead of bringing him to the Society, he had simply said that all creatures have their destiny and that The Monkey would find his wherever he was. He had also given him the fourteen sticks which had been in his possession since he was a child in Cambodia, they had been given to him by an American soldier.

It seems that our unwanted visitors at the house had been breakaway members of the Society sent to retrieve the sticks. It was believed, by this splinter group, that if The Monkey did not have the sticks then he could be left to his own devices but it seems they didn't realise how difficult it is to get something from a monkey who doesn't want to give it up... The black hole had fucked with their juju and things had definitely not gone as planned. All of this had been done without the full agreement of the Green and Red Society, and I got the impression that all was not right in paradise with their organisation. Then, the Mao Shan had received a message from an old lady in a country house on the moors and they realised that The Monkey was coming to them. So now they wanted to know which side The Monkey was on, and I got the distinct impression that a good number of their assembly were of the assassin persuasion. The Monkey explained to them that he didn't give a flying fuck about secret societies but that he felt drawn to the temple in the jungle and that he was going there to find out about himself, not to help anyone else. I thought that might have resulted in a whole lot of stabbing and shooting but it seemed to please the Mao Shan dudes and they nodded lots amongst themselves and the lead one said, 'The monkey god will follow his nature,' very cryptic I'm sure, and then invited us to take tea with them and talk further. Everything suddenly relaxed, in fact I didn't realise how tense it had been. They said that we should spend the night with them in their camp just inside the tree line, and that they would try to answer any questions we had and provide any help that they could.

I looked back at the Huey as they started to walk towards the trees with The Monkey and there was Hambone sitting by the door gun. The barrel had been pointing at were the Mao Shan sorcerers had been standing and I could swear that he flipped the safety on and gave a massive sigh of relief. I asked him if he was coming and he said no that he would stay with the chopper but that he would take us where we needed to go in the morning. I nodded and followed the others into the trees...

9 April

Hi, Tony again – this is what we got earlier...

Last night we heard how the Green and Red Society had fought the agents of the Illuminati for hundreds of years, and how those agents had extended their control across the planet through the financial institutions, the major corporations, governments, the church and the press. This stuff went on for ages, I think there was a big hearts and minds exercise going on to make sure that The Monkey was on the right side. We also learnt that the Society had more than its fair share of Triads, Tongs, Yakuza gangs and other eastern criminal groups, plus a whole shit load of assassins not affiliated to anyone in particular. Seems that they are not angels by any stretch of the imagination, and it was the Yakuza branch that had recently begun to go against the wishes of the main council of the society. Most of the Mao Shan dismissed it as just internal power politics but I noticed that the sorcerer who had greeted us and done most of the initial talking lowered his eyes and looked for a long time into the fire.

This morning we went back to the chopper accompanied by two of their men who they said were to go with us to, 'Keep us safe.' Amazingly The Monkey didn't have a strop and just let them tag along. At the Huey, Hambone looked suspiciously at the two goons in tow and waved us on board. We took off immediately as if Hambone didn't want to hang around and headed east. He shouted back that inside the hour we would be at the temple site and that the Society had given him the heads up about a flat rock outcrop above the temple that we should be able to set down on.

I kept an eye on The Monkey – even though he hadn't thrown his toys out of the pram there was no guarantee that he wouldn't throw the goons out of the chopper. But we got to the temple site with no incident and Hambone set the Huey down on a flat rock area level with the treetops. The Monkey went straight over the ledge and disappeared amongst the green. After about twenty minutes he scampered back up with a massive grin on his face. He says that the monkey temple is directly below us and that there is a passage through the mouth that leads into the cliff and down. I am sending this update now as even the satellite phone can't work underground. We are tooling up and taking food and water with us so we are prepared for whatever we find in there (hopefully), and we are all going – Hambone says that he wants in, so now there are five of us. I will try to send further updates later...

Tony again – there has been nothing else yet...

10 April

Hi, Tony again. We have had no communication since yesterday and we are starting to get a bit concerned – about a couple of things actually...

We are worried that we haven't heard from the guys in Cambodia but it could be that they are still underground, and The Monkey does seem to be more than capable. Closer to home – we received a call late last night from JudyZ, she is the friend who managed to hack the US Army classified site. She was worried because she was getting unexpected activity on her WiFi router and her laptop began to behave in a way she described as, 'Unusual.' Then, at around 4.30 this morning we get a call from her saying that she had woken up to find that the camera light on her laptop (she sleeps with her laptop on in her room) was on and she couldn't close the camera app window down. She was sure that the camera was being controlled by someone remotely. It freaked her out and she switched off the laptop – something she never does. We told her to get back to sleep and that we would call her around breakfast time. We called and got no answer. We have been trying ever since, and texting and emailing but nothing. There is none of her usual on-line activity and we even contacted a couple of her friends, but they said that they hadn't seen her today. Dave has decided to drive up to her flat in Reading to see if she is okay, he left about an hour ago. We will keep trying to get hold of her and let him know if we get her within the next couple of hours. Must admit it has spooked us a bit. JudyZ is the best hacker we know, and after we thought that someone was trying to back track us during our attempt to hack the classified sites, we think she may be in trouble...

I have also been doing some more work on the Arno Whitaker thing. The AI search has produced quite a few image hits that now span nearly one hundred and eighty years including one from LinkedIn! I had got so focused on the image search that it took a suggestion from Kev before I Googled his name, and there he is – Arno Whitaker, CEO of a US company called Brightstorm, who are involved in bioengineering and have links with US military contractors. He has a bloody LinkedIn profile and everything! His profile picture is that same smooth, oddly twisted face with the fixed grin that we have seen in the other photos, as if he has been severely burned and had a not very successful skin graft. I found a biography for him on a corporate business site and it claims he is forty-seven years old and was bitten on the face by a rattle snake in his late teens which has left his face disfigured and partially paralysed. He is a philanthropist, collector of antiquities, and all-round good guy – apparently...

*

Just heard from Dave, JudyZ's flat is completely empty, not even wallpaper on the walls! Completely empty. Dave is not hanging about; he is on his way back...

11 April

This is Kev. The hyper temporal gateway/black hole has started rhythmically pulsing. We are monitoring it, and the electromagnetic cage we built seems to be preventing any overspill from its event horizon.

Dave is totally spooked by the absence of anything JudyZ at her flat – he says it's like she never existed. He also thinks that someone followed him from her flat. He is sure he managed to give them the slip by diverting through the rush hour carnage of Bristol city centre and then sneaking back onto the M5 via a service road to Sedgemoor Services, but we are keeping a close eye on the road.

Probably more disturbing is the fact that the Monster Highs have just turned up. They say they awoke because they got the feeling something was wrong, and they have come to protect us. We have no idea what that means but now we have two really hot, scantily dressed, partially dead girls in the house who have taken up residence in the boss's darkened bedroom. Frightening and arousing at the same time (all those episodes of Buffy etc are coming back)!

Still nothing from Cambodia...

*

Kev again – at last, news from Cambodia. It doesn't sound good...

I have been shot. It was a fucking blood bath.

We rappelled over the cliff edge. I had never done it before, but the others went over like it was an everyday occurrence, except for The Monkey, who doesn't need ropes. The others were down on the ground quickly but The Monkey stayed next to me as I bounced uneasily down the rock and as we descended, he told me in hushed tones that he had spoken to the monkeys who live around the temple and they had warned him that there were other humans hiding amongst the trees.

On the ground I got my first proper look at the temple and it is just like the drawing in the journal, a few more vines and leaves but the same monkey face staring out of the rock. Either side were the seven-pointed stars and through the monkey's open mouth the dark interior of the temple. It was immediately obvious that the goons had been here before. Hambone gave us a knowing look and The Monkey made a couple of subtle hand signals of the sort you see spec ops dudes do in movies, and Hambone shifted his attention to the surrounding jungle. The Monkey led us through the mouth of his giant counterpart, and we clicked on LED torches to show us our surroundings.

It was obvious that the temple was ancient and that anything of value had been removed a long time ago. Vines had encroached through the entrance and cracks in the cliff, and dead leaves and a few small animal bones littered the floor. We moved deeper inside, and an intricately carved arch framed a tunnel that led downwards in a gentle slope. As we moved down, I noticed that Hambone had positioned himself at the rear and kept checking back the way we had come.

After about ten minutes of walking along a tunnel painted with scenes of monkeys dressed in armour and carrying flaming swords fighting with demon creatures with wings we came to a chamber which, after a quick count, I realised had seven sides. In the centre of the floor was a smooth circular indentation about eight feet across and on either side stood a statue of an armoured monkey with its paws cupped and raised as if offering something towards the indentation. As I got closer, I could see that the cupped paws had grooves cut into them, grooves in the shape of a seven-pointed star.

I glanced around the room and saw that the goons had gone to the left side where The Monkey had gone, and that Hambone had stationed himself by the entrance. I also noticed that Hambone had slid a handgun out of its holster and was holding it down against his right leg. The Monkey waved me around to the top side of the indentation and glared at the goons when they made to follow until they stayed put. From his backpack he took two small bundles and gave one to me – the lolly sticks.

What happened next was a blur. The goons spotted the bundles and one of them grabbed for his sidearm before the other could stop him. I hadn't noticed that The Monkey had his Glock under the backpack and suddenly the bag jumped as two rounds ripped through it and smashed into the goon's chest. Goon number two had started to move towards us with frightening speed but next thing I knew he was lifted off the ground and smashed into the wall by a shot from the tunnel entrance. Hambone came over still covering the downed goon, but he didn't need to worry as the bullet from his Colt Double Eagle had put a massive hole in his upper back. That's when it all went a bit special. Bullets started ripping out of the tunnel and ricocheting everywhere. We dived for cover behind a large stone dais at the back of the room and found ourselves amongst a pile of very old human remains.

The others who had been hiding in the jungle must have just opened up from halfway down the tunnel, it's the only way I can explain us not getting hit in the first volley. I returned fire with the Remington that had been slung along the side of my pack and was pleasantly satisfied with the screams that followed. The Monkey and Hambone fired into the tunnel as well, The Monkey putting down short bursts with his H&K as dark shapes crowded the entrance. There were a lot of them, fucking loads, and they kept on coming. It was obvious that we weren't going to have enough ammo. The Monkey stopped firing and I watched as he pulled the pin from a grenade and with narrowed eyes lobbed it over the dais. We ducked down and heard shouting and then the blast as the grenade ripped through the enclosed area. We all opened up again and for a moment drove them back. The Monkey pulled a couple more pins and sent two more grenades clattering down the tunnel, and when they went off there was a massive crash and a cloud of dust filled the chamber. When it had cleared, and we had finished coughing, we could see that the tunnel had collapsed about ten feet from the chamber.

We had a bit of a breather after The Monkey had cut the throats of three wounded black pyjama wearing attackers and took stock of the situation. There were obviously more of them out there but they couldn't get to us even though we could hear them digging. I asked The Monkey what our plan was and he took out the journal and said that there was another chamber at the back of the room if he could find the mechanism to open it. After about half an hour of searching he took the monkey pendant from round his neck and pushed it into a small opening in the wall, and with a grinding noise a large slab of stone slid back into the wall revealing the other chamber. We went inside and shone the torches around. It was almost identical to the first chamber and I asked The Monkey what was going on. He said that the first chamber was a fake to trick those who didn't know and that he had taken out the sticks to force the hand of the goons. This, he said was the real deal.

We assembled the two stars and took one each to the monkey statues. Just as we put the stars into the cupped paws there was an almighty explosion from the other chamber and Hambone shouted that he thought it was an RPG. We heard rocks falling and men shouting, and then the guns started popping again.

At this point it felt as if I had been hit in the side with a hot sledgehammer. The force of the blow spun me round and as I fell, I saw that the indentation had turned into a swirling bowl of energy; then I made contact with the statue and blackness.

I am now lying in the Huey and Hambone has applied another quick clot bag to my wound. He says it's a through and through and missed all the good stuff so I should be okay. I asked him how we got out, but he says that the morphine will kick in soon and that they will fill me in later. I asked him where The Monkey is and he just nodded to the cliff edge we had gone over – I could swear he is shaking. There are explosions and shots in the jungle down there, and there is screaming – lots and lots of screaming. I can feel the morphine fingers in my head now, got to stop...

12 April

Hello, it's Tony. Haven't heard anything else from the guys yet.

The black hole is still pulsing strongly. The Monster Highs are still shut up in the bedroom. Kev thinks he may have spotted someone scoping out our house down the road. To be honest we are more or less living in The Monkey's house at the moment, so we are going to keep an eye out and keep our heads down...

13 April

Hey, Dave here. There is no word again from Cambodia. Don't know what is going on, and to be honest don't know what's going on here either.

The black hole has stopped pulsing and now looks more like a lens through which we can see a desert. The Monster Highs have come out of the bedroom and gone out through the back door into the garden. Tony asked them what they were doing, and they sort of smiled and in perfect unison said, 'Going hunting.' We are really freaked out right now, everything seems to be going to shit. Still can't find any info on JudyZ. None of her friends can find out anything and there is no longer any online trace of her. It's as if she doesn't exist – correction, never existed...

14 April

Its Dave here – we got a message over the sat phone...

Awake for long enough at last to do an update. They have stopped giving me morphine now and I'm no longer on a drip. I lost a lot of blood even though the wound wasn't life threatening. Apparently getting me up the cliff face was done at a run with no time for niceties and that resulted in me pissing blood everywhere...

Seems we are in Vietnam. We were more or less on the boarder anyway and Hambone just flew us to the nearest friendly place he could think of that had medical facilities and wouldn't ask questions.

The Monkey and Hambone have filled me in on what happened at the temple. What a cluster fuck...

When I got shot, I bounced off the nearest monkey statue (that explains the large head wound and concussion) and was knocked unconscious. Hambone grabbed the Remington and opened up on the men streaming into the outer chamber and it seems that The Monkey went straight over to the indentation in the centre of the room and stepped into the swirling energy I had seen just before I blacked out. Hambone was forced to retreat into the room and that was when he looked around for The Monkey and saw him in the indentation. He says that The Monkey was changed – bigger, golden fur, ancient armour like that on the tunnel paintings, and eyes that blazed like the sun (I am guessing like the pendant had glowed). He was so shocked that he had stopped firing and the attackers had almost overrun them. Then The Monkey had stepped out of the energy field and, in Hambone's words, gone ape shit. Everyone in the doorway had died in seconds and the rest had fled back towards the surface as The Monkey pursued them, tearing apart everyone he caught.

Hambone had then looked after me as best he could. Morphine and quick clot from his field medic kit and a dressing for my head wound. He realised that he would need to get me back to the chopper and that while The Monkey was wreaking havoc in the tunnel and temple entrance and beyond, he would have a chance to get me back to the surface. He had given me a fireman's lift and carried me cautiously back up to the temple. He said that it looked like someone had gone through there with a giant weed whacker as there were just bits of the enemy sprayed around the tunnel walls. The Monkey had gone out of the temple and was chasing the enemy through the jungle, it seems he had no intention of leaving anyone alive. Hambone says that's when he started to hear explosions and realised that our attackers had found the old mine fields that were dotted about the area of the temple. He could see The Monkey's blazing form leaping from tree to tree and driving all before him as the temple monkeys screamed and jumped up and down. Hambone got me to the cliff face and fastened a harness under my arms then he used another rope to go up the cliff himself. He then dragged me up the cliff hand over hand and manhandled me into the Huey. That was where I had briefly regained consciousness.

The slaughter had continued for the rest of the day until there was no one left to kill and then The Monkey had scaled the cliff and crouched on the edge in the dying rays of the sun, looking, in Hambones words again, like a hairy medieval butcher. Gradually the bloodlust had left him and he had returned to his own form and then he had come over to see if I was alright. The Monkey tells me that when I had been shot, he thought I was dead and that had been the trigger for his berserk frenzy – nice to know he cares. Hambone had explained that they needed to get me to a medical facility ASAP, or I might just bleed out but The Monkey told him he needed another 15 minutes and then went back over the cliff. When he reappeared he said that we should take off immediately and Hambone says that the look in his eyes said immediately might not be quick enough. Just as the skids had left the rock there was a massive explosion and the ledge where we had sat down collapsed.

We had flown across the border in darkness to a medium size village and this is where we have been for the last few days. I have had a fair bit of morphine and a couple of transfusions as well as stitches in my head. Hambone has got drunk a lot and The Monkey has spent quite a bit of time sitting by my bed and reading the journal (and getting drunk). He says some of the stuff in there makes sense now and he will tell me when I am in better shape to understand it. I asked him why he blew up the temple and he says that he only blew up the tunnel and the first chamber after removing the pendant and sealing the door. This, he says, is to keep people away from the power source that is now active in there along with the two stars. He says that he doesn't need to be in it to tap into the power as a useable portion of it is now with him all the time if he needs it. I asked him if it meant he would change into an armoured monkey of death at the drop of a hat and he said, 'You are a wanker! But quite possibly, who knows?'

This is Dave again and wow, we are happy to know that the guys are alive! This would explain why the black hole seems to have 'tuned in'. We had speculated that the stars had formed a link with the gateway – some sort of morphic resonance Tony thinks, although Kev and myself are leaning towards a chaos theory-based answer (although Tony keeps reminding us that the two theories have similarities that may mean we are talking about the same thing).

The Monster Highs drifted back from their hunting trip with some disturbing news. There are people looking for me and they have ill intent, although it seems that two of them have now *gone away...*

Veterinary grade antibiotics and spooks

15 April

Hello, Tony here – more from Cambodia...

Been out of bed today. Spent some time sat outside on the veranda with The Monkey and Hambone.

Hambone has been doing a bit of maintenance on the chopper and on the scrounge for some fuel, he also borrowed the sat phone and made a call to the Green and Red bunch to find out what the fuck they are up to. He says that he sympathises with their cause and has done a few jobs for them in the past and that is how he ended up taking us to the meeting with them. He kept apologising for the resulting carnage though, and said he would never have agreed to take the goons had he known what would happen. Having said all that though he came back from the sat phone call looking very confused. He was told that the goons were never supposed to have acted in the way they had, and he believes that they were double agents. Agents for who? That is where it gets even more convoluted. They informed him that the small army which had been hidden in the jungle around the temple were linked to the Society but were part of the breakaway Yakuza group posing as Vietnamese bandits. Ah, that's all a bit crap then... Hambone notified one of his CIA contacts still operating in the region that he thought some of Kim Jong's finest North Korean commandos were running riot and they thanked him very much and said they would have a look-see. Hambone thinks that should keep the Yakuza out of our hair for the time being as they dodge black ops' kill squads.

The Monkey has been talking me through some of the stuff from the journal – if my head hadn't already been hurting this would have done the trick. The journal says that after the explorers had reached the temple and made their way inside, they had been greeted by a handful of very old priests whose task it was to preserve the temple. There was, it appears, a difference of opinion between the explorers and the priests over whether they should have access to the inner chamber and the priests ended up getting shot by AW – this explains the pile of human bones behind the dais. They had kept one alive and AW had *persuaded* him to show them how to get into the inner chamber. Inside the inner chamber they had found the sticks in two piles beside the statues and after further questioning the priest had revealed that they formed stars that magnified the power of the monkey god. They had asked him to make the stars, but he had refused and said that only when the alignment occurred could the stars' true purpose be seen. After further pressure it seems that the old priest had given up the ghost and died. Then it all got even weirder because during the night the soldier who had guided them had disappeared with the sticks; he had not been happy with the treatment of the priests, thus leaving them to find their own way out of the jungle.

Obviously, his lordship from the manor house had managed to find his way home with the monkey pendant but there was no mention as to what had happened to his compatriots. The Monkey thought there must have been another journal that followed on from this one but we both reckon the old woman has put that one in the fire. As for the soldier – The Monkey has been having dreams or flashbacks to his previous life and says he remembers helping a young boy who was fleeing from his village towards the Thai border, and he is sure he gave the child a small bundle tied with a red braided cord. If that is right then The Monkey and the soldier are/were one and the same, and the small boy became the Buddhist monk who freed The Monkey from the breeding centre and gave him the sticks. We left the photos that came with the notebook at home for Tony's research, but the one with the soldier, that must have been THE soldier... Bloody hell! That breaks my head!

Oh right, just to make things even more complicated, Hambone has been listening to all this and has just chipped in with the fact that he is sure that the soldier who was The Monkey was one of a covert kill squad he dropped behind enemy lines during the last months of the war. He remembered talking to one of the soldiers the evening before the mission over a bottle of JD who had told him about having searched in the jungle for lost temples a couple of years earlier when he had been paid by an anonymous group to go AWOL for a while. Hambone had thought the cigar smoking trooper had been a bit crazy; he says that he had the eyes of a shark. The unit had been compromised soon after leaving the LZ and although he had turned back immediately to pick them up only two made it back to the LZ and both died on the return flight – one had been the cigar smoker. Hambone says he has carried around a feeling of guilt that they died even though he could do nothing to save them...

16 April

Yo, Dave here again bringing more news from Cambodia...

I have mainly spent the day watching The Monkey and Hambone get drunk and reminisce about Nam (their Nam not the one we are currently in – their Nam sounds like a properly fucked up place!). I am not allowed to drink at the moment so I can't join in – not that I could really add much to the conversation – but it has made me laugh out loud at some of the crazy adventures, and also made me sad as they recount stories of young men turning into killers and losing their best friends in a world where literally anything was possible if you had the balls and the mindset. Hambone explained how, after the fateful mission he had plunged himself recklessly into everything he was assigned, even volunteering for missions which should have been suicide. Every time he made it back while those around him died and he felt guiltier and guiltier. It wasn't until he met a local jungle wizard who told him that he was fated not to die because he had a job to complete and karma to pay back that he began to lose the guilt, then he became just plain crazy as he put himself into more and more dangerous situations until eventually, he just accepted his fate.

They are both quite drunk now and the poker game they started is looking more like fifty-two card pickup. I am getting sleepy – still on some heavy pain killers and they keep making me nod off. The Monkey keeps calling me *granddad* and tucking me in – cheeky little bastard. Looks like there is some stuff going on back home, but I will let the Nerds fill you in...

Yes, it's got a bit strange here. Tony called us into the loft room this morning and we watched two black helicopters landing at the local airbase in the distance. Then later one of the choppers began flying up and down the valley doing slow passes across the houses and the fields around us for a couple of miles. Kev went out to pick up some supplies and when he came back, he was very excited. He was shouting about 'The men in black' having turned up and when we got him to calm down, he explained that a black Range Rover had stopped in the village and a couple of men in black suits and shades had got out. He thinks one had been trying to get a phone signal but there is absolutely no coverage down in the valley. Anyway, they had a bit of a look around and then got back in the car and drove off. We have unlocked the gun cabinet and told the Monster Highs (they told Tony to come into the bedroom, but he just shouted through the door and then ran away – they frighten him quite badly!) ...

17 April

Hi, Dave again. The other two have gone out looking for *The men in black* so I get to do the update again as I can't show my face outside in case I get recognised, not easy being the only black dude in the village!...

Off the painkillers today so a bit sore but okay. The bullet apparently passed right through my left side missing anything of value by about an inch. Made a largish exit wound though so that is full of packing and they are shovelling me full of veterinary grade antibiotics – hooray for science!

Hambone had a visit from a couple of aid workers, sort of International Mission Abroad type thing who are working with local groups and trying to convert them at the same time, he says they were asking a few questions about where we had come from and what had happened to result in me getting shot. Hambone thinks they are CIA payroll and he made up some bullshit about a hunting accident in the hills to the north. He doesn't think they were convinced, and he reckons we ought to be making tracks back across the border tonight now that I am able to get around. He says he knows a vet for my medication and can also get me some rabies shots while we are there. Open season on taking the piss then...

The Monkey is concerned about the news from home. He doesn't like the idea of the Nerds going all Quentin Tarantino with his weapons stash, and neither do I. They have been warned and they know the consequences of pissing off The Monkey. We just have to hope they are sensible/scared enough to keep out of the way.

We are going to pack up our shit ready to get the fuck out of Dodge. I will of course be taking a mainly supervisory role...

Dave again. Yes, we are being careful. We are all pretty worried about shooting each other by accident so we will keep guns as a last resort. The Monster Highs have been doing some sort of cloaking thing as well, not like a Romulan Bird of Prey or Harry Potters cloak but some sort of thing that makes it difficult to focus on the house – sort of like fog but not! Difficult to explain but Tony couldn't find the house after going for a look around this morning. Kev had to go and guide him in! The Monster Highs say it's how they avoid unwanted attention. To be honest they could do that by not dressing like they are just off to a fetish club – not that I am complaining you understand...

18 April

We are back at Hambone's place and I am being looked after by his lovely local staff.

On the flight back we came under small arms fire just after crossing the border into Cambodia. The Monkey returned the favour with the door gun and it all went remarkably quiet after that. Hambone reckons it was probably local bandits as he does get shot at every now and then when he is flying jobs over remote areas – we think it's just because he is so popular!

Hambone got a call from a friendly at the Vietnamese village we vacated to say that a couple of black choppers circled the village at dawn. Coincidence? I think not. Linked to the black choppers back home? Hambone says it's unlikely as most of the covert groups that he has dealings with, including the Agency, all seem to favour black nowadays. He thinks that our missionary/spook friends were responsible and is happy that we were gone before they came-a-looking. I told Hambone he should paint his Huey black as it is very slimming – he called me a cunt.

A local doc has had a look at my wounds and thinks I should be okay to travel in a couple of days so we are going to start thinking about heading home. Me and The Monkey are getting twitchy about events unravelling in Cornwall and it would be good to be on the scene, although I don't particularly want to get shot at again for a while. The Monster Highs seem to have done a good job of masking the house and it seems that they extended it to the Nerds' house last night to give them a chance to go and recover their important stuff without being seen. The general consensus is that it wouldn't be a good idea to hide their house all the time as the men in black have already been poking about around there and if the house suddenly disappeared it would arouse suspicion. Our house, on the other hand, was never the focus of their attention so the fact that it is now just part of the scenery should be okay. I hope we can find it when we get back! I did ask how the postman managed and was given a very convoluted explanation about opening paths through the cloak at various times – Nerds!

The Monkey seems in a much better mood now we are back in Cambodia. I think there was a lot of previous history weighing on him in Vietnam and that whole business about his past life and the twisted connections with the explorers and the temple and also with Hambone, were playing on him a bit. I have just seen him heading off upstairs with three of the young local ladies and a bottle of Jack…

19 April

We have been doing some sightseeing today – more to get me up and moving than to be tourists. Hambone took us to some local temples and a couple of markets and then to a Thai boxing match. The Monkey enjoyed watching knees making violent contact with heads while handfuls of notes changed hands. At one point he gave me a wistful look and said that it was a shame I wasn't healed yet. He is determined to see me get my head kicked in.

When we got back Hambone was told that there had been a visitor who had gone away and said he would be back later this evening or maybe in the morning. The visitor had been American, and the girls thought he looked like a spook. Hambone says he is not surprised. There will probably be questions as to what he knows about the 'North Koreans', and he thinks that is enough of a potential international incident to detract from me and The

Monkey but he wants us to stay out of the way when the visitor returns.

The Nerds are keeping a low profile. The men in black have gone to ground and they have only seen the black chopper on one occasion, and then it was heading out towards the Atlantic. They have been keeping busy working on why the black hole has stabilised and is still showing the desert image. Their latest explanation is something called quantum entanglement – all about stuff being linked together somehow. They believe that it is like a series of doors and the monkey temple with the stars was like the key in the lock. Good for them...

20 April

Hambone's 'visitor' turned up this morning, so we made ourselves scarce. A couple of his girls took us to do some more sightseeing and for a change we had quite a civilised day out.

When we got back Hambone was not happy. The man who visited was someone he has had occasional contact with in the past, a very dangerous someone, and he wanted to know how Hambone had known about the 'North Koreans'. Hambone had worked out an alibi that consisted of him being tipped off by some Vietnamese war lords that he was doing some transporting of goods for. But he wasn't sure that the Agency type bought it. There were a couple of probing questions as to who he had been ferrying around that had got shot and his monkey companion, and then some casually dropped in comments about reports of a major firefight on the border. Anyway, the man more or less invited himself to lunch and hung around most of the day making more casual conversation until Hambone said he had to go and pick some stuff up. He drove around for a while and when he was sure that he hadn't been tailed he called up another of his more official contacts and asked about his visitor. There was a lot of deflection but eventually he managed to establish that said visitor has gone freelance and has slipped outside the radar of the Agency, in fact they were very keen that Hambone let them know if he turned up again.

In conclusion – we need to leave. Hambone is going to drive us back south to Phnom Penh tomorrow. It will be a much quicker journey than the slow cruise upriver and he reckons it's more about getting us safely out of the country now than being too discreet. We will set off at dawn and should be there around midday, then a quick visit to Mr Guns R Us to offload the hardware that Hambone doesn't want to keep and we will look at flying out the following day.

So tonight we are saying goodbye properly. I may not be supposed to be drinking yet but fuck that – this needs to be an epic farewell. The Monkey is wearing an afro wig and some large, round sunglasses he has found in one of the girls' rooms. I think this is going to hurt...

21 April

Hurt, it did...

Getting up at dawn and then being driven through the stunning Cambodian dawn while trying not to be sick and constantly groaning is a different way to start the day. Fortunately, there was very little on the roads and Hambone had sobered up a bit by the time we got halfway up the main highway. We passed around a large thermos of incredibly strong coffee and attempted to force ourselves into normality.

Reaching Phnom Penh, Hambone drove us to the hotel we had booked, and we dropped off our basic kit. Then he took us to the central market and the office of our arms dealer friend. He said that he was very glad to see us again and he had a sort of awed look on his face as if we had pulled off the impossible. We sold him back the guns and any other kit we didn't need (we had given the night vision goggles to Hambone as a present) all at a loss of course and then we headed back to the hotel. We tried to get Hambone to stay for another drink but he looked at us like we were fucking retarded and said that he wasn't one for long goodbyes and that if he left he could be back by early evening. Man and monkey hugs all around and then we waved Hambone goodbye. He didn't look back and neither did The Monkey.

I think secretly we are both glad he didn't agree to another drink as it might just have finished me off and The Monkey still has a stinking headache. We are sitting on the veranda overlooking the lights of Phnom Penh and eating some sort of rice dish whilst washing it down with something called Klang Beer – well, it's not a proper drink, is it? We have a flight at 17.10 tomorrow and then it will be back to whatever chaos awaits back home. We will miss Hambone...

Don't talk to strangers

22 April

Hambone is dead. Sniper round through the head as he sat on his balcony last night.

The Green and Red Society contacted us first thing to let us know. We are not going home now – there will be a funeral tomorrow and we are being driven back to Kampong Cham City later tonight. I asked about police involvement and was told that the Society would take care of everything. They weren't sure it was a good idea us going back but there was no way we weren't going to so there will be bodyguards assigned to us.

We went back to the central market and got our guns back. The dealer had heard the news as well and seemed genuinely sorry.

The Monkey has gone very quiet...

23 April

We watched as Hambone burned.

There were quite a few people present. His girls wailed constantly in the background as Buddhist prayers were chanted and incense carried the prayers to heaven. Scanning the mourners there were quite a few veterans who, like Hambone, had never managed to make it home. Various Orientals paid their respects, many of them were probably from the Society. One figure attracted my attention and I realised that The Monkey had fixed on him as well. Black bomber jacket, sand-coloured tactical trousers, wrap round Oakley sunglasses, his look screamed operator, and he didn't seem to care who knew. The Mao Shan sorcerer we had met in the jungle clearing led us away accompanied by our bodyguards before The Monkey's staring match could turn into something more inappropriate for a funeral.

We asked him what had happened and all he could tell us was that Hambone had returned home and gone to sit on the balcony to eat dinner. When one of the girls had returned with his food, she had found him hanging over the back of the chair with a massive hole in his head and one of the other less distraught girls had contacted a friend who had immediately called the Society. We asked him who the dick in the Oakley's was and he said that it was the man who had visited Hambone the day before we had left. Was there any connection? The look the sorcerer gave us spoke volumes and I had to grip The Monkey's shoulder to stop him turning round and going back. 'There will be a reckoning,' I told him, and he glowered evilly towards the crowd.

The sorcerer has asked The Monkey if he would like to meet the monk who freed him from the research facility. This is a somewhat unexpected offer and I am wondering if it is an attempt to stop The Monkey going all angry god again. The sorcerer keeps saying that today is not the time for revenge and for the moment The Monkey is complying – it is quite scary how quiet and controlled he is being. It makes me more nervous than when he is angry.

So, a meeting is set for tomorrow with the monk and in the meantime, we are the guests of the Society. I need a drink...

24 April

Didn't meet the monk today but we did travel north for hours until we finally crossed the Thai border. We think that a large part of this has been a ruse to get us out of the way of snipers and to prevent The Monkey going nuclear in a built-up area. Apparently the monk is going to be at a nearby temple complex in the morning and The

Monkey will get to see him then.

The Monkey wasn't happy about leaving Kampong Cham City without having a 'chat' with our Oakley-wearing friend but the sorcerer said that Mr Oakley would not be that far away while we were still in country. He thought it wise that the reunion should be somewhere a little more remote.

So now playing cards with our bodyguards and drinking Chang beer and something called Sang Som which is made from sugar cane. Both of us are caught up with thoughts of Hambone – this isn't a pleasant drinking session...

25 April

The Monkey met the monk. They went and sat in one of the courtyards of a cavernous temple. I watched as they sat down opposite each other and just stared. Then the sorcerer led me away saying that it was The Monkey's meeting not mine and that he wanted to talk to me.

We walked through the temple grounds and I asked him who these Illuminati actually are. 'You must understand that the world is not how you imagine it to be,' he said. 'Is this where you offer me the red or blue pill?' I replied, and immediately knew that my future as a comedian in Southeast Asia was dead. He stared at me with amusement and said, 'Let me tell you about reality.

'This existence is but a dream. It is a dream that we have all agreed upon and therefore it is a dream with form. But we are not the dreamers of the dream, we are the dreamt acting out our roles in a story written before the Universe was born.

'Like the Green and Red Society, the Illuminati have for centuries understood the nature of this cosmic dream, and although they are powerless to change it they can manipulate those who are as yet unaware. They pull the strings of finance, government, the military, major corporations, and organised religion. They would make themselves lords of the earth and have their descendants follow them for time immemorial. Your poet Milton said "It is better to reign in hell than to serve in heaven," this is their goal.'

'Okay, but where do the Green and Red fit into this, what's their agenda?'

'We realised over a thousand years ago that the only hope for humanity was for them to awake within the dream, to become aware. As mankind wakes, so the Universe becomes aware and the cycle can come to its end and then begin again but closer to its goal – stillness.'

'Stillness? Surely that is just stagnation and death?'

'Not stillness as you imagine it. Not emptiness as you imagine it. From out of the void all things are possible and into the void all things will return.'

'So like the Big Bang?'

'Yes, like the Big Bang.'

'Okay, this is making my head hurt. Can I ask about the monkey temple and the energy vortex thingy? What is it and what does it do and why is it connected to The Monkey?'

'Placed around the Earth are centres of power. Sometimes they exist naturally and sometimes they have been fashioned by humans, but they all have one thing in common – they are linked together. Like a series of corridors that pass through matter, they allow for the movement of organic and inorganic material from one location to another. Once, there were those who knew how to open and focus the vortexes so that they could travel across the Earth at will, even beyond the Earth. But that is an ancient knowledge that has been lost, and in many cases, purposefully destroyed.'

'So, is this like magic then?'

'To the primitive mind all science is magic.' I think he noticed my indignation and moved quickly on, 'The connection to the monkey god is a not entirely clear. From the mixture of myth that surrounds him it would appear that he may have arrived in this world via one of the vortexes and become an unofficial guardian of the energy force. After all, it is the well from which he draws his power.'

'So how come we have a black hole, vortex thing in our spare bedroom?'

'It would seem that the monkey god has the ability to create his own portals, although from what we can tell, they are not that stable.'

I avoided saying *Just like him*, and went back to the Illuminati. 'So, it wouldn't be a good thing if the Illuminati gained control of one of the gateways.'

'No, it would not. We believe, once the vortexes begin to become live again, that many ancient weapons that are hidden across the Earth will become active. They are not stupid, it would not take them long to work out how to trace the energy signatures, after all, they have immense wealth and technological resources at their disposal. All of the mythical objects that make up such large parts of human culture and storytelling are linked, they come from a single source, an ancient science, and they all draw their power, like the monkey god, from what you witnessed in the jungle temple.'

Then another thought occurred to me. Did he know of an Arno Whitaker? He turned his head slowly towards me and fixed me with those eyes made blacker by the white eyebrows. For the first time since meeting him I saw a flicker of uncertainty pass across his face.

'Yes, we know of Arno Whitaker. We were wondering when he would make his presence felt to the monkey god.' He stared straight into my eyes, as if he was searching for something, then he looked up at an ancient temple spire that poked through the all-invading creepers. 'He is an extremely dangerous adversary.'

I explained about being hacked, the photos we found with the notebook and the research that had placed an Arno Whitaker in the American Civil War, and someone who looks a lot like him in other historically important settings. Plus, his LinkedIn profile and association to the company Brightstorm. The sorcerer seemed amused by the LinkedIn profile, he nodded, 'You know more about him than he would like you to.

'He was a Southern Baptist snake handler. A preacher turned Illuminati initiate and head of their dirty deed's operations, with family connections from the time of the first American settlers that put him a long way up the Illuminati pecking order. And yes, it is the same Arno Whitaker in all of these scenarios.'

I made to object at the ridiculousness of that idea, but he held up his hand and said, 'After everything you have witnessed so far you find that hard to believe?' He had a point, so I shut up and let him continue.

'When he was bitten by his snakes and passed through the death state he was changed forever, both physically and mentally. You will find that, for appearances sake, he disappears and reappears every few decades, each time with a variation of the snakebite story. We lost sight of him in the 1960's for a while and then he reappeared after apparently having been in a coma for four years, after suffering massive poisoning from multiple rattlesnake bites to his face received during a Sunday church service.' He went on to explain how his facial muscles were paralysed into a lunatic smile as a result of snake venom – like a real life *Joker*, the venom also caused serious tissue damage and scaring resulting in a sort of scorched look. That explains why he has a face like a burning clown looking in a fun house mirror...

'Some questions were asked, and two investigative reporters died in unusual circumstances while following up the story. Then the story faded away amidst news of plane crashes and right-wing extremist shootings that conveniently occurred at the same time. He flaunts his deathlessness because he is aware that the rational world will pass over it because they choose not to believe, and if anyone looks too deeply then they can always be silenced... Be wary of Arno Whitaker my friend, he has an ancient and all-pervasive power behind him and now he knows that the monkey god has awoken he will stop at nothing to gain control over the power that awakening brings and seduce the monkey god to the will of the Illuminati.'

We had talked for a couple of hours, and to be honest, I lost track of time. We found ourselves sitting on the side of a hill amongst trees and looking out towards a modern city in the far distance as the sun was beginning to set. He looked at me with those black eyes and said, 'The monkey god has returned. In our pride we believed we would be able to control him, but he is a mixture of East and West that we never could have imagined. And it is good. He should be under the control of no man – but you have more sway over him than any human could ever have. You must help him control his power because if he loses control completely, he could tear the world apart.'

'I thought you said that we are all just bit part players in some drama written billions of years ago. How can The Monkey affect that?'

'Because he is the essence of chaos, the one unpredictable thread in the whole story. He could even choose to side with the Illuminati and then all the visions of hell on earth would be realised.'

'Did the Illuminati have anything to do with Hambone's death?'

'Yes, undoubtedly.'

'Then there's no way The Monkey is going to get matey with them.'

'Shall we go back now? You have a busy day tomorrow – you have vengeance to take.'

For chilled-out philosopher types these Mao Shan are dead pragmatic when it comes to taking life, I asked him how come? 'When it is a man's time, it is his time,' was his answer. Glad we got that one sorted!

As we approached the courtyard where The Monkey waited for us, the Mao Shan sorcerer put a slim, long fingered hand on my arm, He looked at me with a strange intensity and said, 'You must not let the night fall on the future,' and then he turned his head again and entered the courtyard. No pressure then!

We collected The Monkey and left the temple. The monk watched us go but The Monkey never looked back. He was quiet on the way back to the hotel but when we got there he lit up a big old cigar, gave me a shit eating grin and said, 'Let's have a drink 'cuz tomorrow I am going to kill that fucker who was at the funeral.' My head is spinning from all the stuff I have been told but I am up for a drink. I seem to know that it was Hambone's time to die and I can live with that, and I also know that it is going to be good to slot that shit head in the Oakleys...

26 April

So, this is how it happened...

Our Mr Sorcerer had managed to get word out that we would be at a disused factory site on the edge of the nearby city at around midday. He had made sure that Mr Sunglasses would have every chance to hear this rumour and, he said, the rest was up to us.

So early this morning we headed for the factory with its derelict buildings and rusting storage tanks and made our way through the rubble into the darkened loading bay. We would have no idea which way he would approach so we would try and force him into a kill zone when he entered the factory – at least that was the plan. Turns out Mr Sunglasses was particularly good at his job and he got into the factory complex without us knowing. But he had no clue where we were either so it was a surprise for all concerned when I literally bumped into him as I rounded the corner of a corridor between sections of the building.

He body slammed me backwards into the wall. I did some JKD and Thai boxing when I was younger and wasn't bad but I knew just by looking at this fucker that he was going to snap me like a twig, so I went for my Glock. He responded by grabbing my right wrist with both of his hands and smashing his shoulder into my chest so that for the second time in as many seconds I was crushed against the wall. As part of the kit I got for this little adventure I bought two knives, the big old K-Bar combat blade in the back sheath that I would never be able to reach, and a small knife hanging on a chain around my neck. With a burst of sheer desperation, I grabbed the small blade with my left hand, dragged it from its Kydex sheath and continued the motion downwards in a slash across Oakley Boy's shoulder and upper back. He didn't really make much noise, but he responded immediately by jumping back and throwing out his right arm to block the follow up thrust of the blade to his kidney that he was anticipating. Think he was a bit bemused when he realised that the thrust wasn't coming because I was obviously an amateur. But he was hurt. As he went for his gun, he used his left hand to support his right wrist. Hurt or not he was still damn quick and as the gun began to come out of the holster, I could see the void opening up before me. Then The Monkey hit him with all fours right in the chest and sent him crashing backwards. I had caught the movement out of the corner of my eye as The Monkey sort of parkoured off the wall beside me and rebounded into the bastard's chest and then landed on his feet in front of me. Gun and Oakleys went flying but he rolled and was back on his feet immediately, a combat blade in his hand. We saw his eyes for the first time – cold, hard, grey-blue.

At this point The Monkey burst into flames. The cold, hard, grey-blue eyes went wide – it was as if he was finally seeing The Monkey for the first time. I had missed his party trick at the temple, so I too stood there stupidly staring as he physically grew and the flames licked over his fur and seemed to form into glowing, burning armour. Then, as if time had slowed to a crawl I watched as The Monkey punched his fist into Mr Sunglasses' chest with a sound like someone whacking a raw Christmas turkey with a cricket bat, and I watched as the hole he made flared with fire and blackened. Then as Mr Sunglasses' face contorted with fear and pain, the creature that The Monkey had become ripped out blackened lungs and heart from the crater in the chest and stared into the now pleading cold, hard, grey eyes as the life went out of them...

*

We are now in Bangkok. We are going to fly from here to Kuala Lumpur tomorrow to pick up our flight home. The Society have taken care of the flight and our guns, and they would have taken care of the body except that The Monkey reduced it to ash with his fire. Fierce shit...

Remarkably, I survived my hand-to-hand combat session without the wound in my side opening so now we have a chance to party in one of the craziest cities on earth. One night in Bangkok – what could possibly go wrong...?

27 April

Woke up skydiving on the hotel bed wearing someone else's trousers. The Monkey was asleep upright in a swivel chair with sick all down his front.

After quick showers we poured ourselves into a taxi and headed for the airport. We had said our goodbyes to the sorcerer and the other Society members yesterday, so it was just me and The Monkey again. In the taxi he looked at me with bloodshot eyes and said that he didn't think all those girls were girls last night – I really, really, really don't want to know...

At the airport we headed for the baggage drop and this guy comes walking towards us. We saw him from quite a way off and there was something about the way he moved through the crowd like no one wanted to touch him. He had this big, praise Jesus grin on his scared, twisted face and he looked like the Mormons who come knocking at your door, if the Mormons were all slightly out of focus. I wanted to punch him in the face the moment I saw him. He stopped right in front of us and something about his watery green eyes was just creepy as fuck. He opened his gash of a mouth and this soft, southern states of America drawl came out. 'Well, it's nice to meet you at last. Snakebite has missed our web chats.' He seemed to grin even harder at his own cleverness, 'And I've been hearing so much about you this past week.' He held out his hand and we both just looked at it and then back at his creepy face. The hand stayed there for a moment longer before being lowered but the smile remained unchanged. 'It seems Sergeant Maguire underestimated you. I take it you have killed him?' It was more a statement of fact than a question. 'So, he was your man then?' I asked. 'They are all ours in the end whether they know it or not.' The sickly smile seemed to grow larger and more sickly, 'You will be too – you just don't know it yet.' The Monkey moved ever so slightly forward and growled, and I quickly pointed out that there were too many people and too much airport security with guns. This was quite obviously why Arno Whitaker had decided to introduce himself to us here. 'Why don't you go fuck yourself,' I said very politely. He stared straight into my eyes and it felt as if he was trying to crawl into my head. It was as if my brain was itching and I could almost imagine spiders running around inside my skull. The Monkey put his finger on the thin, suit jacketed chest and said 'Stop.' Eye contact was broken, and the smile intensified even more. 'You will join us; it is only a matter of time now that we are aware of you. You have no real choice.' I looked at The Monkey and said that we should go and check our bags, and then I looked at the man and thanked him for his creepy offer but that my mum had told me not to talk to weird cunts at airports, and then I swung my bag round and onto my shoulder making sure to hit him in the balls as I did so. He doubled up and dropped to his knees, the smile sliding slightly off his face. I made lots of 'Oh, terribly sorry. How awful, I do apologise,' noises as we moved away from him and towards the airline desk. I could hear strangled curses and threats, but they were drowned out by The Monkey laughing...

That was this morning and we now have quite a few hours' wait here at Kuala Lumpur airport before the long haul back home. The Society upgraded us to first class, and we have use of the executive lounge and its complimentary bar, we suspect that the Society may also have some of their men stationed around for our safety. If these Illuminati dudes don't get us, then I suspect I will die of liver failure...

28 April

Man, I'm knackered.

At Leigh Delamere services on the M4. We stopped for a break because we were so tired and have now checked into the Travelodge because I don't think it's going to be safe to drive the rest of the way home tonight. Flight got delayed a couple of hours and then I found out that I had lost the sleeping pills so had a mostly awake 20-hour flight.

The Monkey is passed out on the sofa bed and every now and then a glow passes over him like he is just about to ignite. He has been making grunting noises and he has just rolled over and shouted, 'Not the ripe ones!' I have no idea what that is about but I am trying not to piss myself laughing.

God, I need sleep...

Area 51

29 April

Spent the day catching up with the Nerds and the Monster Highs. Had to phone ahead to get the camouflage lifted for us to find the house but we got in with no problems.

It has been an interesting few weeks! And it looks like the Nerds have had their fair share of fun. The presence of the men in black has dropped off – they haven't seen the black choppers for over a week and there has been no sign of black suits for the last couple of days. There has still been no word of JudyZ, and both me and The Monkey feel bad about that, we don't need any more collateral damage.

The black hole is showing a vision of a desert, just as the Nerds said, and apparently the Monster Highs have taken to stepping in and out of it! With the Nerds watching, they passed through the black hole into the desert when it was night there and came back again. They took a GPS locator with them which the Nerds have pinged, and the location came back as the Nevada desert in the good old US of A. They are very excited (again) as they believe that we have a door in the spare bedroom that leads into Area 51...

I asked the girls what they thought of the photos of Arno Whitaker and his history. They looked at each other and then reiterated that we must be very careful how we deal with the grinning dickhead – my words, not theirs. I got the impression that there was more to it than that but they wouldn't be pressed into giving anything away so I guess I will just bide my time. They can be very cryptic (in all senses of the word), but like The Monkey said, they seem to have good reasons to keep some things to themselves and they have never let us down yet.

30 April

The Monkey went out and did a recce today and it seems that the Nerds' house has been bugged but there doesn't seem to be anyone spying on the road so we are thinking that the spooks may believe any persons of interest have skipped the area. The Monster Highs are going to keep the cloaking thing in place just in case – it doesn't seem to cause them any bother to do it so we might as well have it there for the time being. Apparently next door's dog has been having fits because he knows that the house should be there but keeps losing it, he has almost lost his voice barking. The Monkey thinks it is very funny.

We need to work out why the black hole has started showing panoramic views of the Nevada desert. I talked the Nerds through what the Mao Shan sorcerer had explained to me about the vortexes and they are very pleased with themselves because it matches up with their theory that it is a series of linked tunnels through the space time continuum which line up when the master door is opened in the monkey temple. That sounds about right, and it looks like we might be up for another trip although the thought of stepping into something we have been calling *the black hole* does put the shits up me a bit. The Monkey is questioning my sexuality and saying that the Monster Highs were fine when they went for a look around through the black hole, but I have pointed out that they are not technically fully alive anyway. He just makes chicken noises and says I am splitting hairs – bastard! But we are both agreed that we can't go anywhere *serious* until my gunshot wound is more fully healed, should be another week or so. In the meantime, The Monkey may go and have a little look around to see what we will be walking into and continue to take the piss out of me at every chance. Yeah, you need look at me over your JD with your cigar stuck in your mouth – fucker...

1 May

Lovey sunny day today (obviously not as hot as Cambodia – but hey, don't knock it!).

Dave has managed to grow an acceptable beard over the last couple of weeks, so with the addition of a hat and some shades he has been camouflaged enough to come out with the rest of us. All except the Monster Highs that is, they don't really do sun.

We took a drive past the airbase but there was no sign of black Range Rovers or black helicopters, so we swung back to the beach, or more accurately, the pub on the beach. Great to be sitting outside not smothered in 100% Deet and nice to taste a Rattler again. Ah, simple pleasures. After a couple we had a game of footie on the beach that degenerated into some sort of medieval ball game. I had to sit out after a bit so I didn't open up my wound, but it was funny as fuck watching the others charge about like complete idiots.

Had some grub and a couple more pints then Tony, who had drawn the short straw as designated driver, drove us back to the house and now we are sitting in the beer garden of the local and Tony is playing catch-up. When it is dark enough for the Monster Highs to remain pale and interesting, they are going to join us and we may just get a taxi into town and see what trouble we can get into...

2 May

Found a lap dancing club last night and the Monster Highs put on a show – disturbing...

Finally got round to asking The Monkey what he had talked to the monk about. He said that they had talked about the nature of reality and the paths that we all must follow in life. I told him that it was pretty much what the sorcerer had talked to me about although I hadn't been told I had the potential to be the destroyer of worlds. But the monk had told him that all creatures will follow their nature regardless so what will be, will be – so that's alright then? I asked if the monk had mentioned getting the lolly stick stars and he said that as soon as the monk had started releasing the monkeys from the research facility, he had known that the soul of the American soldier had been in The Monkey. He said that he recognised the man who had given him the bundle of sticks in the Cambodian jungle when he was a child, that was why he kept The Monkey and gave him to the seaman along with the sticks. I asked if he had thought about finding out who the soldier had been, and he just shrugged and said that there were other things more important to sort out at the moment, although I did catch him staring long and hard at the jungle group photo featuring the soldier.

The Monkey thinks the journal is played out, so he is putting that on one side for the moment. Now we have to decide what we are going to do when we get into Area 51, if that's where the black hole leads. Doing research on one of the most secure places on the planet is difficult. There does seem to be a consensus that it is ringed with cameras and motion sensors, and that if you stray in there you get shot. All reassuring. And then there is the stuff about alien autopsies and crashed space craft. Well, at least it's close to Vegas...

3 May

We have sat in the sun today and drunk beer (of course) while looking at countless pages of stuff on the internet about Area 51. Pages and pages of so-called insider information, pages and pages of conspiracy theories, pages and pages of de bunking of said theories. YouTube videos that range from the well-constructed to the fucking mental. Hundreds of sane/bonkers/scientific/radical/hysterical arguments. But to be honest none of them are a patch on the story of a burning monkey god in the jungles of South East Asia...

This, I think, is going to be like pulling teeth, but at least the Nerds are having a lovely time...

4 May

The Nerds have picked up some odd activity on their computers. It seems to be the same sort of thing as when they went looking at the classified military files. They have set up all sorts of rerouting thingies and dead ends and firewalls, and all that other shit that computer geeks talk about, and they were pretty sure they had gotten themselves hidden but then the little tracking signs started to show up again. The Monster Highs took it upon themselves to sort it out – they sat at a laptop and put their hands on the keyboard and the screen went a pearly white for a few seconds and then came back to normal. Tony asked them what they had done and as they headed back to the darkened bedroom, they answered, 'Someone somewhere is screaming.'

That's not the only activity the Nerds have picked up. There has been movement in the desert that has been picked up by the tech that the Monster Highs dropped off there – seems to be a few days old but they hadn't noticed in the general fun of us being back. Vehicles have patrolled the area without finding anything and the Nerds are wondering if there are movement sensors close enough to have picked up the sightseeing trips.

We are now watching *American Dad* – The Monkey is fascinated by Roger...

Charlie don't surf

5 May

The Nerds' computer problem seems to have gone away, I don't know what the Monster Highs did but it seems to have done the trick...

Something had been bothering me about the disappearance of JudyZ, and the business with the men in black. 1: Why, if they found JudyZ did they not trace the messages that the Nerds had been sending to her? 2: If they followed Dave why have they not traced the Nerds' identity through their vehicle and the house up the road? When we all sat down in the pub at lunchtime, I decided to ask them and the answers were quite surprising. It seems that they are clever little buggers when it comes to hiding their identities. The programming work they do to earn money is all paid into an offshore account and then routed through a couple of different accounts in assumed names. Their email messages are bounced around multiple servers and go through encryption and coding so that they can't be traced or read by anyone who doesn't know how, and apparently they self-scramble after they have been read so that no one at all can access them. The house up the road is rented in another assumed identity and paid for through yet another account that cannot be traced back to a real person. Their vehicles are, again, registered to false identities and they have a tendency to swap number plates for some phantom ones if they have to go anywhere they might need double anonymity (Dave had done this on his trip to Reading). Dave had also ditched the car on the other side of the village and switched the plates again and he thinks that the only reason that their house was compromised was that his tail must have had a back-up who drove past the house as he was going in. Although their house was bugged (which The Monkey has taken care of) we believe that whoever these men in black types are, they are going on guess work, and with the juju that the Monster Highs have been spreading around it must have caused a massive amount of confusion amongst them.

It seems that even before they were at uni the Nerds had decided to make themselves non people and they set about erasing their identities in the way that only idealistic and intelligent youth have the knowhow and stamina to do. They had smug little smiles on their faces by the time they had finished telling us and even The Monkey was forced to admit a new respect for them. Although not for their drinking...

6 May

What a beautiful day. We all hit the beach, except for the Monster Highs, and surfing was attempted. I had to sit this one out as my wound is not quite healed enough to risk it opening up again due to some over enthusiastic wipe-out, doc reckons by the end of the week I should be back in the game. So, I sat and watched as The Monkey ripped it up – being light and highly mobile does have its advantages – and the Nerds crashed and burned. Everyone had a great time; we are BBQing on the beach and the Monster Highs have just joined us – they are much happier out of bright sunlight and I am trying to work out whether it is because they are ghouls or they don't want a tan to ruin their Goth image! Still, good to have them here now. Sausages and burgers are always better on the beach washed down with Rattler.

Good to chill for a bit and let off some steam. Tomorrow The Monkey wants to take a jump through the black hole to do a quick recce and I think the Monster Highs are going to go with him to mess up any sensors that might be spying. He promises it will be a very quick look as he just wants to get a feel for what the surrounding area is like.

But now if I'm not mistaken, I can see a human pyramid taking shape and even the girls are joining in...

7 May

Well – The Monkey went in with Monster Highs in tow and came out again two hours later dusty but none the worse for wear. He says that there is nothing around for miles, and they did go for a bit of a stroll to make sure. They found a few sensor posts, which the girls messed with in their own special way, and tyre tracks but no buildings or anything else, except, on a distant range of hills they could see the outline of what they think might be a transmitter tower. No real details as they were viewing it against a starlit sky but definitely a tower of some sort. Could be a place to start but The Monkey says that we aren't going to be quickly in and out when we get there, not without transport. This has begun a whole new train of thought...

8 May

So, consensus seems to be that we get motorbikes and ride them through the black hole into Area 51... Doesn't matter how many times I hear that sentence it still gives me the biggest grin!

We are going to buy two trials bikes, take them up into the spare room and then ride them into a black hole – holy shit! Nope – still grinning. I will ride one with The Monkey as pillion and one of the Nerds will ride the other with a Monster High as pillion. This will allow us to disrupt sensors and lay down covering fire. Tony had suggested Segways as being quieter, but The Monkey told him to fuck right off just before I had the chance to. They might be quiet, but they are nowhere near as fast or as cool.

Right, I have just ordered the bikes, and I see the doc tomorrow for a final check-up, so the next adventure is on the cards.

9 May

We have had debates until the early hours of the morning about why the black hole is pointing at Area 51, and the only thing we can agree on is that if the gateway controlled by the monkey temple is an ancient one, then if it points to that place in the Nevada desert there must have been something there a long time ago to draw the energy to that point. There is a second argument that, as our black hole was created by The Monkey, maybe it responds to need – the need of The Monkey – so perhaps there is something there that he requires.

Needless to say, all of these debates have been fuelled by alcohol and have included drunken fights and a couple of arm-wrestling matches, the most memorable of which was when one of the girls beat all three Nerds one after another! I have noticed that the Nerds have now started exercising but the more I learn about the Monster Highs the more I am convinced that even if the boys start taking steroids they are still going to lose...

10 May

Signed off by the doc. Hurray! Although he has advised me to ease myself gently back into physical activity...

Spent the afternoon combat training with the Nerds as The Monkey cast an expert eye over the proceedings. That little scuffle with the Oakley kid in Thailand opened my eyes to just how out of shape and practice I have got, so plenty of sparring and bag work, with The Monkey throwing in the military close quarter combat side of it.

Knackered now. We have all crashed out in the living room to watch *300* for the three hundredth time and rehydrate with JD – the only real sports drink you need...

Just noticed how the Monster Highs are staring at *300* – they are almost drooling, and it's not at the fit Spartans. No, they really are salivating at the piles of dead bodies...

11 May

Ooh, sore today but back for more training. Kev is not bad and learns quick, and he can ride a bike so it looks like he has drawn the short straw and gets to go with us.

We have spent much of the afternoon cleaning and checking guns. The Monkey wants to do some shooting tomorrow to make sure we have all got our shit together, so that should be fun. We are now having a nice group craft session in the living room as we learn to make pipe bombs to take with us.

The Nerds have found a video on YouTube of a chimp riding a Segway accompanied by an annoying theme tune. Fairly amusing but I fear it may wear thin quickly.

I was right about the chimp and Segway video. After it had been played about fifty times The Monkey no longer saw the funny side and threatened to choke out the next person who played it or sang the song. Tony had an early bath...

12 May

A day of rainy muddy shooting at make-shift targets in the woods. Got a lot of gun cleaning to do again. The Monkey is happy though and we have quite a stash of pipe bombs.

Now for a drink...

Bat out of Hell

13 May

The Monster Highs disappeared last night. They were back again this morning, slipping silently into the bedroom. I am guessing that they needed to eat and all the bodies piled up in the film the other night must have given them a proper appetite (shit – it is so weird that it doesn't freak me out, my tolerance for the bizarre has gone through the roof!). No idea where they went and to be honest, I'm not going to ask, and The Monkey just doesn't want to know. I just hope we don't see any stories about grave robbing on the local news...

*

Collected the bikes today! Tony drove me, The Monkey and Kev to the dealer and we rode back on two 250cc XR-

F Enduros. The Green and Red Society have offered us all the funding we need to bankroll our shenanigans, so I paid for the bikes in cash and left behind a very happy salesman. Haven't been on a bike for a while and I'd forgotten what a buzz it is! The Monkey loved it and insisted on flipping the finger at every car we passed.

This afternoon we manhandled the bikes up the stairs and into the spare room. After we got our breath back, we did some more training and then checked out the night vision goggles etc. It looks like we are going in either tomorrow or Wednesday. We won't know for sure until the girls wake up – they are a bit like snakes and sleep a lot after a big feed...

14 May

Boooo! The girls are still asleep so no adventure today...

It's been a fucking horrible day – wind, rain, cold. It's May for fuck sake! Ended up doing bag work and oiling our guns (and that's not a euphemism). Now we are in the midst of a *Buffy the Vampire Slayer* marathon courtesy of the Nerds. Ah Spike, the Billy Idol of vampires, always so much cooler than Angel – I blame Angel for the rise of the shiny, angst, pretty boy vampires... bastard! Anyway fucking off now, JD has just been topped up and Buffy is back on screen...

15 May

The Monster Highs are up and about again – hooray! But they didn't wake up until the middle of the afternoon which was too late for us to go through the black hole. We stood and watched the sun's rays gradually creeping over the desert through the window of the black hole, very picturesque but totally the wrong side of the day for our purposes. We need to go in when it is still night there so that we have a chance of not being observed and also because the girls don't do well in broad daylight. So we will be setting the alarm for 5am tomorrow and that should give us plenty of hours of darkness to go romping round the desert.

Of course, this has meant more training and gun cleaning, although the sun did come out today, so we got to play outside. Now, once again, we are drinking and watching TV. This time The Monkey has chosen, and we are watching *Black Hawk Down*. Not sure if this is doing Kev much good. He has to go into a possible firefight tomorrow, and as we watch the US Rangers aren't doing so well, and there is a lot of arterial spray.

I think we may call it a night earlier than usual and see if we can be a bit more professional tomorrow morning – maybe without too much of a hangover, those guns are loud...

16 May

What an anticlimax going through the black hole was! I was expecting mad sensations and crazy warping effects or something – too much TV. Instead, it was just like stepping through a doorway into another room, except we were on motorbikes and there were two blokes, a monkey and a ghoul, all armed to the teeth. I like to think that in some small way it looked like the cover of Meatloaf's *Bat out of Hell* album – but probably not.

Anyway, we were in the Nevada desert, Area 51 to be precise, and we were stoked.

I looked back at the black hole expecting to see the other two Nerds and the remaining Monster High looking at us out of mid-air but the only sign was a ripple in the air, a bit like heat haze but in the dark. I asked how the hell we were going to find it again but apparently to the Monster Highs it looks like a whirling light show so no problems there then.

We set off across the desert in the direction The Monkey said the tower thing was. It's so cool riding a bike through the desert at night! The moon was still off its first quarter so it was pretty dark although there were no clouds, so the starlight was awesome. Riding in night vision goggles is interesting as well, it takes a little time to get used to the change in depth perception. We stopped on a ridge and The Monkey pointed out the outline of the tower on the distant hills and we did a quick estimate and decided that they were about a ten-minute ride away.

Twelve minutes later and we were at the foot of the hills and looking for a way up. We rode along the lower slope for a couple of miles and then found a wide track leading upwards. There were tyre tracks visible, but they didn't look recent, so we powered up the twisting track to the top. The tower looked a bit like a radio transmitter tower but it had a dome shaped thing at the top and a series of spiral antenna radiating out from its sides most of the way up the forty-odd foot of its height. It all looked a bit old school Sci Fi and I was half expecting a robot to appear shouting *Danger Will Robinson*! We had a good look round and Kev took some photos but there was nothing else there; no buildings and nothing leading to or from the tower. Kev thinks that the central pole running the height of the tower must go down into the earth and he hazarded a guess that it might be some sort of seismic monitoring tower.

We rode along the top of the hills until we came to the western end, and in the distance we could see lights out on the desert floor. It looked from that distance like a compound of some sort, and stretching into the distance behind it we could see more towers. The slope down the other side of the hills was fairly gentle so we rode down to the desert again and headed off towards were the lights where although we could no longer see them as it looked like there was a ridge in the way. After another ten minutes we reached the ridge, got off the bikes, and crawled up to the top to peek over. The compound was closer, and we could see tall lights all the way around the outside, and low concrete structures behind tall wire fences and razor wire. The inside of the compound seemed to be separated by further fences and it looked as if there were people squatting or sitting in each of the separated sections. Then something truly bizarre happened. One of the figures turned towards us and seemed to be looking directly at us even though we should have been too far away and in too much darkness to be seen. Then it started to howl. We could hear it even at that distance. More lights came on and searchlights began to scan the desert around the compound; after a couple of minutes the gates opened and a Humvee came tearing out onto the road and towards us. We scrambled down the ridge and took off on the bikes. We took the same route back as it looked like the quickest, and as we were heading back down the hills after passing the tower, we could hear a deep hum that seemed to be coming from underground. The Monkey told me afterwards that when he looked over his shoulder he saw the tower flickering with lights that looked like static and we all felt our hair beginning to stand on end.

Back on the desert floor we kicked it as fast as we dared, and the Monster High guided us back to the black hole. We slowed enough to ride through safely and all of a sudden, we were back in the spare room.

Dave and Tony kept an eye on the black hole and reported that they had seen a vehicle driving round the area of the black hole and when the sun came up soldiers on foot checking where the motion sensors are. We will need to be more careful next time but now at least we have a target – find out what the fuck is going on in that compound.

The Nerds have spent the rest of the day looking at Kev's photos and discussing what they think the towers are. We have left them to it…

17 May

Even though the Monster High used her skills to mask us in yesterday's adventure they still managed to track us back to the black hole – or at least they picked a big enough area that we might have been in and saturated it with soldiers. Patrols have been spotted through the black hole over the past 24 hours and there have been sightings of helicopters as well. They seem to be going round in circles, but they are worryingly close so no more incursions until everything settles down again.

The Nerds are now thinking that the tower we found might be some form of energy generating structure. Their favourite pin-up Tesla is being mentioned again and they think that we should avoid towers when we go back in – just to be on the safe side. More worryingly the Monster Highs have been discussing the figures in the compound and they think they might be *super normal* humans. Not quite sure what that is but they reckon we need to be careful if we are anywhere around them. After being spotted by one in the dark at extreme distance I tend to agree.

The Monkey thinks we should go back in ASAP and have a good look at the compound. He agrees with what everyone is saying but also contends that this was never going to be a picnic so we should just get on with it. He sent a message to the Green and Red Society today telling them what we had seen and asking if they had any idea what it might be, but we have heard nothing back from them yet. Plan is now to wait until the patrols slack off and head directly for the compound.

Tonight though, we are wearing sombreros, eating chilli, drinking tequila and watching Danny Trejo in *Machete*. This is what happens when the supermarket has a special on tortilla chips – things get out of hand...

18 May

The Nerds spent a good two hours showing us a PowerPoint presentation they had put together outlining why they think the towers are some sort of Tesla coil – with diagrams and photos. No typewriter sound effects but a few checkerboard transitions. If they are correct, and despite the use of Comic Sans they made a compelling argument in favour, then we could be in trouble. They think nobody had trespassed into the area for so long (ever?) that the towers weren't activated and now they are probably up and running at full tilt. And what does that mean, I hear you ask? It means that we will get fried to fuck by a billion volts if we stray within the killing zone of the towers and from what we have seen there are a lot of towers by the compound. Thank fuck for complacency as that probably saved our arses the other day but now they know someone has been on their patch of sand we won't be as lucky next time.

More choppers were spotted through the black hole again today and a patrol with dogs was seen moving through the area. The Monster Highs did something and the dogs went mental and bit their handlers before sprinting off into the desert. It was pretty funny until the handlers started opening up on the fleeing dogs with automatic fire. High velocity rounds can apparently take a dog's leg right off...

The Monkey has been chatting to some of his contacts and thinks he can score some claymore mines. He is talking about setting them around the area of the black hole so that when we are on the run back, we can smash the fuck out of anyone pursuing. He has the best ideas...

19 May

Claymores arrived today, delivered by a bloke called Johno in a silver and black Mitsubishi Barbarian with what look worryingly like real shrunken heads hanging off the rear-view mirror. I don't know how The Monkey meets these people, but it seems that Johno is an ex South African paratrooper turned mercenary. We sat and talked about our little issue and Johno suggested that we should take out one of the patrols and then infiltrate the compound in their vehicle. Sounds like a good idea and I suggested to The Monkey that Johno might like to come along and play. The Monkey gave me a look that said, *You really don't want* that, so I kept my mouth shut.

We are all going out to dinner at Señor Dicks in town (more Mexican) and while we wait for a couple of taxis, I have just asked Johno where he got the realistic shrunken heads from. 'Two realistic non shrunken bodies my friend,' was not the answer I particularly wanted...

Hen Party

20 May

Johno ended up going off with two women from a hen party – fair play. We guess he will come back for his Barbarian when he has finished shrinking their heads or whatever passes for fun with him!

This has left us pondering the idea of taking over a patrol. It would need to be at night, or at least dusk for the Monster Highs, and there are less of those patrols. It would also need to be a patrol with its own transport not one just dropped off. The Monkey has been back through again this morning to plant a few claymores in a gully area to the south of the black hole and he says that there were no patrols in the immediate vicinity but he could see lights out in the desert to the east. It is more than likely that they have spread their search pattern out in that direction as they can't find anything else in the area where we just disappeared into thin air...

21 May

All of us sat for hours staring through the black hole and at the Nerds monitoring devices. No patrols came anywhere near. Oh they were out there, but too far away for us to get at them quickly and quietly. In the end we started taking shifts to watch but we are all still knackered – lots of adrenalin with no place to go just wipes you out!

The Barbarian is still parked down the road. Johno must have become a feature of the hen party or he has got himself thrown in jail for drunk and disorderly...

23 May

Right, we have had enough of waiting. The Monkey went through again this morning and hid some little strobe lights in a dip in the desert floor about 200 metres to the west of the black hole. We are going to wait until tomorrow morning when we pick up one of their night patrols in suitable proximity and then set off the strobes to attract them to the dip. Then it's game on and we are going to the compound no matter what.

A friend of ours in town phoned this evening and asked if we knew a South African bloke. He had found Johno sitting in the sand dunes at the back of one of the beaches. Just sitting and staring. And he has puncture wounds on his neck. I said we would come and pick him up. I explained what had happened to the others and the Monster Highs laughed and said what did he expect if he went off with vampires? Vampires? They clarified by saying that the women he had gone off with were vampires – hadn't we realised? We all looked at each other and agreed that we hadn't. They say that at least 10% of the supposed hen parties in town are made up of vamps – it's an easy way for them to hunt. So why had they not warned Johno or at least given us a heads up? Well, they didn't particularly like Johno, and they knew the women wouldn't kill him, and they hadn't realised that we didn't see through the glamour they were putting out.

Me and The Monkey are going to pick up Johno and I have said that when we get back we need to have a serious conversation about exactly what is wandering around out there...

24 May

Taking out the patrol went like clockwork and within half an hour we were heading back towards the compound in an armoured Humvee with some new toys to play with. Felt a bit sorry for the patrol, they were obviously just hired grunts who were doing a glorified security job but there you go...

Not much radio chatter so we just rolled back in and they waved us through, the night vision goggles we were all wearing covered enough face to keep us anonymous. We swung through a double row of gates and pulled up beside one of the low concrete buildings. The whole place was pretty well lit so we just decided to bluff it out, although we could no longer hide behind the night vision kit, the stolen uniforms helped us blend in especially with the fog type thing that the Monster Highs can do, just enough to make it hard for anyone to really stare at us.

It was immediately obvious that the people we had seen in the separated areas of the compound weren't soldiers. They looked more like zoo animals. They stood, or sat, or lay, many of them paced around exhibiting symptoms of stress like caged wild animals do. They looked malnourished and haunted and it reminded me of photos taken in concentration camps by the Russian forces as they swept across eastern Europe at the end of World War Two. We got close to one of the smaller enclosures and a dishevelled young man standing just the other side of the wire spoke to us, 'Kill me please,' he said without taking his eyes from the night sky. As we moved quickly on, others also took up the pitiful chant begging for death. It had attracted the attention of the guards on the perimeter, and the team of lab coats who were doing the rounds of the cages. The Monkey motioned us back towards the buildings and our Humvee and our Monster High increased the glamour to give us more cover but now the eyes of all the inmates were fixed on us and their demands became louder and louder. It was difficult not to break into a run, but we got back into the area in front of the buildings with no one challenging us.

At this point I looked up at the only two-storey building in the compound and at the lighted window, and there was the smiling freak from the airport in Thailand, Arno Whitaker, looking directly at us and grinning like a loon. As I watched, he gabbled something to others in the room although he didn't take his eyes off us. Other, military faces joined him at the window and there was a lot of puzzled looks, but the freak obviously got his point over and all of a sudden an alarm went off and everyone started running. We bolted for the Humvee and made it just as the cage doors clicked open and the inmates came out. They had changed. They no longer looked like tortured animals, now they had a focused look and that look was turned on us. Then they began to run, and I mean run. What went through my head was scenes from the film *28 Days* and as we fumbled to get into the vehicle, I could see The Monkey cocking the assault rifle he had taken from the patrol. We got the engine started as they reached us and began to clamber over the vehicle. I threw it into reverse and hit a few of them as I swung it in a wide arc to face the gates. For a moment I sat horrified. Not all of the lab coats had made it to safety, and I saw at least three cornered by a fence. The inmates didn't tear them to pieces like some zombie movie, they beat them down with precision and I watched one get choked out from behind as if they were all highly trained martial artists. One thing was for sure – the lab coats weren't ever getting up again.

I smashed the Humvee through the gates and accelerated into the desert. I swear I could see the smile of that fucker like some massive Cheshire Cat in the window as I glanced in the side mirror. Then Kev was screaming about the towers and I saw massive arcing flashes of lightning begin to run around the perimeter of the compound. The

Monkey looked at me and said, 'They're to keep them in!' and it was immediately obvious. The inmates had all halted at the wire and suddenly the alarm stopped and they all began to mill aimlessly around, some even dropped to the floor in obvious distress. Vehicles began to stream out of another gate, and we started to hear bullets pinging off the Humvee's armour. And the race back began.

We knew we couldn't dump the Humvee right by the black hole so I did a drive by and Kev and Monster High jumped, then Me and The Monkey drove back to the gully at the south and left the vehicle going as we leapt out and ran like fuck back to the others. It seemed like seconds before the chasing vehicles came roaring past and down into the gully and then The Monkey set off the claymores and the night got very bright and bloody. We came back through the black hole as dawn was breaking and The Monkey told the Nerds to close it up, so they turned on their net thing again and the desert image faded to a ghostly shadow.

Damn it, what the fuck was that?

Kev is rocking in the corner – he is still not a happy bunny. The Monster Highs have been trying to calm him down with some of their mad mind stuff but even they are having a hard job. That spooked the fuck out of us all. Even the girls are shaking their pretty heads – there is something very, very wrong with what they are doing to the inmates in that compound. Going to need a stiff drink to shut off the images of those staring faces and that grinning lunatic...

25 May

We have spent the day massaging our wounded minds. Still too shocked about yesterday to try to make sense out of it. Kev has spent the day in bed, I think we had all forgotten that on top of everything else he had never seen combat before, and there was a lot of blood.

Johno is beginning to come round again. He is massively confused, and it might take some time to get a sensible conversation out of him. In lieu of therapy we are pouring alcohol down him and ourselves – doesn't make you forget, just takes the edge off it...

26 May

It's a bank holiday weekend and the sun is shining and no one was in the mood to celebrate – except maybe Johno who doesn't have the slightest idea what has been going on and is wandering around in a strangely euphoric daze.

We checked out what was happening on the other side of the black hole this morning and there has been a lot of activity in the surrounding area. Helicopters have been in and out, and armoured patrols have been scouring the desert. There has obviously been much clearing up of the mess we made but I do get the feeling that they don't really care about the men who died, more about the fact that we discovered their compound and got away seemingly into thin air.

The Monkey has been in touch with the Green and Red Society to try and get some advice and they have gone away to have a think and do whatever Mao Shan sorcerers do. Until we get some feedback, we need to cool our jets. I have had to talk The Monkey down from going back through the black hole in burning monkey god mode and laying waste to whatever comes across his path. I keep reiterating the fact that we have a door into Area 51 for a reason and that reason must be more than just killing the fuck out of a load of things. Mustn't it?

*

Finally, we got down to the beach for a BBQ. I think it will do us all good to be out of the house for a while. Even the Monster Highs are here before the sun has gone down – with very large hats it has to be said. Kev looks a bit haunted still, but the other Nerds are doing a good job of geeing him up. Johno has come down with us and we have got him ferrying beer from the shop down to the beach while we get the BBQ going so, we can burn some meat in a manly fashion. The Monkey is smoking a cigar and building a massive sandcastle with the Monster Highs while I spray lighter fluid about and use his Zippo to try and get the charcoal burning...

HAARP

27 May

Our oriental friends have come back with some worrying thoughts regarding the compound. It seems they have been hearing rumours about this for some time.

After the super soldier experiment got shut down in south east Asia it restarted in the Nevada desert but this time using ex-soldiers recruited by none other than Brightstorm. But the rumours are that the DMT-fuelled test subjects began to experience a different reality that began to impinge upon their everyday reality, and this made them uncontrollable. It was believed that the programme had been scraped but it seems that the test subjects are still alive and kicking, and weird. The Mao Shan did some remote viewing strangeness and they reckon that the test subjects are being kept under control by some sort of hypnotic drug and then they are *switched* on or off by a stimulus – the alarm in this case. They also believe that the experiment is continuing although with a different focus and the potential for releasing these remote-controlled human bombs into society has not escaped us. If you need a false flag attack, an assassination or any number of other possible scenarios then what better than to have a puppet do it for you?

There is also something else in the desert that they are concerned about. A Chinese *communication* satellite has been sending back high-resolution images of the desert to the east of the compound. There is an antenna array there that covers approximately a square mile, but it doesn't show up in all of the photos. They are going to remote view this as well but already believe that it could be more important than the compound. The Monkey is planning another raid but this time he is talking about leaving nothing behind...

28 May

Johno went home today with a shopping list from The Monkey. He is still not quite sure what has happened over the past few days and I don't think he is safe to drive long distances but hey – I'm not his mom...

*

The Monster Highs have been giving us the lowdown on the dangers of a night out in town. Apparently, there are all sorts of non-humans on the prowl out there that like to prey on drunk, horny boys and girls. Fortunately, most of them just want a taste rather than to devour their victim but even so it does leave a residual effect. The Monkey reminded the girls they had manipulated their meeting with us, and they replied that there are, of course, no coincidences but surely it was us who had rescued them – sly smiles all around. After seeing them in action I doubt very much that they needed our protection.

It's just a good job that we are such models of restraint and decorum – fuck off with your laughter! The Monkey has drunk a bottle of Jack and is currently throwing shit at *Britain's Got Talent*...

29 May

The Mao Shan came back to us today with the result of their remote viewing. The antenna array that the satellite photographed is really troubling them. They believe it is a HAARP installation and they are convinced it is being used to manipulate the weather for very specific purposes – the devastation of crops across vast regions of the planet. I had to get the Nerds to explain to us what exactly HAARP is – High Frequency Active Auroral Research Program – supposed to be for ionosphere research but linked by some people to earthquakes, wildlife death, abnormal weather, and a list of other stuff both feasible and totally mental.

We are waiting now for Johno to come back with The Monkey's latest goodies, if he remembers, given the state of his head that is. In the meantime, we sit and look at slightly bonkers conspiracy theories on the web…

30 May

We have been keeping up with the training and it is really starting to pay off – not just in terms of our ability to fight – we are also starting to get decent beach bodies, so if we don't die or get anything shot off, we might not look like fat bastards this year. Of course, The Monkey doesn't worry about that shit and is convinced that all you need is cigars and JD to look cool. Maybe he's right… But then he is an incarnate monkey god…

31 May

Johno called to say he has got most of the stuff that The Monkey has ordered. He is still waiting for something called an MPS AA-12 Sledgehammer, The Monkey has asked for two of these and he says one is for me and one for Kev. I had absolutely no idea what an AA-12 was but when Kev heard he went all wide eyed and the other Nerds looked at him like he had been voted mayor of Maplins. He then proceeded to show me clips of *The Expendables* where the MPS AA-12 Sledgehammer – an automatic shotgun – is used to blow most of a building and a shit load of bad guys to bits. Awesome!

We are coming for you Mr Arno Whitaker and your little dog too, and we are coming bearing the gifts of fire and death. Now I need a drink and to watch the rest of *The Expendables* to get warmed up for my new toy…

1 June

Training today was tough but at least we have some sun. We went back out to the woods and shot some more random targets with random firearms. The Monkey also practised bringing on a small portion of his god self and the Nerds looked on in awe as he flickered with fire and punched holes in trees. He seems to be controlling it quite well, but I worry about what his self-control will be like when we are in full on combat.

BBQ and beer in the back garden this evening. The Monster Highs have gradually relaxed the cloaking thing they put on the house and we can talk to the neighbours again although they do look a bit surprised, as if they were not at all sure that we actually existed.

The Monkey found some lawn darts in the shed and we are now battling it out in epic style – doing shots between throws is making it interesting and quite lethal…

2 June

Dave came back from the minor injuries unit around midday. We thought that the lawn dart wound in his leg was superficial but then we were very drunk, and we didn't want to wake him up. When he came round this morning and we had a good look we all agreed that he should get it looked at, plus the dart was pretty dirty. They cleaned him up and irrigated and packed the wound and then gave him quite a lot of antibiotics. They wanted him to explain how it had happened and when he said lawn dart, they all nodded sagely...

*

Johno phoned again and he says he will have all the stuff tomorrow morning and can deliver later on in the day. Looks like we are going to go back in on Tuesday morning...

Like turning a combination lock...

3 June

AA-12s are the fuckin' bollocks! We set up some chunky wooden targets in the woods and watched them disintegrate. We all had a go, The Monkey wedged himself against a tree and shot from the hip so he wouldn't get knocked on his arse, and we all came away with massive grins.

Johno has offered to go through the black hole with us and dig in to cover our escape. The Monkey has agreed despite expressing reservations about Johno before the last time we went through. I think that is an indication of just how rough it is going to get.

We need to be ready for the morning so we are having an unusually dry evening – just a few beers – while we watch *Jacob's Ladder*...

4 June

Boom baby! Oh yeah!

First we went east to the HAARP installation leaving Johno and one of the girls to guard the black hole on the desert side. There were a few sentries patrolling but using the Monster High fog and The Monkey's stealth training we took them out without any problem. Checking over the bodies it was obvious that they were private contractors not regular army and that made us realise just how off the grid this whole thing was.

We liberally sprinkled the magic pixy dust of thermite charges The Monkey had ordered around the antenna array. It was vast so we couldn't cover all of it but we hit a good cross section including the generators. Kev was fascinated by the fine mesh that arced over the whole site; it was almost invisible in the dark. He believes it is some sort of invisibility cloak, a bit like what the Monster Highs do but using technology to reflect the surrounding empty desert over the installation. That will be why the Chinese satellite couldn't keep constant images of it. We set timers and then booby trapped the timers and headed west towards the compound.

The Nerds had done some research and they reckoned that the Tesla coils in the towers ran in series, their reasoning being that there was no way that anyone could control that much power if they were linked up any other way – and after all, they decided, the towers had been put there to keep something in and they had never expected an attack on the towers themselves. So, we needed to take out one of the towers to break the chain and the one on the ridge seemed favourite. Me and The Monkey gunned the bike up to the top of the ridge and set a pretty large charge at the base of the tower. We had two reasons for wanting them out of the way – one, they are fucking lethal, and two, without the towers we were hoping that those in charge in the compound would not risk releasing the test subjects.

Back down on the desert floor we regrouped and pushed the bikes behind a rock outcrop to wait for the fun to begin. A series of massive explosions lit up the sky to the east as the HAARP installation went to meet its maker. Even more lights came on in the compound and very quickly armoured vehicles began to race through the gates heading in the direction of the firework display. When the last one had disappeared, we watched the towers around the compound begin to flicker into life. The Monkey gave it a couple more minutes and then pressed the remote detonator and we watched a ball of fire erupt on the ridge and then one by one the towers around the compound went quiet.

This was our moment and we belted at full tilt towards the compound. With me and Kev steering, our pillion passengers opened up with automatic fire, and The Monkey took out a watchtower with the grenade launcher on his weapon, then he took out a whole section of fence and we were through and into the compound. I looked over and saw that Kev had clipped a section of the trailing wire and skidded the bike onto its side but as I watched the Monster High rolled gracefully and sprang back to her feet like nothing had happened while Kev scrambled back up and they both took cover behind a row of metal tanks. I threw our bike along the side of one of the low buildings and almost before it had stopped The Monkey was off and throwing pipe bombs. Then I heard Kev's AA-12 and I unslung mine and the massacre began.

We shot and blew up anything that moved or stood still. With all of the decent fire power heading off into the desert we had no real competition and we had guessed right – no one had the guts to activate the test subjects with the towers down. Only one real disappointment, when we blasted our way into the large building there was no sign of Arno Whitaker. I am pretty sure that if he had been there then he would just have set off the inmates regardless of consequence. So as the buildings disintegrated, and the compound fences collapsed the test subjects actively walked into the fires or stood in the way of the exchanges in gunfire. I have no idea what horrors they had been through, but they had no intention of passing up this chance of ending their pitiful existences. That just made us angry and we hunted down anyone who was responsible for their plight – lab coats or private military – they all died.

Kev found a fuel store and we set some charges and then got the fuck out of there. As we raced back through the desert, we were illuminated by the fireball that had been the compound. The Monkey was flickering with his own fire and he leaned close to me and whispered, 'No survivors,' and we headed back in the direction of the HAARP antennas. We could soon see the still-burning wreckage from the thermite charges and the lights from the armoured vehicles, that was when The Monkey pressed his other remote detonator and the arc of claymore mines he had set tore into the patrol. Once again, we opened up with everything we had, and The Monkey's armour piercing rounds rattled through the vehicles while the AA-12s turned human beings to pudding.

Back at the black hole we found that Johno and the Monster High had been having fun. Looks like it had been sussed that we were using the area as a staging post; perhaps they thought it was some sort of chopper landing zone, anyway they had sent a couple of vehicles to secure the area and cut off our retreat. These had been dealt with in no uncertain terms by RPG and assault rifles. As we surveyed the damage done, the girls suddenly got very agitated and said that we needed to go back through the black hole immediately. So, through we went, and there the other two Nerds were jumping up and down (Dave sort of hopping because of his bad leg) as they pointed back at the hole. Everything was turning into a swirling vortex and the image of the desert with its burning wreckage and mangled bodies disappeared to be replaced by blackness. We got the Nerds to seal it up again with their grid thing and then we all just sort of collapsed.

The adrenalin has well and truly worn off now and I just ache. We have checked each other over and apart from some fairly minor cuts, bruises and burns we are all in pretty good shape. In fact, Dave's lawn dart wound is still the most serious. Not sure how this is all going to play out mentally, especially for Kev. I think he has partitioned it into a game of *Call of Duty* and is treating it as such, I hope he can keep that reasoning going. I think a stiff drink is called for and I am fairly sure I just saw The Monkey rolling a spliff...

5 June

Sent a message to the Green and Red Society today, not so much to tell them what we did as I'm sure they are well aware, but to ask their advice on the shift in the black hole. It is still showing just black and their feedback would be helpful. Apart from that we have tried to chill out and get the sight and scent of death out of our minds.

Going in the sea and then having a mad game of football on the beach has helped. The Monkey and Johno don't suffer the post combat stress of us non-military types. In fact Johno has homed in on some more ladies on the beach and has wandered off to seduce them with tales of daring-do and his apparently irresistible abattoir worker's charm.

In the meantime me and The Monkey are sitting in the sun outside Coasta Coffee – the little coffee shop by the beach – while The Monkey smokes cigars and we drink large Americanos that we have heavily laced with Jack, and eat massive ice creams. What? It's healthy to vary your diet...

6 June

The Green and Red have responded to our questions saying they believe the black hole has shifted in line with some cosmic pattern. It's like turning a combination lock and each time it clicks it opens up a new pathway – apparently. They think that at the moment it is still turning and that's why it is black. They have sent some of their men to check the monkey temple just in case anyone has managed to blast their way into it but they are pretty sure their theory of it as a turning lock is accurate...

*

Johno is AWOL again. Probably not vampires this time as the women were sunbathing. The Nerds are testing their own theories on the black hole and the Monster Highs are sleeping a lot – they had no problem with the mass slaughter, but I think they need to eat again.

Me and The Monkey? Well, we are just enjoying the sun and placing bets on where the hole will stop next. As we have no real idea, we have taken to throwing darts blindfold at a map of the world, and it seems The Monkey has the hole coming to rest in Tanzania while I am odds on for mid Pacific. Who needs science...?

7 June

Johno has gone back wherever he goes. He turned up late last night with a very self-satisfied look on his face and helped us drink a bunch more Jack while he told us tales of manly daring-do as a contractor working in the world's worst trouble spots. He obviously has vast experience and isn't just all talk but I can't get over the fact that The Monkey is not totally comfortable with him.

Spent a good deal of today asleep in the garden. It's all gone very quiet – but The Monkey keeps saying it's the lull before the storm...

8 June

The Monster Highs have decided to go home for a bit. I think there is more grave robbing afoot. And the Nerds have moved back into their house up the road after the girls gave it one more going over and fried any electric device that was in the house (mind you, they will still be at our house at least 70% of the time).

The Green and Red sent us another message saying that they had seen pictures from the Chinese satellite showing the carnage in the desert. We really wrecked the HAARP installation, that won't be fucking with our nice weather anymore.

Seems a bit odd not getting ready to kill the shit out of anything. We did a couple of hours training this morning and I can tell that The Monkey is still edgy, he wants to be getting on with whatever comes next. Lots of cigar smoke and JD as we wait for *Terminator 2* to start. Is it wrong to fancy Sarah Connor? No, of course it's not...

9 June

Went out for a run today. Can't shake the feeling we are being watched – even in the house. Had a good look around, The Monkey had a good look around, the Nerds searched high and low. Didn't see anyone or anything unusual... Still got the feeling. The Monkey isn't discounting it but thinks it could be a touch of post combat stress...

Sweet dreams aren't made of this

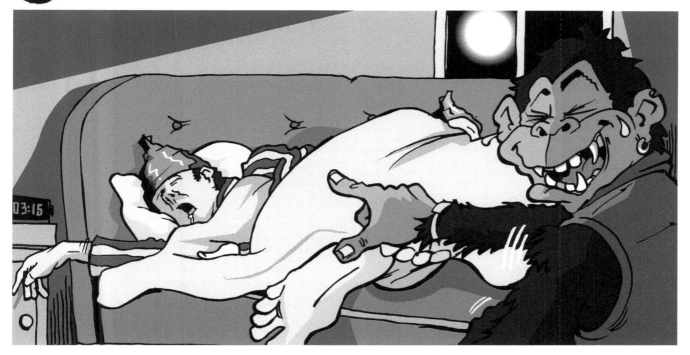

10 June

We were in a bar in town and I got a text message – 'Leave NOW!' I quickly showed it to The Monkey and we legged it. We went into one of the shops a few hundred metres away and watched as two police vans pulled up outside the bar and a whole squad of riot-gear-wearing cops exited and rushed in. Other cops secured the street and we saw them begin to bring out everyone in the bar in handcuffs and put them into the back of two more wagons that had arrived shortly after the others. They took everyone, including the staff, and then sealed the bar and left a couple of officers outside while the others all piled back into their vans and drove off. Whole thing took no more than twenty minutes. The Monkey pointed out that some of the cops had sidearms...

We left town and went to a bar on the beach closer to home. I checked out the message, but it had scrambled into a meaningless bunch of characters and numbers, plus the number it had been sent from was showing as blocked. We have no idea who sent it or what the raid was about. When we got home, we asked the Nerds to take a look at the message and they are still scratching their heads over how it could be effectively erased like that, it's the sort of thing they set up with their covert emails. We are all wondering if me and The Monkey were the targets of the raid or whether we were just in the right place at the right time...

11 June

The Monkey did a bit of asking around to find out what the story is with the bar raid yesterday. The informed rumour is that it was a drugs raid and possible firearms seizure. From our experience that bar has never been like that – The Monkey says he would love to be able to get all that good stuff close to home. Looks like an excuse to me. Were they after us?

Black hole still showing nothing but black. The Green and Red have reported that there is no evidence of digging at the monkey temple although they did say that it is so badly smashed in it is hard to tell.

House feels empty with the girls and the Nerds gone. Oh well, looks like a drunken Xbox session is on the cards...

13 June

Bad dreams. We have all been having them. Darkness, and an overwhelming sense of dread. Being chased or rather hunted. Arno Whitaker's demented grin... I asked The Monkey if he had been having them and he just said that we shouldn't eat cheese before going to bed. Wanker... The Nerds have been particularly bad with Kev suffering the most. I phoned the Monster Highs to find out if they were okay, but they said that they never dream.

Tried to do some physical stuff today to chase away the nightmares but because we hadn't slept much it didn't last long. The training session was a bit half-hearted and in the end The Monkey suggested that we just go for a drink at the local and then those who needed it could try to get some shut eye. Sound idea but when the Nerds nodded off, they were awake pretty quickly having had the same sort of dreams again.

I think this evening The Monkey has a film fest planned along with booze, curry, and I believe there may be a bong involved. He has a very practical, simplistic way of dealing with problems like this – if you can't kill it then render it comatose with drink and/or drugs...

14 June

Tired...

Chemicals didn't work well, just sort of gave all the crazy nightmare images a glowing edge. We spent hours watching *Adventure Time* – okay, it's a kid's cartoon but it's pretty cool and very weird. The Monkey stayed up with us for moral support, and of course to drink…

Today we have mostly drunk coffee and tried to work out what the connection (if any) is between my sense of being watched, the message warning us about the raid, and the bad dreams. Tony thinks it is all coincidence but like The Monkey always says – there is no such thing as coincidence. The other Nerds have a different theory. Seems they have heard of a remote observation system that involves the use of focused energy beams to view/listen in on a target. This is a bone of contention between the three of them as it seems to be highly experimental and there are apparently many valid reasons why it shouldn't work. But if it does work then it could be disrupting our sleep patterns and causing my paranoia. There is also rumour that it could be used to project images into people's brains… Doesn't explain why The Monkey isn't affected though but that could be the whole monkey god thing again.

Dave suggested that we should ask the neighbours if they were having problems, so we have just done a quick *casual* round of the houses nearby and guess what – those closest to us are having problems sleeping…

15 June

Just in case you need to know – it's hard to sleep in a tin foil hat and you look like a twat. The Monkey has just about shat himself laughing…

16 June

Another anonymous text, this one said, 'Do not drive past the base.' I picked it up just as we were driving away from home and had turned down the road that runs alongside the airfield. We pulled over and after a quick discussion decided to drop the car back at the house and then go on foot along the path through the woods that runs parallel to the road.

We got to opposite the service road that intersects the main road and there, through the trees, we could see two black Range Rovers. Looked like a couple of guys on foot talking to the occupants of a car they had flagged down. These guys weren't in black suits but were wearing black tactical gear. After a couple of minutes, they waved the car on and flagged down the next one that was coming from the same direction. We watched for about three quarters of an hour and then suddenly they were listening to the earpieces they wore and talking into their radio mics and then they jumped back into the Range Rovers and headed off down the road.

The Monkey sat for quite a while just staring after the black vehicles, eventually he lit up a cigar and we trudged back along the path in silence. When he spoke, he simply said 'Pity we didn't have the AA-12s.'

We drove out of the back of the village and went the long way avoiding the base perimeter. We had been going down to Falmouth and didn't see any reason to change our plans. We met a contact of The Monkey's at the docks and he passed us a bit of kit in a large black waterproof dry sack. We dropped it off in the car and then found somewhere to eat and drink. The bit of kit we are told, is a micro frequency disruptor that is used for fucking up listening and other surveillance equipment. The Monkey has *borrowed* it from some Russian *friends*. The tin foil hats were just a comedy of errors. They sort of worked but were hard to keep on and keep intact. There were various attempts including wearing one under a woolly hat (very sweaty) and gaffa taping one on (painful, painful removal process), but they did provide for a better night's sleep until they got ripped and mangled. I think that The Monkey couldn't take another night of laughing that hard – nob head.

I was intrigued to know how The Monkey had Russian *friends*, especially the type of friends who could supply high tech jamming kit. He asked me if I remembered that time he went out clubbing and I got all special needs when he came back pissed, 'Yes...' I said, trying not to rise to the bait. Well, it seems he met a bunch of Russian sailors in the club and when they found out he had grown up onboard ship they just adopted him. After many drinks and much trouble making, they all agreed that they were best mates and that if The Monkey ever needed anything, especially anything military grade, he should give them a call. They said that they would be stationed down at Falmouth for the foreseeable future as they had some projects to be getting on with. So, they typed their numbers into his phone and there you go. The Monkey showed me the numbers and a few photos of the night out on his phone. Christ on a bike, I rarely get to see his phone and as he scrolled through some of the pictures on there I am quite glad that I have been blissfully ignorant! The one of him in porn star mode with his teddy bear will haunt me for quite a while.

We have switched the disruptor on and are relaxing in front of *Tears of the Sun* with a Jack or two. Hopefully I will get a better night's sleep tonight if I can blot out those phone images. Oh, and the text message scrambled itself again...

Space Conkers

17 June

That helped! The Russian tech messed with whatever is being beamed at us and for the first time in a week we all got a decent night's sleep. We aren't going to be able to keep the tech forever and to be honest we need to find out who is zapping us and where it is coming from so that we can end it – and them.

The Nerds have begun a project – capture the signal and track its source. There are oscilloscopes set up in the loft and one of the Nerds' satellite dishes has been commandeered to collect and amplify anything incoming. Looks like a bad 1950s science fiction movie set up there, just needs some women with ridiculously pointed bras and giant beehive hairdos.

The Monkey has been in touch with the Green and Red again about the black hole. They have been plotting the possible permutations for the black hole based on various star charts, readings of the I Ching, and a lot of intelligent guess work. We know that the hole opens up to various power centres on the planet but at the moment there seems to be no logic to it. They speculate that the reason we will find our enemies (and maybe our friends) there is that they will be attracted to these spots because of the power emanating from them – whether they know it or not. But most of them will know it and will be looking to exploit it. The Mao Shan sorcerers reckon that the cosmic wheels are aligning again and that very soon the black hole will open up to a different location...

18 June

Another decent night's sleep had by all.

The Nerds have been scratching their heads over the incoming signal they have isolated. General consensus amongst them had been that it would be coming from somewhere quite nearby, possibly the airbase, but that doesn't seem to be the case. They think now that it is coming from a satellite but it would have to be a satellite in geostationary orbit and the implications of that are quite scary – there would have to be some serious, serious players involved to get a satellite tasked just to fuck with us! But we know that the Illuminati are serious players, so maybe Arno Whitaker is searching for us again.

The Monkey has started to ask questions about how we bring down a satellite and I definitely heard the word laser used with absolutely no irony. The Nerds do seem to think that it is more likely that they can scramble the signal and cause it to shut down – The Monkey's disappointment is palpable and he says that the Nerds aren't trying hard enough. I foresee more drinking, smoking and arguing...

Following some late-night whiteboard scribbling the Nerds are now elbow deep in the NASA intranet and hunting for another satellite to play space conkers with, the premise being that if you can reroute an orbiting satellite and make it crash into the geostationary one then bye bye nasty mind fuck signal.

The Monkey on the other hand is scouring the internet for an industrial laser and has also found instructions for making a home-made railgun – he is obsessed. I am leaving them all to it and hitting the Jack...

20 June

Kessler syndrome – who would have thought?

We have been warned by an astrophysics contact of the Nerds (he had an email screaming fit when they asked his advice) about the possible implications of crashing one satellite into another. Seems there is something called

Kessler syndrome which basically means that if we smash stuff together in Earth's orbit it could have a knock-on effect that causes all the other stuff floating about up there to bash into each other causing such a car wreck around the planet that all other satellites and any space travel will be bolloxed. That perked The Monkey up, he would be up for a bit of orbital Armageddon, he thinks it might level the playing field...

*

The Monkey has stolen Dave from the Nerds to work with him on his railgun project. He also has me carrying heavy things. He has gone off the laser idea for the moment as the components and power required are a bit out there, but the railgun seems to be more of a possibility. If the thing can be built it could theoretically blow a neat hole through the offending satellite putting it out of action without smashing it to bits. The aiming would be the interesting part but the Nerds all agree that it should be possible to get a lock on it in the same way they would if they were going to crash it by using a back door through NASA's own tracking system.

Just finished carrying large coils of wire up to the loft. Dave has decided that a coil gun might be easier and more efficient. He has been online ordering infrared sensors and other stuff. The Monkey doesn't care as long as it's destructive. I have a feeling that next quarter's electricity bill is going to be massive...

22 June

The monkey pendant has started to glow again...

The black hole has started spinning and flickering with purple lightning, and The Monkey has blown a massive hole in a caravan standing in a field about two miles away with a small version of the coil gun. Things are happening...

23 June

There is now a vista of mountains and sea visible through the black hole. Tony dropped a little GPS tracker through, and we gathered round the laptop screen to see where it had landed. From the view I would have said Scotland and I would have been right. Seems our latest doorway leads to a mountainside in the far north west of Scotland. Why? How the fuck do I know?

The Nerds are wondering whether they can send a drone with a GoPro on board through the hole. They think it should be possible to steer it from this side of the hole and if not, we just lose a toy or two. The Monkey is online ordering OS maps of the area.

The Green and Red Society have asked us to hold off doing anything crazy with the satellite as they think they might be able to get a Chinese satellite assigned to *deal* with it. They are more than a little concerned about the prospect of the Kessler syndrome if it all gets a bit out of hand – I don't know where they get that idea from...

Can you hear me, Mother?

24 June

The Monkey contacted the Monster Highs last night and asked them to come back and help with the latest gateway. They said they were on their way and would be with us by the early hours of the morning. At two in the morning I was woken by the text alert on my phone – Roadblock A30. Diversion Roche. Trap. NOW!

Fuck! The Nerds piled into their van and me and The Monkey jumped onto one of the bikes and we tore off towards Roche which is about fifteen minutes away at normal speed. Fortunately, we hadn't been drinking... that much. We knew that subtlety wasn't going to be an option, so The Monkey rode pillion with night vision goggles and H&K while I had my AA-12 slung along the side of the bike. We were quicker than the van and we had told the Nerds to cover the retreat, so it was just us who came upon the scene of carnage.

Two black Range Rovers were parked across the road, one of them on fire. Through the smoke and flames we could see the Monster Highs, their hair flowing in some invisible wind almost like they were under water. Their eyes glowed white like flares and they were tearing black clad figures apart. I saw one of the girls get hit with a taser and drop to one knee then I skidded the bike to a halt between the Range Rovers, and The Monkey was off and firing. I dropped the bike and started with the AA-12, I could see another vehicle behind the girls' car, and I put a couple of rounds into it. It went boom.

We took down the rest of the tactical team in quick order, they hadn't been expecting us, then I backed the non-burning vehicle off the road and The Monkey got the girls into their car and they drove past. I could see flashing blues in the distance, so I blocked the road with the vehicle again, and as I pulled away on the bike I made that one go boom as well. Further up the road the Nerds were parked in a side road with the back doors open and weapons trained. They waved me past and then followed me up the dark lane.

The Monster Highs are okay – not even shook up, just pissed off. I took a drive up to Roche earlier and to my surprise the road was open, passable by one lane only, but open. I asked one of the local plod who was waving traffic through what had happened and he said that a lorry had clipped the railway bridge and caught fire. And sure enough, there was a burnt-out lorry cab and trailer. These fuckers move real quick... it's like they bend reality...

25 June

The reports of gunfire in the early hours of the morning have been explained away as a freak electrical storm complete with localised thunder! At least that's what the local news reports are saying, and the burnt-out lorry story is running as a minor news item. Way to cover up...

The warning text scrambled again – I wish we knew who was helping us out. The Monkey reckons it must be someone inside the enemy camp. How else would they know what was going to happen?

There is news from the Green and Red Society – a Chinese satellite is going to be rerouted to deal with our little problem. I asked them about our window onto Scotland and they have told us to be on the lookout for submarines...

Tonight, with the Monster Highs providing some covering fog, we will go through the black hole again and have a scout around the immediate vicinity. Don't think we are likely to find a submarine on the mountainside but judging by the way things are going I am reserving judgment...

26 June

No submarines – at least not where we came out. Undercover of the Monster High's spells of confusion we stepped out onto a heather covered Scottish mountainside under a beautiful starlit sky with the huge full moon casting a pale glow over everything. It soon became obvious that we were all alone. Not a person or habitation to be seen, not even a crofter's cottage.

We did ever expanding circuits of the area and found a cromlech on the flat summit above us. Standing there we could see far out across the darkly glimmering loch below us and in the distance the moonlit sea. We took photos and planted some mini cameras and sensors that the Nerds had acquired around the mountain and then we came back through the hole. Because of the location and apparent lack of anyone around we should be able to do some daytime insertions and maybe go for a bit of a wander but we will see what the tech we have left there picks up first – if anything.

The Russians are starting to make noises about wanting their jamming device back – I hope the Chinese come up with the satellite goodies soon or we could be back to sleepless nights and rampant paranoia. Anyway, in the meantime The Monkey wants to party. We can't risk going into town at the moment so there is much takeaway and drink and he has found the disco lights from our New Year's party. He has also asked a couple of the neighbours around – unusually sociable for The Monkey...

27 June

Well, The Monkey spiked the neighbour's drinks with acid and when they were tripping their tits off, he proceeded to interrogate them. After several hours of weird he was convinced that none of the neighbours had anything to do with the roadblocks and set-ups that had been happening. I asked at one point how far he was going to go, and he said that if he hadn't had LSD then it would have been the jigsaw. The neighbours have got off lightly... Apart from that the evening went wonderfully and we all got very pissed and had a good laugh although much of that was at the expense of our heavily tripping *friends*.

This morning the South West news reported that a mansion up on Dartmoor had been gutted by fire overnight – no one survived. While the reporter droned on about possible arson a helicopter camera crew circled overhead filming the scene. The Monkey sat with his spoon of Cookie Crisp breakfast cereal two inches from his open mouth and stared at the smoking devastation that was all that was left of the house where we had got the notebook. Coincidence? There are – you know the rest...

The sensors and cameras picked up low flying jets blasting down the valley above the loch. There were several passes, so it looks like the area is used by the RAF for training. That shouldn't be a problem, they won't fly every day so we will just keep tabs on what sort of regularity there is to the flights.

So, what's on for tonight? There is a strong possibility that we will be playing Kerplunk for money. The Monster Highs have produced a Ouija board which they claim belonged to Aleister Crowley (although that might have been just to mess with the Nerds), and they are talking about trying to contact the old lady from the mansion to find out if she knows what happened. Really? The Nerds are sceptical but also more than a little scared. The Monkey is up for anything as usual, and me, well I've been sleeping with partially dead girls so what right have I got to kick off? Going to keep an eye on my drink though just in case The Monkey has any acid left...

28 June

I won big time on Kerplunk – I now have everyone's loose change and whatever notes they had on them, plus a whole bunch of IOUs and Tesco vouchers. That's how I roll.

The Ouija board, well, what can I say... At first there were just random twitches from the planchette but then it began to slide around the board at some speed. As we spelled out the words it formed there was an obvious theme – men in black bursting into the house and ransacking it. Then something about a faceless man and questions about notebooks and a monkey, and then fire and silence. Creepy, I can still feel my goose bumps. Well we know who the faceless man has to be, and he is close...

29 June

Today a satellite somewhere up there went pop as a Chinese satellite carrying an energy beam weapons platform went off its normal orbit and kicked ass. Get in! Disappointed, The Monkey blew up another caravan with his coil gun from the loft room window – he really did want to fire that into space...

The Monkey contacted his Russian buddies and told them they could have their kit back; we will go and drop it off tomorrow. In the meantime, we went back through the black hole and had another mooch around. Actually, very pleasant. Along with the firearms we took a disposable BBQ and some beer and ended up having a picnic amongst the heather. Made a nice change from killing shit...

30 June

Back down to Falmouth docks to drop off the Russian toys and then a spot of lunch and a few beers. I kept expecting to get a text warning of impending doom and for us to have to leg it, but nothing happened, and we just had a chilled time. The Monkey thinks that maybe it was the satellite that was spying on us as well as messing with our sleep – I hope that is true, although it would still mean they know who and where we are...

This has been a topic of discussion amongst all of us – if they have been targeting us with their sat then why haven't they just come and picked us up? The Monster Highs' take on it is that they are shot gunning the area because they don't really know where we are. They are convinced that the residue from their magic fog will still be causing a general level of confusion that will prevent anyone from physically homing in on us until we leave the *fog*. They are pissed that they were able to be targeted and we are now examining the possibility that our phones are being tapped. If the noose is tightening it isn't tightening very quickly or very effectively – perhaps the Illuminati are just a bit crap?

We will take the bikes through the hole tomorrow and head down towards the loch and then out towards the coast. Maybe then we can at least work out what that bit is all about. In the meantime – Jack...

Nostrovia!

1 July

Took the bikes and off-roaded down to the shore of the loch. Bit damp and misty but glorious all the same. We smashed it round to the north west end of the loch and the ruins of a tower house castle that hangs broodingly over the water. It took us about three quarters of an hour to have a good look round – nada. Then we tore off further west to the coast, some big waves – should have brought the boards. We sat on a sand bar and watched the seals but didn't see anything else that might have caused the black hole to open up here. We saddled up and started back but this time around the other shore of the loch. As we rode up the slope to the top of the cliff The Monkey grabbed my shoulder and told me to stop. Looking down at the next cove we saw it – the submarine.

Actually, the wreck of a submarine, a U-boat, mostly submerged in the incoming tide. Rust red and twisted into the rock formation where it had finally come to rest. Kev took some photos of the sub and of the surrounding beach. It was obvious that we weren't going to get near it as the incoming big surf would have royally fucked us if we had attempted anything heroic. We need to go back at low tide, with diving gear and also some climbing gear to get down to the cove.

We rode back around the loch and as we hit the mountain slope a lone jet fighter screamed past above us at a couple of hundred feet. As we reached the black hole, we could hear the jet returning – if the pilot was looking for us on the way back, he must have been freaked out that we had just disappeared...

Tragedy has struck! In all the excitement of the last few days we have totally overlooked shopping and we are out of Jack. So, we are drinking vodka until emergency supplies can be acquired...

2 July

The Nerds did some interneting and searched all sorts of resources and shit for references to the U-Boat. There were reports of a U-boat being sunk off the west coast of Scotland in the last days of World War Two and subsequently various sightings of wreckage by fishing boats, and then numerous attempts by salvage crews to locate it. All to no avail. It became a bit of a legend – The Nazi Ghost Submarine – and treasure hunters still go searching for it. There is probably a Discovery Chanel programme about it... The Monkey also got the Nerds to doublecheck the map reference for the exit point of the black hole to make sure that we are not popping out in a restricted military testing area. The last thing we need is the RAF doing low level bombing runs over us by accident or sending out patrols because we are in a restricted area. The Nerds stick by their assertion that everything is fine and that the jets are just flying exercises over what are usually deserted valleys.

The Monkey has been back onto the Russians and they have agreed to lend us some dive gear. We can pick it up tomorrow evening (apparently they are using it at the moment...) and as it won't be a deep dive, we won't need nitrogen – whatever that means – so the gear will be quite simple. That is a good thing as the bikes are not equipped for taking loads of luggage and going off road. We went into Truro earlier as well and picked up some climbing gear from an outdoor shop – all very outward bound! And we hit the supermarket and got essentials. A boot full of JD bottles makes a very musical sound as you drive.

There has been a general consensus that we watch *Das Boot* this evening to get us in the mood...

4 July

Got drunk with the Russians last night. What was going to be just a visit to collect the diving equipment turned into a full-blown drinking session on board the Russian cargo ship. Must have been prophetic that we were drinking vodka the other night because we sure as hell drank a lot of it until the early hours of the morning! Even had a worried call from the Nerds asking if we were all right – bless 'em. Am aching like a bastard today as The Monkey once more got me into a fight, although this one was friendlier and called *wrestling* apparently – despite the fact that my opponent was the size of a Transit van. The Monkey said it was bound to happen so he just pre-empted it. Well thanks for that! Anyway, we are now all great friends and my head feels like Thor has been smashing it with his hammer. Had to sleep it off in some borrowed hammocks and have just got home. The Nerds look a bit jealous even though I have a black eye and swollen lip and The Monkey has scorched fur on his shoulder from trying to breath fire with vodka and cigars.

We will not be going through the black hole today. I need to sit still until the Norse god has finished his drum solo...

5 July

Big swell equals no go. The Russians had warned us, based on our description, against trying to get into the sub if the swell was big, and looking down off the cliff it just looked like a death trap. It's not that deep or even fully submerged most of the time but us not being bona fide Jacques Cousteau lookalikes it's all a bit wing and a prayer. The Russians have offered to come along and help but we really don't want to start explaining about black holes and all that shit.

Anyway, Scotland was rainy, and Cornwall is sunny, so it wasn't a major hardship to come back. We spent the rest of the day training and lounging on the beach. The forecast tomorrow is looking a little better for the Scottish surf so we will aim to be in the water at low tide. Dave will have to come with us to help Kev with the beach support – basically hanging onto safety lines.

And now? We haven't used the old laptop since we found it was hacked and The Monkey has stayed off the dark web chatboards that he had been frequenting. But today, after Tony had well and truly set it up so that the IP address couldn't be traced, he decided to log onto the laptop and check his message account on his favourite board and see if there was any chatter, and there amongst the usual right wing, conspiracy, gun for hire lunacy that passes for conversation there was a message request from Snakebite. It simply said, 'You have probably got questions...' and contained a link. The Monkey clicked it and off we went down the rabbit hole to a video. Nicely made, lots of high production values like a corporate sales pitch. In a tastefully lit boardroom with the fronds of several green, leafy plants casting shadows on the back wall, sat Arno Whitaker with his back to the camera. He turned his swivel chair towards the camera with a theatrical swirl and smiled into the lens as if he was trying to crack it. 'Hello monkey, and friends. I have been hoping to speak with you and maybe clear up a few misunderstandings, but we seem to never get the chance to have a civilised chat. When we met at the airport, that would have been an ideal time to get to know each other, and saved a great deal of fuss, but your companion seemed unduly aggressive and to be honest you did both seem a little upset.' The Monkey's paws clenched into fists on the arms of the chair and I grumbled something about shooting him in the mouth, but we kept watching.

'For millennium there have been men of vision who would shape the destiny of mankind in order to lead it into a better, collective future. Ancient rulers, prophets, mythical heroes, great thinkers, and great doers. Men who would sacrifice everything to see the world united under one leadership. No more wars, no more struggle. A single great machine, powered by the people and directed by those who have the will to make the hard decisions.' As he spoke an inset video window opened and imagery played out, supporting what he described.

'You have something unique. You have a power that, if focused under our guidance, could usher in a new age for mankind. A new start in which all the peoples of earth, the lower classes, the disenfranchised, the migrants and refugees could be integrated and merged into one. Then they can be directed to productive labour, and they will be happy in their role.' There was much muttering of, 'Totalitarian wanker,' from the Nerds at this point and you definitely got the impression that Whitaker and his Illuminati fan boys saw themselves as a different race, dare I say a master race. More supporting imagery rolled in the inset, it looked like it had been pulled from every news reel since 1900 and showed mankind at its very worst.

'It is only a matter of time before the world realises that there is only one solution to hunger, war, disease, and the destructive impulses of the masses. It will only take one major catastrophe for the governments of the world to lose control. Unstoppable climate change, a nuclear war, a pandemic... When it comes, we will be riding the wave not swept away by it. It is we who they will beg to assume control, whether they know it yet or not. You can be with us, guiding the future, shaping the destiny of mankind.' As the supporting images changed to happy, smiling crowds beneath a dawn sky and then faded away the camera zoomed in slowly to his eyes, like stagnant green pools of water.

'Reach out to us before it is too late.' The video faded to black and The Monkey said, 'It was always too late mutha fucker.'

Belly of the Beast

8 July

Into the belly of the beast.

In a much calmer swell we clambered up onto the hull of the U-boat and wadded waist deep to the conning tower. The ladder was rusted and broken away in places and it soon became obvious that we had as much chance of getting tetanus as drowning. The Monkey clambered up easily enough and lowered down a rope to help me climb. Once up there we used the mini oxyacetylene cutter to loosen up the hatch and then we popped it open with a couple of pry bars.

Looking down through the hatch we could see that the sub was pretty much flooded, and we took it for granted that the hull must have been holed, maybe by Allied fire. We put on our masks and mouthpieces and started down the inside ladder. Neither me nor The Monkey are dive experts. We have pissed about a bit doing some spear fishing around the Cornish coast but nothing as freaky as this. Turning on the dive lights just made everything even stranger. The U-boat must have been wedged there for a good few years as there are quite large rocky formations even on the inside – it's very much like diving into an underwater cave. As we swam further in, we could make out the control panels and seating. No skeletons sitting at the controls. All of the bones were scattered around the deck.

It took us an age to swim about in that underwater crypt, trying not to get snagged, trying to find something that might have pointed the black hole here. It was strange. All the bulkhead doors were open. Why would that be the case if they were taking on water? Then we got to the torpedo room and saw that the hatch doors on the tubes were all open and when we looked down them, we could see daylight filtering in. Scuttled; the sub had been scuttled.

We used our rudimentary knowledge of U-boats gained from watching *Das Boot* to locate the captain's cabin and there we found a locked box – the only thing vaguely interesting in the whole place. Between us we got the box back to the conning tower and started up. I got the most unpleasant feeling that something was following us and I couldn't get up the fucking ladder fast enough. I looked back at the top and maybe, just maybe, I saw a shadow at the bottom of the ladder. We took off our masks and I looked at The Monkey and knew that he had felt something too.

Anyway, we got the fuck off that sub doubletime and made it back to the black hole without incident. The Nerds were very excited about having Nazi goodies and had to be dissuaded from trying to open the box there and then. We got all the kit through the hole and then ourselves. The Monster Highs stood and stared through the hole for a long time after we were all through. The Monkey asked them if everything was okay and they said that they didn't know...

The box. We haven't been able to open it. It seems to have some sort of puzzle for a lock and the Nerds have been desperately trying to keep The Monkey from shooting it off. They believe that it may be rigged to destroy the contents or even those trying to open it – even after all these years. So they want us to see a friend of theirs who is very, very good with puzzles. Nerd!

9 July

The girls sat and stared at the black hole all night. This morning they told the Nerds to set up the protection grid and wouldn't leave the room until they had done it. I asked them what was wrong and if we had anything to worry about but again, they said that they didn't know...

The Nerds puzzle guru is a lecturer at Bristol Uni. Me and The Monkey have reservations about bringing someone else into the house, but it might be safer than travelling with the box. So – Prof Brian is driving down this evening after he gets through with some Uni business. The Nerds had him on speaker phone when they told him about the box, and he went from very professional to excited schoolboy in a heartbeat. Cute, in a geeky way. Everyone has been warned not to talk about the black hole or any of that crazy shit. The Nerds might think the Prof is a good guy but until The Monkey has vetted him, he is only getting to see the box.

Just waiting for the Prof now. Not smashing it this evening – probably better to be mostly sober when he arrives...

10 July

Prof Brian – early 40s, sporting the dress sense of a much older don but with a Stone Roses T-shirt under his tweed jacket and an almost Daliesque moustache. The Nerds introduced him to everyone, and he was fine until the Monster Highs walked in, at which point he started to stammer a bit – they have that effect on some people. Anyway, he soon forgot about that when we brought out the box. He stared at the lock for a long, long time before he even touched it and then he ran his hands around all of the box's edges. We watched him expectantly for a while and then The Monkey got bored and wandered off followed by the girls and then me, leaving just a little clump of Nerds (what is the collective noun for Nerds?).

We went into the back garden and The Monkey sparked up a cigar and produced a bottle of Jack and we chatted with the girls and passed the bottle around. After about an hour Kev came out and said that the Prof was convinced that although the box had been made in Nazi Germany the lock was much older, possibly Russian, and had been retrofitted to the box. But could he open it? Yes, but it was going to take time. I asked Kev what made the Prof such an expert in puzzles and he said that he had been interested in puzzles since he was a very small child and had even appeared on kids' TV shows solving Rubik's Cubes in record time. Then he had got into programming and in his late teens, cryptography. He had worked for some of the big software companies writing encryption algorithms but became disillusioned when he saw how they got into bed with military and government agencies to capture and share information on ordinary people. Consequently, he burnt out by his late 20s. So, he left and got back into puzzles in a big way, travelling the globe looking for ancient and not so ancient pieces and then lecturing in programming at Uni to support his passion. This is how the Nerds had met him and become good friends.

We went back in and The Monkey asked if we could just shoot the lock off at which the Prof became horrified at the prospect of his new toy being vandalised. He literally pleaded with The Monkey to not do anything hasty saying that, as the Nerds suspected, there may be a vial of acid or similar inside the box which would be broken and released should the lock be forcibly opened, thus destroying the contents. The Monkey shrugged and we went back to drinking.

Today the Prof has been minutely examining the intricate designs around the lock that all slide in different directions – bit like one of those sliding block puzzles. To be honest, he may get his jollies that way but me and The Monkey find it tedious so we left the Nerds gathered round him again like some geeky witches' coven and we headed back down to Falmouth to drop off the diving gear to the Ruskies.

Wow! Just got back and the Prof has conjured up a flipchart from somewhere. The living room is now covered with abnormally large sheets of paper which in turn are covered with the arcane scribblings of a man on a mission. He says that he has seen something similar to these sliding patterns before in a temple in Tibet. This has caused him to rethink the origin of the lock and sent him off on a different unlocking tangent. I asked him how he does what he does, and he replied that he *sees* the patterns that the puzzles create and that allows him to work through them. Dave said that this is the way many mathematicians see equations, and all the Nerds nodded sagely. Me, I don't do hard sums...

11 July

Breakthrough...

In the early hours of the morning the Prof managed to open the lock. Unfortunately, it was only an outer lock so now there is a secondary set of intricately patterned metal bits – a puzzle within a puzzle. He has gone to bed now as I think it has fried even his brain...

14 July

Okay – shit has been happening...

Prof Brian woke from his slumber and got back on it. He was in the groove after getting through the first layer of the lock and it was early evening when the Nerds came running out to the back garden where me and The Monkey were in the process of burning meat over charcoal. We all piled back into the living room and there was the Prof holding up the box minus the lock. As The Monkey took the box, I thanked the Prof and then we all gathered around as The Monkey opened the lid.

There in the box was a small, cuddly, stuffed rabbit toy. We looked at each other and the Nerds laughed but The Monkey stretched out his paw and as his finger approached the rabbit, we could clearly see flickering fire running across his fur. The Monkey withdrew his paw to avoid burning the rabbit and the girls lifted it between them and examined it. They produced a small, curved blade from a mini skirt waistband and slit the rabbit along its stitches. With a little squeezing out slid a brownish black stick like object. We all gathered a little closer and that's when the Prof said, 'It's a finger bone!'

In the night I was woken from a restless sleep by a Monster High sitting bolt upright in bed. 'What's up?' sez I. She just looked at me, grabbed my hand and dragged me out onto the landing. Almost simultaneously the other Monster High burst out of The Monkey's room dragging him behind her. For a split second they looked at the spare room door and then they were through it, hissing like cats. In we went after them and there we saw a shape, a human figure, bulging through the protective web covering the black hole. The Monkey burst into flames and he punched the shape right in its head. There was a strange distant scream and the shape disappeared from the black hole.

Then followed hours of us running around the Scottish mountainside after whatever was trying to push through. I had managed to grab some shorts, but the girls were stark naked, which was kinda cool, and The Monkey was all covered in monkey god fire. Haven't seen him like that for a while and it was obvious something serious was up. I had also grabbed night vision goggles and the Glock. By the time the sun started to rise we had found nothing, except for me, I had found loads of mozzie bites...

We came back through the black hole before the sun was fully up and I went round to the Nerds and got them to come and seal the hole again while we got some sleep. The girls reckon it is something from the sub, the same something they sensed when we came back with the box. After a couple of hours sleep, we went back through on the bikes while the girls guarded the hole from the spare room. We were all tooled up, AA-12s, the works. I had persuaded The Monkey to *flame off* as I didn't want him setting me on fire as he rode pillion, so he was carrying his trusty H&K. Nothing. An entire day of nothing.

Some more sleep followed by another all-night search session – me, The Monkey and the girls (disappointingly dressed this time), but once again, nothing. And then sleep followed by another day on the bikes. Whatever it is, it is very good at hide and seek. The girls have suggested that we play it another way, so tonight we will leave the hole open and wait in the dark of the spare room for our *friend* to poke its head through and then cut it off. In the meantime, Tony and Prof Brian have been examining the bone. Seems the Prof is pretty good at the old *Time Team* stuff as well after his years of searching for ancient puzzles and he has some lab contacts who he is making full use of. They think the bone may be some holy relic, which, given the Nazis penchant for collecting occult paraphernalia, is quite probable. It makes The Monkey light up though so it must be some strong juju.

We are getting ready for a night of watching the black hole with more fire power than you can shake a stick at, and we also have some sticks...

Fucking hell! it's Ghandi!

18 July

At long last the girls can feel the presence of whatever it is, and it is very close. We are getting tooled up again and tonight we are going hunting. Tally ho!...

The girls picked up the scent almost immediately and we scrambled across the steep slope to our left and then fanned out into a loose semicircle and pushed down into the valley. For the first time since we started chasing it, we could make out a shadow amongst the other shadows darting ahead of us. The moon, although not yet full, was doing a very good job of lighting up the slope below us and the valley sides and I gave up with the night vision goggles as I couldn't make out the shadowy figure with them on anyway.

At the loch shore we picked up speed and we knew that this time we were going to run down whatever it was. But it kept to cover as much as it could and we were forced to run across a mix of difficult terrain – thank fuck for all the training we have been doing! Finally, we saw the shadow dart into the ruins of the castle, and we knew that there was no easy way out. The Monkey's fire had started, and he gave off a bluish glow in the darkness. The Monster Highs led us unerringly through to the back of the ruins and there it was – waiting.

My first thought was, 'Fucking hell! It's Ghandi!' But it wasn't Ghandi... Very thin, bald head, wearing a long mouldering overcoat on top of a tatty orange robe and what looked like the remains of green gloves, but the massive glowing eyes were not the result of National Health specs. It still had vaguely oriental features and the string of prayer beads around its neck immediately made me think of the Buddhist monk that The Monkey had met in Thailand. The girls closed in and it began to lash out, but it was no contest and they pinned it to the wall by its bony arms. It looked quite pathetic as it struggled against the girls and gnashed what was left of its teeth. 'What is it?' asked The Monkey and the girls told us that this was a sort of zombie creature that had died but its life force had never truly left its body – probably the result of some magic ritual. They also said that they thought us taking the box and bringing it home had woken the thing up and it had been trying to get the box back.

The Monkey stared long and hard at the squirming zombie thing and lifted the beads around its neck. 'He was a monk,' The Monkey stated, confirming my thoughts. What was a Buddhist monk doing on a U-boat off the shore of Scotland with a holy relic stuffed inside a soft toy? But we would not get any answers from the monk, even if he still had a tongue in his head, because The Monkey's fire touched the shrivelled body as he handled the beads and the undead monk was consumed in blue fire. The girls jumped back releasing the monk as they did so and it staggered round in a small circle as the flames ate through its body until there was nothing left but a pile of ash. Ah... The Monkey crouched down by the smouldering heap and fished something out of the remains. It was a metal object, sort of like a really ornate egg whisk. He dropped it into his belt pouch and that was it.

We started to retrace our steps and when we got to the edge of the ruins, we could see the first glow of dawn. So we started running again. The Monster Highs don't burst into flames or anything stupid in sunlight, they just don't like being out in the open in it – winter is a much better time of year for them. Running up steep hillsides is not fun though so eventually me and The Monkey waved them on, and we sat on a convenient rock while I got my breath back. The girls had soon disappeared out of sight and so we just had a gentle stroll back up to the black hole and we made it there just as the sun was rising.

Spent the rest of the day in bed and we have reconvened with the Nerds and the Prof to find out if there is any news on what the finger bone might be...

19 July

We told the Nerds and the Prof what had happened with the zombie monk and The Monkey showed them the metal thing he had picked up. Prof Brian recognised it as a vajra, a Tibetan prayer object in the form of a stylised lightning bolt. A Tibetan monk on a Nazi U-boat? Tony got very excited by this. He is heavily into conspiracy theories and weird history stuff and he said that there are stories of Tibetan monks in Berlin at the end of WW2. He immediately offered to get together all the stuff he could find on the subject – he loves a project...

The Prof's lab buddies want to run some tests on the finger, so we agreed to run it up to Bristol. They have been doing a bit of research into what was collected by the Nazis during the war and there are some rumours that have got the lab geeks hot under the collar...

20 July

In Bristol. Me, The Monkey and the Prof that is...

We drove up this morning against the flow of holiday makers heading for the Cornish beaches. Prof Brian guided us to the labs, and we met a couple of truly nerdy nerds. There was much excitement and we were ushered further into the lab and into the presence of a more senior nerd. The Prof and the other Prof man-hugged and then it was all about the finger bone.

We let them get on with it after The Monkey impressed upon them how potentially lethal it would be for them if the bone went missing, then Prof Brian took us to his house where we will be staying tonight while the lab boys go mental. The place is full of puzzles and code and shit. There are stacks of books all over the floor and cabinets full of ancient and not so ancient puzzles, although to be honest I only really recognised the Rubik Cube. The Prof offered us a guided tour of his obsession, but we asked him where the nearest boozer was and now we are getting happily pissed while the lab geeks do their thang...

21 July

Was expecting some answers but the lab guys have gone to great lengths to explain that overnight they have carefully taken minute samples which they are now processing but that it will take several days for the results to be ready. They especially went to great lengths when they saw The Monkey's expression and offered us some possibilities to placate him...

Among the rumours circulating about Nazi occult collecting are tales of the German army, a French castle, the Knights Templar, and holy relics brought back from the Crusades. Amongst those relics was rumoured to be the finger of John the Baptist and it was considered to be the greatest treasure of the Templars. Well, we won't know if that is a possibility until the results come back, and then we will only have an approximate age and ethnic grouping. Interesting. Doesn't explain zombie monk boy though...

So, we drove back home. The Prof came with us, he said that he wanted to but he also had no real choice as his car is parked outside our house. Right then, take away curry, lots of Jack, beer, cigars, and new *Family Guy* on the TV. Things are looking up...

Man or Superman

22 July

'Many high-ranking members of the Nazi regime, including Hitler, but especially Himmler and Hess, held convoluted occult beliefs. Prompted by those beliefs, the Germans sent an official expedition to Tibet between 1938 and 1939 at the invitation of the Tibetan Government to attend the Losar (New Year) celebrations.

'The head of the Tibetan Monks that Hitler imported to help him lead Germany was known as The Man with the Green Gloves. The monks were posted in Berlin, Munich, and Nuremberg.

'During the final days of the war, Soviets advancing on Berlin discovered the bodies of several Tibetan monks wearing green gloves in a cellar, "as part of some arcane ritual", and over the next few days, hundreds more were discovered, all lifeless, in green gloves and SS uniforms, but lacking identifying papers.'

As you can see, Tony has been busy searching all known sources of the weird and wonderful. We have no idea how much of this is factual or just mental but given the stuff that has been happening over the past few months I for one am discounting nothing. The Prof has suggested that maybe we need to go back to the U-boat. The black hole is still open into the Scottish mountains so maybe there is a reason to go for another look around. Will need to pester the Russians again...

23 July

The Monkey is tucked up in the armchair with the iPad resting on his hairy knees. He has decided to do a bit of digging for information himself and has downloaded the PDF versions of a few hard to come by books and is using a clever little app designed by Kev that allows him to search PDFs based on keywords.

Update from The Monkey's searching: A large element of Nazi occult belief was Hyperborea-Thule, a mythical land believed to be located at the North Pole according to the Swedish author Olaf Rubeck, writing in 1679. During a period of the earth's cataclysmic history, it split to form two islands – Thule and Ultima Thule – which some people believe to be Iceland and Greenland. Then there is the hollow earth theory, the idea that the earth is formed of four concentric spheres. This was the basis of Jules Verne's *Voyage to the Centre of the Earth* published in 1864.

The books – *The Coming Race*, *The Sons of God* and *The Indo-European Traditions*, published 1871, 1873 and 1876 respectively, describe a superior race called the Vril-ya who live beneath the surface of the earth and aim to conquer it with their psychokinetic energy, called vril. This is all linked (supposedly) to the Thuleans who will use the power of vril to become supermen and rule the world.

Are you keeping up? There is more...

Nietzsche talked about Hyperboreans and, although he never mentioned vril, in *The Will to* Power he writes about the common people 'the herd', and how supermen, instead of striving for security, have an inner vital force that drives them to go beyond the herd. This necessitates and drives them to lie to the herd so that they can remain free from 'herd mentality'.

Then, in 1903, the Thuleans began to be linked to the origin of the Aryan race and many Germans of that era identified with the Aryan/Hyperborea-Thule, believing that they were descended from them and were destined to become the master race of supermen. Hitler was among them...

The Thule Society was founded by Felix Niedner in 1910 and in 1918, Rudolf Freiherr von Sebottendorf created the Munich branch which he based heavily on his own secret society which combined esoteric Sufism and Freemasonry.

The Thule Society's creed became assassination, genocide, anti-Semitism, and anti-Communism. In 1919, the German Workers' Party was spawned from the Thule Society and Hitler was initiated into the Thule Society and trained in the occult before, in 1920, he became head of the German Workers Party, renamed the National Socialist German Workers' Party, AKA the Nazi Party.

Seems possible that the Nazis sent further expeditions to Tibet in search of the hidden subterranean cities of Shambhala and Agharti. These were supposedly repositories of secret occult power, especially vril, and may well have come back with a few *trinkets* to help their war effort.

So, maybe the Illuminati are buying into all this superman shite as well. They certainly like to keep *the herd* in the dark. Their need to recreate society in their own image, at least the parts of society that matters to them, and the complete disregard they have for everyone else fits in well with the jolly mentality of the totalitarian movements of the last century. It's almost as if they had been waiting for those ideologies to arise. They seem to want to make us all cogs in their machine, and they have a proper hard on for The Monkey. The Prof quoted something he had committed to memory years ago, 'To these people (and they are more numerous in any large city than we like to admit) the totalitarian hell proves only that the power of man is greater than they ever dared to think, and that man can realise hellish fantasies without making the sky fall or the earth open.' Well, I think that The Monkey has other ideas about that...

24 July

We have some more diving gear, not the same as last time as we don't need such complex kit – and also the Russians are a bit full on with their underwater cable exploration...

We also have results from the lab. It isn't the finger of John the Baptist. It isn't even a human finger. It's a monkey finger...

So, the finger is a monkey finger, and it's old – over a thousand years old. The lab results couldn't tell us a great deal more and to be honest I think the lab dudes were a bit disappointed – they really wanted a bit of John the Baptist. They think that the monkey finger may have been passed off as a relic of one of the saints and have written it off as a con job. But they haven't seen how The Monkey's fire starts up when he gets near it. We have sent messages to the Green and Red Society to get their take on it and in the meantime, we are off to play Jacques Cousteau again...

27 July

Been a heavy 24 hours...

We went back into the U-boat in rougher conditions than the last time. Harder to get up the conning tower and just generally unpleasant all round. We spent a while hunting around in the guts of the sub, and back in the captain's cabin, under a layer of shite on the floor we found a black screw top tube, the sort of thing that important documents get sealed in. On the way out there was a massive shock wave and a loose bulkhead door fell on The Monkey and trapped him. It took an age but I managed to manoeuvre a steel bar under the side of the door and then gradually wedge bits of crap in there until I had made enough room to drag him free. He was out cold.

I got us back up the conning tower despite a couple more shocks that shook the sub and when we got to the top, I found out what the cause was. Two jet fighters were flying low level passes across the beach and the sonic booms were rattling everything. It was just me and The Monkey on this mission, so no back up. I roped him down the outside of the tower and into the surf, it was getting big. I followed him down and then basically just managed to drag us both back to the beach. I couldn't wake him up. I ditched the scuba gear and gaffer taped The Monkey to my back and making sure the tube was secure I got us on the bike, and we got the fuck out of Dodge. At least that was the plan. As we tore along the loch shore the fighters low levelled past again and I could see the pilots checking us out, I could also see that the jets had no insignia. Then, before we had made the lower slope, a helicopter rose over the crest of hills to our left. A fucking Apache and I could hear the mini guns starting to whir.

I thought we were dead. There was no way we could evade or fight back. We were about to become a red smear on a Scottish mountainside. But then I saw the air ripple above us and we were knocked off the bike by a blast wave going past and then a massive explosion behind us lit up the valley. The Apache, now a fireball, crashed into the loch and I got us onto the bike, and we started back up.

At the black hole, the Nerds helped us through and untaped The Monkey from my back. It was then I noticed The Monkey's coil gun. The mad buggers had spotted the jets through the black hole and later they saw the chopper land over the hill so they dragged the coil gun down from the loft room and set it up pointing through the hole, 'Just in case.' They were pretty pleased with themselves – good for them. We got The Monkey onto his bed and the Monster Highs were there, hands either side of his head and doing whatever it is they do. After a while they got up and said that he would be okay and that we should let him sleep. First time I have seen The Monkey out of it – weird...

We won't open the tube until he comes round so in the meantime, I am having a Jack or two in his honour. Oh, and I have drawn a moustache and glasses on him with a Sharpie – well I'm not a fucking girl am I...

28 July

The Monkey is fine. He took long enough to wake up though! The girls stayed with him to make sure his spirit didn't stray from his body – at least that's what they said – and it was around midday when he finally kicked the living room door open and called me a nob head. He hasn't tried to clean off the face graffiti or stab me, he said it's only what he would have done...

We gathered round and opened the seal on the document tube. It has done its job well and the rolled-up papers inside are dry and intact. There are official documents of the Wehrmacht as you would expect but there are also documents written on Wehrmacht headed paper in an alien script. Prof Brian proved his worth again by identifying the script as Tibetan court script – he can't read it but has seen it before. He also has another contact who can read it (once again his puzzle hunting career has come up trumps), seems Google Translate isn't going to cut it for this one. Dave is giving his A Level German a whirl with the other stuff but he reckons large portions of it could be in code so he is transcribing it so that the Prof can have a crack at it.

The Prof hasn't managed to contact his translator yet, he thinks maybe tomorrow. We will also need to let the Russians know that we lost their diving gear. I don't think it would be too safe to go back through the black hole at the moment, there are bound to be recovery teams after the Apache. On the subject of which... The Monkey wanted to know how the hitech Apache didn't pick up the coil gun firing? 'Simple really', said the Nerds. 'Because they had fired it from this side of the black hole there had been no energy signature for the chopper to pick up, so it had just gone boom.' Obvious apparently...

For he on honey-dew hath fed, and drunk the milk of paradise...

30 July

Finally! The Prof's translator has answered his messages, seems he has just come back from Ibiza. I scanned in the documents and sent them via one of the Nerds' convoluted email routes. He says he needs some time to work through it as it is easy to misread. We are going to give him some space to get on with it...

Dave has translated all the German stuff and the Prof is now playing, *What the fuck does that mean?* with the transcript. Good on him. It's a fucking good job that the Uni has broken up for summer, and also that he is a sad loner with no family life. Bless.

We owe the Russians. They are pretty cool in a, *We have drunk way too much vodka*, kind of way about the lost diving gear but we do feel bad that we had to ditch it, and also the possibility about someone tracing it to the Ruskies. They don't seem bothered and say that there are always Russian boats lurking around the coast of the UK and stuff is always washing up. The Monkey still wants to make it up to them though so it could either mean one hell of a piss up or he is going to kill someone of their choosing...

1 August

The Tibetan writing is basically a warning. All sorts of dire shit about not getting the finger wet and not feeding it after midnight. Not really, but rather a lot about the finger being from a god demon who walked the earth around the time of Kublai Khan. The god demon laid waste to anything that got in its way until it was eventually trapped by the Bon shaman who sealed it in a temple made of volcanic glass high in the Himalayas. The finger is all that remains, but the finger has mad powers. The warnings are very nonspecific, but they do say that it is powerful enough to warp space and time and possibly change the course of history...

And the German bit? Well, the Prof has managed to crack the cypher (he is very good at what he does – nerd) and it all seems to be orders instructing the SS officer who was obviously on board and his men to get the monkey finger to London and let the monk on board with them do his business. Doesn't go into detail what that business might be but knowing that the finger has the potential to alter history it's not that much of a stretch of the imagination to think that Hitler was desperately attempting to change the outcome of the war...

The Monkey is intrigued by the idea that this could be a bit of a previous incarnation. None of the stuff we have says how to use the finger, that part of it was probably the sole domain of the monk, but maybe the Green and Red can give us some ideas. Not entirely sure that letting The Monkey loose with something that can change history is a good idea but what the fuck do I know?

We are playing a drinking game of the Prof's. The Nerds look a bit nervous. There is a massive cloud of cigar smoke hanging over the table which is covered in shot glasses. Hurray! A booze version of Russian roulette...

3 August

That was a pretty epic drinking game. Woke at four in the morning, hanging off the sofa, to find Tony slumped in the corner with the monkey finger pushed up his nose. I seemed to remember some sort of forfeit – this was confirmed later by the others. The Monkey was asleep on top of the bookcase and the girls were curled up together on the sofa behind me. The other Nerds and the Prof were skydiving on the carpet. There was lots of snoring. I got a fit of the giggles, crawled back up with the girls and went back to sleep...

The sorcerers from the Green and Red Society got back to us. Seems there is a whole raft of myths and legends regarding Shambhala which mention the god demon and his glass prison, and the finger. They are not sure of the method used to fuck about with space and time but there are several other hinted at properties, one of which is that the finger acts as a sort of lodestone when in the presence of occult power objects and will point towards them. They think that one reason the finger was being taken to London was to locate one of the ancient magical objects of the Tuatha Dé Danann – the Dagda's Cauldron. Now I don't know much about this Eastern stuff, but I know a bit about Celtic mythology. The Dagda's Cauldron was supposed to be bottomless and would feed all who ate from it until they had all had their fill. Also, and a lot more relevant to the German war effort, the bodies of killed warriors dropped into it were reborn as undead soldiers under the control of the owner of the cauldron. Fact or fiction – I don't know anymore but the Monster Highs think it is quite possible. The Monkey thinks we need to take the finger to London and see what happens. What's the worst that could happen...

Spear of the Sun

5 August

London...

Trains are funny. You can get drunk while travelling at speed. Some of the other passengers in first class didn't appreciate the loud, swearword-based game of Travel Scrabble we played for much of the five-hour journey – bless. They can think themselves lucky that we didn't bring Twister.

We got to Paddington and joined the mass of grumpy bastards going about their daily grumpiness and the hordes of wide-eyed tourists trying frantically not to miss anything. Then we got the tube down to Tower Hill and checked into the Double Tree just around the corner from the station. The Prof and the Nerds all reckon that anything worth looking for is probably going to be in the Tower of London hence our choice of hotel location. Plan is to go there early tomorrow morning before it gets too busy and have a scout around and see if the finger points at anything. Then, if there is anything, we will make some sort of plan to go back later. I have no real idea what that means...

As for now we are going to find somewhere for a quiet drink...

6 August

Yes, we did Stringfellows – man, it never ceases to amaze me how much money you can blow on twins – and a bunch of other boozers and clubs around Covent Garden. No, we didn't get up early and go to the Tower. It was mid-afternoon when we finally had our acts together enough to get down to the Tower and stand in line with the tourists and shuffle zombiefied through the medieval structure. We had decided that I should carry the monkey finger so that The Monkey wouldn't catch fire and give the game away, so I held it loosely in my pocket so that I could feel if it moved.

Nothing. Not a twitch. I ended up passing it over to The Monkey in case it was me but he got nothing either just a bit of blue flame over the fur on his paw. So, we left the Tower and went back to the hotel to have a think and talk to the Nerds and the Prof.

There is a whole argument going on amongst them now as to what to look for and where to go. We are all wondering if there is not some ritual involved which we have no idea about. But the Monster Highs have chipped in with their usual laser intuition. They think the finger will probably just point at what it wants to point at regardless and the whole altering time thing is far more likely to require a convoluted ritual. They also think we should take the finger out with us on a little tour of London. They suggest the tube as a starting place, seems they spent a few years in London during the time of the construction of the Thames Tunnel and they reckon some strange stuff went on that would be worth checking out. I have just Googled the date for the construction of the Thames Tunnel – it was finished in 1843! Raises even more questions about the girls, not sure if I'm worried or aroused, or a bit of both...

We are going to go for a little ride – should be a bit quieter by now...

7 August

We trawled round the tube lines yesterday evening and again today. There was a possible bit of twitchiness from the finger on a couple of occasions but nothing we could really be sure about, and certainly nothing we could get to easily.

Speaking to Kev on the phone this afternoon he said that the black hole is still pointing at the Scottish mountains and this raised the question – is there still something there we need to find? Could it be the thing we have been looking for in London? What if the U-boat was on the way back from London? Bollocks. It would also explain why the Apache turned up and tried to fuck us up. The Green and Red Society did warn us the locations that the black hole takes us to would also be of interest to the Illuminati and their friends.

The Monkey thinks it's funny. We are going to go for a drink again tonight and then think about going home tomorrow. We will take the finger out with us on the off chance that it does something interesting. Oh well, made a change I suppose...

8 August

Holy shit we got bent out of shape last night! We started off in Leicester Square and I remember being in Tiger Tiger for a bit but after that nothing, and The Monkey is pretty sketchy on the whole evening as well. When I finally came to it had gone 1.00pm, I found I was sporting a split lip and The Monkey was curled up hugging an ornate spear point. I woke him up and asked him what the hell it was and where it had come from, and he looked as surprised as I was that he was having a cuddle with the business end of a spear.

As we tried our best to get our shit together to catch our train home at 3.45pm The Monkey started to remember something about a museum. I put the finger on the table about two feet away from the spear head and it span round to point at it. It had obviously signalled us during our drunken rampage and taken us somewhere we shouldn't have been. We speeded up and got out of the broken hotel room as soon as we could, if we had burgled a museum we would need to be away before anyone realised it was us...

The train is nearly back at Truro now and I have just about stopped feeling sick. The Monkey has slept most of the way but still looks well rough. Haven't been able to piece together what happened last night. Don't even know which museum it was although the closest one to where we started was the British Museum. I am trying not to think too hard about it – my head still hurts too much...

10 August

The Nerds first thought was that the spear point was an ornamental one off some railings – probably the ones around the museum – but ornamental railings are generally not sharp enough to shave with and this bad boy is razor sharp as Dave found out when he ran his thumb down its edge. The Monster Highs came in as Dave was shoving his now bleeding thumb in his mouth to try and stem the bleeding. They raised perfectly shaped eyebrows at his predicament and then they saw the spear point lying on the table. I have never seen the girls show fear, but this was something like it. They backed away from the table at a run and stood wide eyed in the doorway, snarls twisting their beautiful lips. We all just stopped and stared at them – this was a bit unexpected.

It took us a while to coax them back into the room and we had to move the spear point over by the window. The Monkey asked them what was up and they asked us what we were doing with the Spear of Lugh. Ah, my interest in Celtic stuff reared its ugly head again. The Spear of Lugh, another of the treasures of the Tuatha Dé Danann, this one was supposed to make whoever carried it invincible in battle – Hitler would have enjoyed that one! But why were the girls so freaked out? Well, seems it could seriously fuck them up if they touch it. Apparently, it is a weapon of the sun, and as we know, they don't play well in the sun. I remembered what the Mao Shan sorcerer had said to me about all the objects of power coming online as the vortexes controlled by the one in the monkey temple flicked on and synced up. I mentioned Joseph Campbell's *The Hero with a Thousand Faces*, which I had read years ago, and how, as the sorcerer had hinted, maybe all of these myths and legends and sacred objects had a common source in human collective history. The girls looked at me as if I had said something so blindingly obvious that I should probably be ashamed of myself, but I ignored them and satisfied myself with the nods of agreement from the Nerds.

We watched the news lots but there was no mention of any daring midnight raids on London museums or even fumbling, pisshead smash and grabs (far more likely). Is it being covered up? Maybe we got in and out without leaving a trail a deaf and blind donkey couldn't miss, and maybe the spear point was in a place where it has not yet been missed? Don't know, and as long as our pissed-up faces aren't all over the news as stills from CCTV I don't much care. We have the spear point now and that's cool, we may well need it when we go back through the black hole to look for the cauldron in the U-boat. Perhaps there is nothing there, perhaps they were on the way to London and never made it, but we need to know if there is anything there that could aid our enemies...

When the wind blows high, and the wind blows low

12 August

We have rented some scuba gear from a dive school in Padstow. Took us ages to fight through the coach parties and OAPs to find a parking space, I had forgotten how busy Padstow gets, especially in the summer. We would never normally go this route, but we didn't think we could impose on the Russians again after losing the last lot of kit. The Monkey still owes them a *favour*.

We also went to see an acquaintance who makes armour and weapons for medieval reenactors and asked him for a suitable shaft and fittings for a spear. We came away with a six-foot spear shaft and a bunch of iron rivets and some basic instructions on how to attach a spear or poleaxe head securely. We also came away with a war hammer which took The Monkey's fancy...

We will go through the black hole again tomorrow for hopefully a last look at the U-boat and we will be taking the spear with us.

14 August

We got medieval on their asses...

Through at dawn and raced on the bikes down to the beach. The girls stationed themselves around the black hole and set up their disruption thingy to give us a fighting chance on the way back. The Monkey said I should carry the spear as it was too big for him to handle comfortably; he slung his new war hammer over his back.

At the beach Kev and Tony dug themselves in with the AA-12s and we scrambled into the scuba gear and waded out into the mild swell. The Russians' dive gear was conspicuous by its absence and we decided it would be a good idea to play it safe going into the U-boat. Fucking good job we did. The Monkey's laser sharp eyesight picked up, well I don't know what it picked up – maybe it was just instinct – but he balanced the stuff sack he was carrying on the edge of the conning tower hatch and we retreated back to the shore line. He waved Tony over and using his Glock he shot the sack so it fell over into the tower. Boom! Bye, bye U-boat.

We picked ourselves up off the sand and looked at the smoking debris that jutted out of the waves like some mangled shark jaws. It was obvious that we weren't going to get anything from the sub because it was now blown to bits and anything that had been left would have been stripped out by our *friends* or vaporised.

Now we needed to run. We quickly got the scuba gear off while the Nerds kept lookout and then we gunned the bikes and tore up the cliff path. At the top it was all a bit shit...

Another Apache hovered in the centre of the valley above the loch and we could see men on foot fanned out along the hillsides, plus there were at least three armoured support vehicles. The Nerds looked over at us and The Monkey just said, 'Well, no chance for subtlety now,' and he laughed his best crazy laugh, and we belted down towards the valley floor. The Nerds bless 'em, must have been absolutely shitting themselves but they joined in the charge without hesitation and as the adrenalin kicked in, they began to shout their own war cries. We were spotted immediately by everyone, but no hail of death came from the Apache and it was obvious that the girls' voodoo was messing with the choppers systems.

'Use the spear!' The Monkey shouted in my ear, so I skidded the bike to a halt and just hefted the spear and threw it. I had no idea what would happen, in fact none of us had yet thrown the thing. Well – that was a revelation. It seemed to come to life and it literally tore out of my hand and screamed (really screamed) through the air and went straight through the Apache as if it was paper. We all looked at each other and I think we all went, 'Fucking hell!' at the same moment. Then the spear came screaming back like some big, pointy boomerang and I found myself laughing like a mental thing. The Apache smashed down into the loch and everything got red...

The Monkey burned and ran amongst the soldiers with his H&K in one hand and war hammer in the other. The Nerds stood back-to-back and fired the AA-12s until the barrels glowed. And me, I threw the spear, caught the spear and threw it again – blood and bodies. Amongst all this, the armoured vehicles began to explode and afterwards we realised that Dave on the other side of the black hole was racking up points with the coil gun. And sweeping down the mountainside came the Monster Highs, their hair blowing in some otherworldly gale and their eyes burning like fireballs as they tore apart those who couldn't run quickly enough.

The hired guns fought back though, and I saw Kev go down with a bullet through his leg and I felt a burning pain as a bullet grazed my shoulder. But by then it was too late, and the berserk rage was upon all of us, and the survivors threw down their weapons and ran. We got back on the bikes and rode up to meet the girls. They kept their distance from the spear which seemed to have a mist of blood around it and together we retreated to the black hole. I looked over my shoulder and the valley was stained red, and smouldering craters marked the end of the armoured vehicles. As I watched, two crew from the Apache crawled from the loch and collapsed on the bank. We got everyone back through and collapsed ourselves.

Kev is being looked after by the Russians' medic. Couldn't really take him to A&E with a high velocity bullet wound – questions may well have been asked. My wound is only a scratch. After cleaning and gluing it just aches a bit – oh well, another scar... The adrenalin dump was massive though – left all us mortals feeling like we had run a marathon and badly needing sleep. Tony asked if we had seen the figures up at the cromlech above the black hole, none of us had, but he is convinced that one of them was Whitaker with some massive goons in tow, and another, ragged looking figure who was capering about as if he was at some private rave party. The Prof looks horrified, he helped us clean up, but he hasn't said much, this was his first sight of combat – I remember what that was like...

15 August

The Green and Red Society picked up a message that was basically being beamed out on some sort of emergency channel that would only be picked up by anyone monitoring those channels. It was from our friend Arno Whitaker and went as follows:

'This is a message for the monkey and his friends. Sorry you didn't get caught in our little surprise, it would have saved so many problems, but there you go. Anyway, we have the cauldron. Surprised? Guess you didn't look hard enough did you? And the mess you made of our men? Well, it has given us a chance to try out the cauldron – I'll let you know how that goes – very soon. Bye, bye for now.'

Mutha fucker...

18 August

Been laying low and licking our wounds. Kev is still with the Russians. His wound was nasty enough to warrant a stay in their sick bay but they reckon he should be okay. The black hole has gone black again so no more views of Scotland. Where will it take us next? – haven't got a clue. The Monkey has hung the pendant up in the living room so that if it starts glowing again we will get a heads up that the black hole is realigning.

Pissed down all day yesterday so we stayed in, got very drunk and played Just Dance on the Xbox – hilarious, and predictably, quite violent. Today the sun is shining so I think the beach may be in order. The Prof is still struggling with the amount of death and carnage he witnessed through the black hole and is saying he might go back to Bristol, for a while at least. Think he has finally realised that it is not just an intellectual exercise, and I think that the crazed looks on our faces when we came back coupled with the insane laughter may have just tipped the balance...

The sky is turning black

20 August

Prof Brian has gone. He was a good bloke, be a shame if we don't see him again but I guess it's a casualty of war.

The Monkey has buried his head in my books of Celtic tales. He is trying to get his furry head around what we might be up against and also what potential the spear might have – although we got a pretty good idea from the battle the other day. I did a little Googling on the iPad as well and there are other mythical spears from cultures all over the world, and to be honest, they all sound very similar to our pointy stick of death. Once again it seems that some sort of ancient science has had a hand in creating all this stuff and we are only just becoming aware of it.

There is a big old cloud of cigar smoke hovering above the pile of books and we are sharing the Jack as usual while the Monster Highs check out my minor wound...

22 August

Text message – 'They will be coming, I don't know when, but you must be ready. The sky is turning black – I don't know how much longer I will be online. This is JudyZ and I am in the dark...'

I showed The Monkey, the Nerds and the girls before the message scrambled itself again. The Nerds are freaking out, they are convinced it is JudyZ. They think there is something different about the way the text is coded this time and they have taken the phone back to their house. The Monster Highs weren't around when we got the last lot of texts and they have a strong feeling that the message didn't come from a human – they can't explain why but we have got used to trusting their instincts...

24 August

The Nerds believe that the scrambled text message contains coordinates that could point to JudyZ's location. They have been trying to get hold of the Prof for some help, but he is not answering – can't say I blame him. They reckon they can work it out but it's going to take longer. The girls are still saying that the message isn't from a human...

We have all been watching the pendant in case the eyes start to glow again. There is a dark air of expectancy, it's like the feeling at the top of the roller coaster just before you plummet down. Even The Monkey is on edge. He is still reading the Celtic tales and is wondering if we ought to take the monkey finger on a road trip to find the other treasures of the Tuatha Dé Danann – there must be a sword and a stone out there somewhere. I think though that he is just looking for something to keep himself occupied while we wait for the impending whatever... The sky is turning black...

25 August

The coordinates seem to be within two miles of us. It puts them on the old military base. The Monkey went for a little ninja style recon and he says that there is nothing there, just a grass hillock. The Nerds are rechecking their workings out...

Tally Ho!

27 August

Seems that the coordinates are correct. The Nerds are looking at satellite imagery and old maps of the area, there has to be something that we are missing if the message definitely came from those coordinates. There was a captain at the airbase who we met some time ago, mad as a barrel of frogs on speed but we got on really well with him – there's a surprise, and I reckon we can track him down and see if he has any info on the base.

30 August

Was my birthday yesterday and we got absolutely fucking battered. Woke up in a field with a whole bunch of other people – a lot of them naked – and the remains of a giant bonfire. To be honest me and The Monkey had been on it from the previous evening and I don't remember much of yesterday at all. The Nerds bailed at some point and the girls joined us again when the sun went down. The Monkey got me a new Glock 17 Gen 4 pistol as a present and that was tucked into my belt when I woke up. The girls reckon I emptied a couple of clips in celebratory gunfire last night – I hope that didn't end badly for anyone...

The Nerds spent today recovering and doing a bit more research, they also put in a call to Captain Bartholomew Tempest-Stewart (Barty to his friends) and he has agreed to meet us tomorrow for a little chat about the old base...

31 August

Barty is the ultimate RAF cliché. He is tall and gangly, has the best handlebar moustache I have ever seen, smokes a pipe, drinks gin constantly (when he's not drinking tea) and is completely bonkers.

We met at Fistral beach bar and sat outside on the terrace under the sun. This gave Barty and The Monkey the opportunity to spark up their respective smokes and see how much fog they could create. We got Barty a very large Bombay and tonic and started on the Rattler ourselves while we asked him some questions.

He was very forthcoming and doesn't have any problem discussing the base. Seems that it was the home of Britain's airborne nuclear deterrent after the missiles left Greenham Common. There are hardened concrete bunkers and underground hangars dotted all over the base and also a warren of tunnels and other nuclear proof storage, admin and living quarters down there. He admitted that there is still some military activity, mostly training, going on there but said that the majority of the installation is shut down. Although he did qualify that by saying that there is a communications hub operating there shared with the US military. We asked if there had been much coming and going of black helicopters of late and he said that after the mad frenzy of a couple of months back it had all gone very quiet. I asked if any prisoners had been held there and Barty got a bit thoughtful. He admitted that renditions had taken place from there in the past and he wasn't very happy about all that, 'Not cricket, old boy.' He never had much to do with the Yanks and the spooks who dealt with all that side of things and said that a whole section of the underground base was given over to that sort of stuff. The Monkey asked if there were any unwilling guests at the base at the moment but Barty thought that was highly unlikely.

So, we spent the rest of the afternoon boozing and exchanging stories. Some of Barty's exploits during the first Gulf War even made The Monkey blow cider out of his nose! It's funny but we trust Barty, he is old school and a proper mad warrior. We even told him some of our Cambodia/Vietnam story and we all raised a glass to Hambone...

1 September

We are now getting ready to take a look at the base tonight. The Monster Highs are going to whip up some bad ass voodoo fog for us all to sneak in under and we have all spent the afternoon cleaning our weapons (no – it's not a euphemism). Seems The Monkey got himself a new toy when he bought my birthday present and tonight he will mostly be packing a SIG-Sauer P226 alongside his war hammer. I think it is a bit big for him – he thinks I should fuck off...

Ghost in the machine

3 September

Just when you think things are weird, they get a little stranger...

It wasn't hard to find an entrance to the underground tunnels and rooms once we knew where to look, but it soon became obvious that it was a proper labyrinth. We had anticipated this and one of the Monster Highs stayed outside on the spot the coordinates had pointed to. The girls know where each other is at all times so even underground we could navigate to an exact spot even though our GPS wouldn't work in the nuke proof complex. We were led unerringly through the tunnels and eerily deserted rooms. Some of them were a bit *Mary Celeste* because they had that look about them like someone had just stopped what they were doing and left.

Some of the doors were locked but none of the ones we needed to go through were, so we made good time. When we reached the spot where the girls unerring sense of each other's location synced up we were in a medium sized room (based on the size of the others we had passed through) that contained several metal cabinets and what looked like an autopsy slab. Sluice drains were dotted around the tiled floor and the only other thing visible in the room was a desktop computer and CRT monitor on a metal table. We split up and checked the cabinets, but they were all empty and the Monster High stood by the slab and said that something very bad had happened in that room.

Dave wandered over to look at the computer and Tony pointed out that the power light was on so Dave switched on the monitor and when it blinked into life there was a message on a black square in the centre of the screen. 'HELP ME. THE SKY IS TURNING BLACK. THIS IS JUDYZ AND I AM IN THE DARK.' Dave said that the text messages I had received must have come from this computer but then he just stopped and stared as more words appeared on the screen. 'I AM HERE. I AM HERE. I AM HERE. I AM HERE. I AM HERE. I AM HERE. I AM HERE. I AM HERE. I AM HERE. I AM HERE. I AM HERE. I AM HERE. I AM HERE. I AM HERE. I AM HERE. I AM HERE. I AM HERE. I AM HERE.' We all looked at each other and The Monkey just said, 'Fuckin' hell!'

The Monster High touched the PC and after a few seconds said, 'She is in there. Or at least what remains of her.' The Monkey told the Nerds to grab the PC but the message on the screen changed, 'NO. NO. NO. IF YOU TURN OFF THE POWER I WILL CEASE TO BE.' The Nerds went into a huddle and after a few minutes Tony pulled out his smartphone and after a couple more minutes of fiddling with cables they had managed to plug it into the PC. Once more the message on the screen changed, 'OKAY. OH SHIT. PLEASE WORK.' Then the screen flickered, the black square scrambled, and the Monster High said, 'She has gone.' Tony held out his phone and she put her hand over it and looked at us with a smile and nodded. A message appeared on the screen, 'Bubble Witch! Oh please!' Tony looked shamefaced and we all sniggered.

We retraced our steps and got out of the base without any incidents. Back at the house we sat down and just looked at each other. Tony's phone had gone quiet but the Monster Highs confirmed Judy was still in there, so he put it on charge...

5 September

Judy is still charging up. Seems she needs a lot of power and she drains the battery of the phone within an hour, so it is plugged in constantly. The Nerds are working on getting a laptop set up to transfer her into and Dave went and got a UPS to make sure nothing happens to the laptop power (that's Uninterruptible Power Supply just in case you don't know – me and The Monkey had to ask).

We have lots of questions that we would like answers to but Tony reckons she needs some more time to integrate and find her way about in the phone, plus the girls think we should just leave her alone for a bit. The Monkey is strangely accepting of this. I think he feels guilty as she has ended up in this state after helping us. He is back on the books, at the moment he is reading *Lebor Gabála Érenn* – The Book of Invasions, he also has the graphic novel version in case he gets bored...

6 September

Ended up watching *Enter the Dragon* again last night – it was on, so like we weren't going to... After a few more drinks the acting out parts of the film got a bit special and some furniture got broken and Kev's leg wound opened up a bit. The Bullshit Mr Han man sequence resulted in a lot of punching and the finale saw The Monkey as Han griping butter knives between his fingers and flailing around like a psychotic windmill. It's surprising how much damage butter knives can do...

7 September

JudyZ is now ensconced in a shiny laptop with a huge processor, loads of RAM, massive battery life and attached to the UPS. The Nerds did the transfer from the phone and she seems to have settled in rapidly to her new digital home. This means that we finally got to have a chat...

We asked JudyZ what had happened to result in her being inside a computer and the answer was predictably strange and very unpleasant:

She told us how she had been sitting in her Reading flat working on the stuff the Nerds had asked her for when she heard the door burst in and something bounced across the floor. It was a while before her senses returned after the blast of the stun grenade and she remembers vomiting and then trying to struggle against the cable ties binding her wrists. She watched as men in black tactical gear and gas masks gathered up her computer equipment, hard drives and USB sticks and then one of them knelt beside her and injected her in the neck and she passed out.

She came round as they frog marched her from a helicopter and into a dark hangar entrance – it was still night. Her head was hooded as she passed into the hangar and then she was strapped to a trolley and wheeled down endless corridors. Next, she was questioned in an interview room by suited men for hours on end. They asked her random questions that she could not possibly answer to disorientate her and then began to question her about why she was hacking classified US military networks. She said she knew she was in deep deep shit and decided that the only thing to do was to tell a version of the truth. She told them she had heard rumours about a secret military project involving psychotropic drugs and had gone looking for information. There was also a screen on the wall, and on the screen she could see a man sitting behind a desk observing the interrogation and occasionally asking questions in a soft American accent. She said the figure on the screen frightened her far more than the men in the room with her, he didn't stop grinning and his face seemed fuzzy.

At some point one of the men was called out of the room and when he returned it was to shout in Judy's face that she might think she was very clever but she was just about to find out how wrong she was. They had discovered that all of Judy's computer equipment had been wiped clean by the degaussing loop that was fitted around the entrance to her flat – and they were pissed. Judy said she knew it was about to get physical and was expecting waterboarding but what happened next was way worse than anything she could have imagined. She was dragged to the room where we had found the computer and stripped naked before being thrown onto the steel table. She was then injected with something that paralysed her but even though she couldn't move she could still talk and feel. Then they went to work on her with cutters, pliers, scalpels, hammers and a blow torch. All she remembers is screaming and screaming until she passed out, but they brought her round again and it continued.

Then JudyZ explained how she had got into the computer. At Uni she had been involved in a bio computer experiment and had a processor implanted in her arm with which she could interface with computers. The fuckers who were torturing her got out the electric cables and started zapping her and she said that she blacked out and when her consciousness returned everything was black and she couldn't feel anything anymore. She thought she was dead and in some sort of limbo. It took her a long time to realise what must have happened, she thinks that her consciousness tried to escape from the horror that was happening to her and somehow the electric shock had caused the processor in her arm to overload and the resulting data surge took her consciousness with it into the nearest computer equipment – the desktop PC. (None of us can come up with a better explanation.)

Time passed in which her body must have been disposed of and the room abandoned. She gradually began to work her way around the operating system and discovered that she could access tracking and communications data within the base, and although she had no internet connection, she found she could piggyback the comms. Then after many hours she began to sense us and that we were close – that's when she worked out how to send texts...

Judy was quite upset by this point and we all agreed we should let her chill out in whatever way she could before we asked any more questions. The Monster Highs are sitting with the laptop and doing some more voodoo stuff to help Judy calm down. The Monkey is chewing on a cigar and there is fire flickering over his fur. He is angry, a cold fury, and we all know what happens when he gets this angry – someone is going to die...

The windmills of your mind...

11 September

We have had a few more chats with Judy and she has told us how she became aware of satellite uplinks attached to the network she had become part of. Even though her terminal was pretty low down the food chain it still had limited access to the overall system. JudyZ was a lot smarter than that and before too long she was *seeing* through the eyes of satellites linked to the military base. She could only see where they were pointing but she could listen in to the communications traffic and that's when she began to pick up chatter about *the hostiles* and it didn't take her long to realise they meant us.

The girls reckon that Judy is broken. Hardly surprising given what she has been through, but they are genuinely worried and want the Nerds to keep an eye on what she is up to.

The Monkey is still scowling. He has been up on the roof a lot with a bottle and a cigar. I have joined him occasionally by hanging out of the loft window, but I can't really navigate the roof – I would end up squashed in the garden. He is building up anger and needs an outlet for it pretty soon. The black hole is still quiet, and I hope he doesn't instigate anything that draws attention to us. We seem to be living a charmed existence at the moment (undoubtedly due to the influence of the Monster Highs) but I sense this could flip at any time.

Blade is on TV in a bit and I have talked The Monkey into coming down to watch it – that and the fact that it has started pissing down. The Nerds have headed back to theirs, I suggested that it might be wise given the violence simmering just below the surface. Actually, that's a point – perhaps *Blade* is not the best choice of movies. Oh well, the girls are watching with us and hopefully they will prevent him from doing me too much harm if he gets carried away...

13 September

We have just come back from the pub and it looked like the living room was on fire. An orange glow flickered through the blinds and spilled out of the doorway when we got in the house. Judy's laptop screen was filled with 'What's happening? What's happening? What's happening?' and there on the wall the monkey pendant was blazing with that orange light.

The Nerds almost killed each other running up the stairs but The Monkey still beat them up there. The black hole is spinning like a whirlpool – round and round it goes, where it stops nobody knows...

14 September

The black hole is still spinning, makes me feel sick to look at it, and the monkey pendant has begun screaming again – we have locked it in a box. We are all feeling weird and I don't think it's just the drink or the monstrous spliff that The Monkey has rolled. There seems to be an odd vibration coming from the black hole and it sort of hits you in the chest and makes you feel uncomfortable – like something is running around in your rib cage, as if your heart is on a hamster wheel.

Like the circles that you find, in the windmills of your mind...

Basking in the glow...

17 September

We have had to leave the house and move into the Nerds' because the overall sensation in the house is overwhelming. Everyone is much calmer here and we nip back every now and then to check on the black hole – as of half an hour ago it was still doing the washing machine spin cycle trick. Been sending messages to the Green and Red to let them know that something is imminent – they said they were aware of a disturbance in the force (they didn't really say that but it amounts to the same thing).

So, at the moment we are all living in a big hamster pile. The digital entity that is JudyZ is pleased to be out of the black hole static and is currently exploring the interweb and looking for ways into satellite systems.

The Monkey is now playing Mousetrap with the Monster Highs and is very excited by the prospect of a small plastic mouse being captured by a crazy ass jumble of plastic bits. I love the fact that he is powerful enough to do the world some serious damage but also still awestruck by the simplest things...

18 September

Rien ne va plus – we have a winner...

The black hole has stopped, and we now have a vista of overgrown and deserted buildings. It is night there so we can't see much – there is a full moon but no light anywhere amongst the buildings. The Nerds are going to send through a GPS thingy and a GoPro attached to a drone, which they have finally managed to work out the technicalities of, so we can get an idea of where it is.

The Monkey has taken the diving man from the Mouse Trap game as a mascot and gaffa taped it to the strap of his webbing harness. The little plastic bastard is going to see some different action...

19 September

The Nerds have pinpointed the location of the new black hole exit point – fuck... We need to pay a visit to our Russian friends again in the hopes they can get us some different kit.

I had to explain to The Monkey what Chernobyl was and why we are all a little concerned...

21 September

The Russians just looked at us when we mentioned radiation suits and called us something which I think translates as *mental*. We thought it best not to mention our destination as we want as few welcoming committees as possible. The Russians seem ambivalent towards us at the moment. They have no love of the Illuminati and keep themselves out of the dealings of the Green and Red Society but we are about get into something right next door to them so we need to keep as low a profile as possible. An interesting challenge for us based on recent experience. Anyway, they say they can provide us with a few sets of military grade Hazmat suits in a day or two. A few vodkas sealed the deal...

The Nerds have done some narrowing down of the GPS signal and it looks like the black hole opens up in the middle of Pripyat, the town next to the reactor. The footage that came back from the GoPro was a mass of deserted buildings and streets that are being reclaimed by nature. A few stray dogs wandered around and to be honest it didn't look much different from some rundown inner-city areas in this country, except that there was no litter or gangs of predatory yooth. We have informed JudyZ what is happening, and she has been trawling the internet for any and all information relating to Chernobyl and its current state of radioactivity. Seems that we might have been unduly worried as the local radiation levels appear to be safe and they even take guided tours around there. The real problem is contamination from dust etc that can attach to you, or from consuming the local vegetation – probably won't be doing that. Tony said that we should rename her *AskJudy* but that resulted in a torrent of abuse and the displaying of some very strange porn which I think was the nearest thing she could come to expressing her feelings about that title and anyone referring to her as that. The Monkey still wants us to have the Hazmat suits just in case; after all, we do tend to make things go boom and that does tend to kick up debris.

We have also asked the Green and Red for their thoughts on the new location and what could be waiting for us. Hopefully we will get some sort of intel before we go blundering in. It would have been cool if JudyZ had sussed out the whole satellite uplink thing, but she is still feeling her way around that.

The Monkey has us back out training. More target practice, more CQC, and more fitness work, all with extensive breaks for pasties and Rattler. It's a closely guarded secret of Olympic athletes – no really – don't give me that look...

Worst End of the World movie EVER!

25 September

The Green and Red Society weren't much help, but they did say that we should take the monkey finger with us and see if it pointed at anything. Good idea. In all the JudyZ excitement we had forgotten about the finger.

But we now have the Hazmat suits and decided that we would carry them through and leave them somewhere safe until nightfall. Until then we decided to do a bit of sightseeing. We popped through the black hole in two groups and tagged onto a guided tour we had seen wandering through the ruined town. The girls used their voodoo again to make us blend in and we spent a day looking around the wrecked remains of other people's lives.

Obviously when the incident occurred everyone just got the fuck out ASAP so they left everything that they couldn't pick up and run with. Since then some people have been back to salvage a few things but mainly the looters have striped anything and everything that was left and vaguely of interest to them or someone else. Consequently, Pripyat is a cross between a ghost town and a salvage yard.

Our highly excitable tour guides led our party of backpackers, thrill seekers, academics and other assorted rubberneckers across the town and eventually to the reactor core and its concrete tomb. Everyone went, 'Ooh,' and, 'Ahh,' and photographs were taken, and questions asked, and then as the tour was coming to an end we detached ourselves from the group at a convenient moment and made our way back to where we had hidden the suits.

It was all a bit odd really, sort of a day trip for the *Whoops Apocalypse* generation. Had we seen anything out of the ordinary? Yes. Everything was out of the ordinary. Had we seen anything of interest to us? Who knows? I had been holding the monkey finger in my pocket and it had made some significant twitches in the vicinity of the rusting amusement park so I guess that will be our starting point.

26 September

All I can say is that I am glad there was no one around to see us. Three adults and a monkey in Hazmat suits wandering around in the dark waving a mummified monkey finger about. We must have looked like a trailer for the worst *end of the world* movie ever made!

The whole place is very eerie in the dark and surprisingly easy to get lost in. We placed little LED lamps on road intersections to mark our route and we blundered about for an hour around the outskirts of the amusement park getting increasingly hot and sweaty until we decided to ditch the suits before making one last sweep of the area. Can't really explain the reason for this logic but I am sure I felt the finger twitch when we were on the tour and that was the only movement it otherwise made. But without the thick Hazmat gloves on it was quite a different story.

Perhaps the finger needs contact with living organic material in order to do its thing but whatever the reason, it started to twist in my hand the instant I picked it back up. We turned to follow the direction that the finger was pointing and found ourselves facing the amusement park once again, a rotting Ferris wheel stood out against the sky and we made our way past rows of swings and the remains of dodgems in their weed overgrown enclosure. It was a strangely sad reminder of the normality that was wrenched away from this city. Through a stand of birch trees at the far side of this was a wall about seven feet high and when we reached it The Monkey leapt easily up to its top and adjusted his night vision goggles. He looked down at me with that monkey grin and I boosted myself up next to him with only minimal scrambling. There, on the other side of another open area stood the black shape of a tower with a dome on top. I looked at the finger and it was pointing directly towards it so we dropped over the wall and watched as a ghoul and a nerd followed us up and over; Monster High with an effortless flowing motion as seen in all the best horror/kung fu movies, and Dave with a series of grunts and curses.

It was obvious as we got closer to the church that it was one of the very few buildings not to have been ransacked. The door was closed but not locked and inside was neat if dusty. As you would expect all of the religious trappings had been removed and most likely carried off to another church by the priest at the time of the meltdown. It wasn't a big church and I was beginning to think that maybe the finger was pointing to something beyond it rather than the church itself when Dave found the crypt. We stood at the top of the stairs and the finger pointed straight down them so down we went.

Monster High led the way as this was her element, and not for the first time I marvelled at how she and her sisters' eyes glowed slightly in the dark. And it was really really fucking dark. We had tried to keep light to a minimum just in case there were any hostiles about but down there we cracked some Cyalume sticks (sort of a big party glow stick) and in the strange chemical glow we got our first glimpse of the obviously medieval crypt. We all looked at the finger and the finger pointed to a stone slab at the far end. It proved difficult to budge but between us we managed to slide it off the top of the sarcophagus enough that we could see inside, and instead of skeletal remains we found a tablet of stone carved with some very Viking-looking runes.

So now we have slab of rock etched with what are definitely runes sitting on the coffee table in the living room and the black hole has gone, well, black again...

27 September

The Prof was a bit reticent when we contacted him today – I think he is still having bad dreams – but we sent him over a photo of a small part of the rune stone and he was immediately hooked. We photographed the rest of the stone and sent the pics over to him, The Monkey had the feeling he wouldn't be able to resist and he was right. It's not the sort of thing Google translate can help with so it's a good job he's interested.

29 September

Getting feedback from the Prof – seems the runes form part of an epic poem. He has some bods checking it out but has only given them small sections each to keep them out of the bigger loop. I asked him why a slab of Viking poetry would be in the crypt of a Ukrainian church? There then followed a lecture on how the Vikings founded Kiev and how they traded along the rivers from the Baltic to the Black Sea. It is a bit too much to relate here, but translates to, 'Why the fuck wouldn't there be Viking artifacts in the Ukraine?' Okay, point taken...

The monkey pendant is glowing again...

Winter draws on...

1 October

Long did the well of the sky grow black,
Until the Bifröst bridge did appear.
And into the shining void we strode to battle, to glory.
Summoned by Óðinn to fight by his side at Ragnarök.
Of ice and fire we were called and made,
Into the shining void where death awaited marching towards Niflheim.
Gladly shall I drink ale in the high seat with the Aesir.
The days of my life are ended. I laugh as I die.

Not the cheeriest poem I have ever read but pretty cool all the same. The Prof's experts are desperate to get hold of the rest of it but that definitely is all she wrote or at least all we have. After having bits of it explained to him The Monkey thinks it refers to something similar to the black hole and the Prof agrees.

What does it all mean? Since last night the black hole is showing ice, snow, volcanoes and the northern lights. Looks like we are going marching towards Niflheim...

2 October

The Nerds have done their GPS beacon trick again and we can now pinpoint our exit to south east Iceland somewhere inside the Vatnajökull National Park. A fly around with the drone is showing a massive icefield, some dark, volcanic looking mountains and lots of snow. JudyZ is gradually insinuating her way into some of the communication satellites that are up there, they are easier to access than the military ones and will give her good practice and us an eye in the sky. She is currently waiting for a particular satellite to sweep across the Arctic circle and give her a view of Iceland so that we can have some more reliable info than Google Maps.

Is this the *Thule* that The Monkey read about? Another of those coincidences that don't exist maybe...

We have had a Skype conversation with the Prof about what he thinks the runic poem means and why the monkey finger would point at it as the stone doesn't appear to be intrinsically magic/ancient tech on its own. General feeling is that it must have been part of something bigger that was full on and this fragment of it is carrying the vestigial traces of that power. The Prof and his experts all think that the poem is about the last stand of a famous band of Viking warriors. The experts think the reference to 'The well of the sky' and 'Bifröst bridge' are all figurative but the Prof is convinced it refers to another occurrence of the black hole possibly summoned by Viking shaman (we told him how The Monkey had managed to make ours using magic ritual) and that is how the Viking band went off to their final fight.

The girls are looking forward to our trip to the frozen north – their kind of place. I am pretty excited as well, always wanted to go to Iceland. We dropped the Hazmat suits back with the Russians, had a couple of sociable vodkas and then went cold weather gear shopping. Thermal pants all round...

4 October

We fucked up. We fucked up bad...

Through the black hole we went, me and The Monkey, the Monster Highs, and Kev. We took weapons, of course we did, and the monkey finger. We had gone through and planted a couple of sensor devices the night before along with a camera and had picked up nothing on the feed but snow and ice. JudyZ had done some aerial scans as well and the surrounding area for miles was just snowfield with the odd volcano dotted around. So, through we went, full of it, and with a clear playing field...

We had on our cold weather gear and at minus ten it felt cold after a very mild day in Cornwall. I held out the monkey finger and it immediately swung to the left and pointed us towards a black outcropping in the middle distance that smoked gently in the light breeze. After we had been walking for about twenty minutes, we realised that the smoking outcrop was much further than it had at first appeared so we stopped to take stock of the situation and I used the sat phone to call Tony and Dave to see if they could give us any distances. We had timed our excursion for when the satellite would be passing overhead again so that JudyZ could keep an eye on proceedings, at least for a while, and we reckoned that she could probably tell us how far we needed to go – if indeed the volcano was our goal.

That's when the shit hit. JudyZ started scanning the area and suddenly the Nerds were shouting about movement up ahead of us. We couldn't see anything. The sun was beginning to set, and the northern lights were starting to flicker over the icefield which made it difficult to tell what was happening in the distance. Then we saw them coming. They were literally erupting from the snow. Stumbling, shambling figures carrying automatic weapons and as they got closer it was obvious that there was something very wrong with them. The Monster Highs gave it a name 'Zombies!' and The Monkey shouted that it was the reanimated dead from our battle in Scotland. And sure enough they were wearing the same sort of paramilitary uniforms as the mercs we had fought by the loch. That grinning freak's threat was coming true, the dead had been dropped into the cauldron and were now walking the earth again and coming for us!

We opened up with everything that we had but the bullets just ripped through the bodies and they kept on coming. They began to return fire, although with no real accuracy, but that would improve as they got closer, and we knew that we couldn't afford to get into a close quarter firefight with them. We turned and ran.

The sat phone was still open and I could hear Tony screaming into it that there were helicopters approaching from the north. They were trying to cut us off. We slid down a long slope that we had recently trudged up and hit a flat icefield with very little cover. The girls began to create a mist that quickly thickened into a fog that followed behind us obscuring us from the zombie troops, but bullets still whistled through it and we knew that our luck couldn't hold forever. The Monkey began to burn, his cold weather gear quickly turning to ash and I could sense that he wanted to turn and fight and then the mortar shells began to land, tearing up the snow and ice all around us so we kept running.

We knew we were close to the black hole, but the choppers were coming with their searchlights sweeping across the snow. It was obvious we had been set up and now the trap was closing on us. Up ahead there was an eruption of gunfire and explosions. I heard Dave's voice on the sat phone shouting that they were coming out to us and that he had the spear. We could hear the distinctive thump of the AA-12s as they attempted to clear a path for us. One of the choppers turned and then exploded as something red and screaming tore through it. We watched as the other chopper veered away and then swept low across the snow and disappeared over a ridge. We were within a couple of hundred metres of the black hole and the Nerds when the fog that had been cloaking us was swept away in a swirling vortex, and we were suddenly in the open again. I looked back and standing in the centre of the vortex was a wild looking figure, arms raised and strange dark robes billowing around him. One of the girls grabbed my arm and pulled me on and as I turned, I saw Dave running towards me holding out the spear shaft and then he disappeared in a cloud of red mist.

The world went into free fall. I dropped to my knees next to Dave's lifeless body. He had been hit by a mini gun burst from the other chopper and it had all but cut him in half. I heard The Monkey roar and saw him attack a shadowy bunch of figures that appeared out of the smoke and mist. He tore them to pieces and the pieces burnt. The girls circled around us striking out at anything that came near and taking at least one bullet. I saw Tony and Kev's faces as they looked at Dave and the horror and grief there was unbearable. I snatched up the spear and hurled it at the oncoming undead and it ripped through them, burning them and ending them forever. Back it came and I threw it again and again and then looked for the chopper to destroy but it had landed out of direct sight and I had to be content with killing the still human soldiers that came at us seemingly from thin air.

Confusion, chaos. Somehow, we got back through the black hole. Several of the reanimated soldiers came through with us and I forced them back with the spear as Kev frantically closed the black hole. We stood staring at each other, all of us carrying wounds, all of us stunned into silence...

The girls had managed to drag Dave's body back through with us and they have taken it off somewhere. We were all horrified at first but they have promised not to eat it – they say that we have to do something with his body to disguise the fact that he was blown apart by high velocity rounds. They say they have a way to remould it to make it look less suspicious – I have been having visions of them dropping it into a wood chipper as some terrible agricultural accident – but the girls swear they will make it as right as they can. We need to give Dave to his parents, it's only right. The girls themselves look worse for wear, both of them took hits and although they appear to be rapidly healing it looks like proper damage to me.

We are all in a state of shock and more than a bit upset. We really did walk right into that one although JudyZ swears that there was no sign of anything around us until it was too late. The zombie troops must have been buried in the snow for some time just waiting for us and if we hadn't stopped to use the sat phone, we would have been right in the middle of them when they came out of the snow. We have tried to piece together our impressions of what happened, and we are all convinced that live troops were dropping out of nowhere as if they were coming through a black hole as well. I think I was the only one who noticed the figure in the fog vortex, he looked like a character from some National Geographic anthropology programme about lost tribes, and after describing him to the others Tony said that it sounded like the figure he saw with Whitaker above the loch in Scotland... The Red and Green Society have been notified – we need some answers.

JudyZ is in a state of shock. She is just sort of babbling, the screen is filling up with what we can only imagine is digital screaming. The Nerds are in a very bad way as well, they had known Dave for a long time – they are drinking heavily and not doing a very good job of it. Me and The Monkey are taking it in turns to guard the black hole, we are both pretty fucked up and don't know what to do for the best. Oh, and by the way, I dropped the monkey finger when we were fighting. The best we can hope for is that it got buried in the snow and lost but I have the nagging feeling that it has fallen into enemy hands...

Hitsuzen

8 October

Today we attended the burial of Dave the Nerd, a top bloke and a brave one who died for something he barely understood but wouldn't let his friends down. Maybe it was hitsuzen...

The Monster Highs managed to make it look as if Dave had skidded off the road in his car and died in the wreckage. Their magical ability to mask and distort reality seems to have done a good job of making the police and the coroner look in the opposite direction and whatever they did to his body has left no awkward questions. His parents are understandably gutted – I think that is a major understatement – and watching them crumble at the funeral was heart-breaking. He was an only child and watching his parents it was obvious nothing was ever going to fill the void. The Nerds went to pieces and I had to work hard not to join them. The Monkey was very quiet, saying nothing until he gave his condolences to the parents. The girls, dressed in less revealing black than usual, shepherded us all through it. They are far more comfortable around death than the rest of us – for obvious reasons...

We went to the wake for a while, I think it was comforting for his parents to know that he had friends. On the drive back everyone was silent. As the sun was setting two massive black Chinook helicopters silently swept past us along the edge of the road and we watched them disappear into the distance. Sometime later, as we crossed Bodmin Moor, they flew back past us again with nose lights chasing away the darkness in front of them. I glanced across at The Monkey and he looked back as he chambered a round in the Glock he had taken from the door pocket. Paranoia? Maybe, but we have learned the hard way about surprises.

We are having our own wake now. We can let lose here and remember Dave in our own way. He began as a keyboard warrior and ended as a real one.

> Lo, There do I see my Father
> Lo, There do I see my Mother and
> My Brothers and my Sisters
> Lo, There do I see the line of my people back to the beginning
> Lo, They do call to me
> They bid me take my place among them in the halls of Valhalla
> Where thine enemies have been vanquished
> Where the brave shall live Forever
> Nor shall we mourn but rejoice for those that have died the glorious death...

Pass the Jack...

9 October

The Mao Shan sorcerers are freaking out in a sort of Zen way – if that's possible. It's all very understated and controlled but they are concerned. They are concerned that I lost the monkey finger, they are concerned that we got ambushed by zombie soldiers, they are concerned that the Illuminati have got themselves a shaman who seems to have the ability to create black holes for them, they are concerned that undead soldiers got through our black hole and into our spare room... I don't give a flying fuck. I am concerned that one of ours died and we couldn't do fuck all about it. I am concerned that The Monkey has done a massive amount of hallucinogens and is siting by the black hole with his war hammer and growling. I am concerned that the Nerds are in bits, JudyZ has gone silent and the girls are shot to bits and need to feed real soon.

I think we might have to go back to Iceland. The black hole hasn't changed. The northern lights are flickering weirdly and colouring The Monkey like a rainbow oil slick. Nothing else is visible through there but then nothing else was visible last time. I told our Shaw Brothers look-a-likes that I wanted to know if the bad guys had led us there or whether they had somehow known that our black hole had opened up in that location. They are going to check the I Ching or whatever it is they do and then I guess we just go back and take care of business...

11 October

Our Oriental benefactors have identified that the mad robed figure that cavorted in the fog vortex is a Siberian shaman – the sort who drinks Amanita muscaria-laced reindeer piss to chat to their thunder gods. They reckon this fucker has opened up a hole and that he can sync it to ours. Well at least we know we weren't led like lambs to the slaughter. No, seems they locked onto the location of the black hole when it opened in Iceland and then just dug in and waited for us. And the Mao Shan are certain that the bad guys have the monkey finger so they will be searching for artefacts now – we could be about to be outgunned. Our main Mao Shan contact called privately on the satellite phone afterwards. He is concerned that the breakaway factions within the Green and Red Society are planning something. He believes that the Yakuza element has been in contact with the Illuminati and is spreading dissent amongst the other members, but he can't prove anything. He is very concerned that we should take care how we proceed and who we trust.

I have managed to get everyone into the living room to discuss what we do next. The Monkey has come down off his massive trip and is now sitting calmly and smiling in a way that is far more worrying than when he was raging. We are all agreed that we have to go back through because the black hole is still pointing at the same location. Are we going to be walking into more of the same – quite probably – but this time we know what to expect and we also know we have little choice.

13 October

JudyZ has got herself into a military satellite and she has moved it into geostationary orbit above Iceland. It seems Dave's death gave her the impetus to make the leap across whatever networks and firewalls she needed to in order to break in. Dave's death has also finally pushed her over the edge. The Monster Highs say that the last of Judy's humanity has finally fled and she has become something *else* and they are concerned... We are getting constant aerial recon at least, and we have seen the dead soldiers digging in again around the area of the black hole and other troops appearing from thin air just to the north. There are helicopters in a staging area on the north east coast, they haven't been camouflaged which seems to be an indication of how confident they are. We have also spotted parties out in the area of the volcano we were heading towards when we got jumped.

Everyone has more or less gotten over their injuries, even the girls who were quite shot up look much better. They disappeared in the night and have obviously eaten which has gone a long way to repairing them. Now we are cleaning weapons, sharpening blades and generally getting our shit together. There is not likely to be a good time to go through but we are watching the sat feed and the *live* soldiers seem to be dug in to the north and they are the ones keeping an eye on our exit point; with a bit of luck we can catch them on a watch change. There is also a circular tented structure which we all agree looks like a yurt, our shaman friend could be in residence.

The Monkey has been trying to get in touch with Johno to see if he can provide some back up but no joy, he seems to have disappeared. The Russians have offered us some toys – seems even they have got wind of what has happened – and they all got on well with Dave even if he couldn't hold his vodka.

Into the cauldron

15 October

A chamber, in the side of the volcano. A bubble in the cooled lava, an obsidian globe, and in the centre a giant stone sarcophagus covered in runes. The side has a piece broken from it and it looks pretty much the same shape as the slab we found in the church in Pripyat. The lid has been removed and inside is a skeleton that is the size of the sarcophagus – fucking huge! It is dressed in rusting scale mail and on its massive skull is a Viking ocular helmet, the sort with eyeholes. Its hand bones have been broken and scattered around the tomb obviously to get something out of them. But I get ahead of myself...

JudyZ alerted us as the guard changed and we opened the black hole and then fired salvo after salvo of steel bars from The Monkey's coil gun through the hole. That ruined quite a few people's day. Then we went through and ran straight at what was left of the northern guard post. We shot the shit out of everything that moved and when we got there, we found four, still serviceable, snowmobiles. We had spotted these on the sat photographs, hidden just behind a ridge. We took three and blew up the fourth, then we twinned up and headed at full tilt towards the volcano.

As we blasted across the snowfield with the girls once again providing voodoo fog, there was a trumpeting from behind us and The Monkey shouted that the shaman was there blowing on some sort of horn thing. Out of the snow in front of us rose up the undead soldiers and our pillion passengers opened up on them with automatic fire. We burst through their lines and hit the ridgeline and then raced down towards the boulder strewn edge of the lava field with the zombies in pursuit.

The sat phone was open and JudyZ, in the freaky sat nav style voice she has appropriated, was warning me that the choppers were airborne, and we had only minutes to get under cover. We headed towards the location she had pinpointed for us and as we bounced over another ridge, we saw a large dome tent with work lights blazing around it. Living soldiers came running out alerted by the gunfire. We slammed on the brakes and skidded to a halt, but The Monkey was already off the back and dealing death. We fought our way into the tent and there in front of us was the entrance to the underground chamber.

We could hear the choppers closing in so we dropped into the entrance – that's when one of the girls got stabbed in the back. We heard a howl and turned to see a length of burning steel coming out of her chest and on the other end of the sword was the shaman. He pulled the sword out and it wasn't difficult to see that it was a magical weapon. Before he could strike again, I swung round the spear and charged but he laughed, a truly crazy laugh, and then he ran out of the tent and we heard the mini guns on the choppers whirring just before they began tearing the tent to ribbons so we dived into the cover of the chamber entrance.

Once again, we found ourselves trapped in a cavern with bad guys shooting at us. The uninjured Monster High cradled her sister, talking to her in a language we couldn't understand. Then she began to scream, a long, terrible, lonely scream and we saw that her sister was dead – properly dead. I looked at the Nerds and they looked back wide eyed as bullets continued to ping around the walls of the entrance. Suddenly the Monster High stopped screaming and looked straight at The Monkey, 'The cauldron,' she said, and began to pick up the body. Then The Monkey looked at me and asked, 'Can you take out the choppers with the spear from here?' I nodded, as long as I could throw the spear out of the entrance it would find stuff to kill and then return. 'Do it,' he said and then to the Monster High, 'I will come with you.' Then he looked at me and said, 'We will be back.' I began to protest but he shook his head and as I watched he burst into blue flames and seemed to become huge then he roared 'THROW THE SPEAR!'

The whole entrance glowed orange as the spear tore through the helicopters circling the shredded tent. Everything shook as the choppers exploded and crashed into the ground above us. After what seemed an age the spear came shrieking back into my hand and with one last look The Monkey stalked out of the opening with the Monster High behind, her sister's body over her shoulder.

The Nerds looked on the verge of panic, so I dragged them further into the cavern until we reached a massive iron door which hung open. We went inside and pulled the door shut behind us.

That was midday and we are still waiting for The Monkey to return. No one has tried to get into us as yet so I think he is keeping them occupied. We explored the cavern and the giant's tomb, and our best guess is that the giant skeleton was holding the sword that the shaman used. The sat phone still works, but JudyZ says that the sky has gone black and she can't see what is happening. The Nerds have been talking; they are truly freaked out by what has happened to the girls and they think that if The Monkey doesn't return by morning we should just go out and do a Butch and Sundance. Bless 'em...

16 October

The shaman came back – well at least his head did, in The Monkey's paw.

He returned around one in the morning, bloody from head to foot, and threw the head across the chamber. We wanted to know where the girls were and he told us how they had found one of the snowmobiles that was still okay and then they had raced back across the icefield towards the location of the shaman's yurt. The zombies had followed but they had managed to outrun them, and the Monster High had made the fog again but this time she set it on fire and everything around them burned. At the yurt they had burst in and there was the cauldron and without a second thought the Monster High dropped her sister in. The Monkey said that the cauldron wasn't very big, but her body had disappeared into it as if it had been a bottomless ocean. There had been a commotion outside the yurt and then the shaman had appeared in the entrance brandishing the sword. The Monkey attacked and drove the shaman back out of the yurt, and he said he looked back at the Monster High and she was lowering herself into the cauldron after her sister and then she disappeared.

The Monkey and the shaman fought out across the ice and snow amongst the burning fog for what seemed like hours. The magic sword gave the shaman superhuman powers and they were evenly matched but in the end The Monkey's ferocity and combat experience tipped the balance and he crushed the shaman's chest with his war hammer. But as he died the shaman threw the sword into the air behind the yurt and it disappeared. The Monkey took his head with his combat knife and went back to check the cauldron – nothing, just dark swirling liquid.

He made his way back to us against very little opposition. The burning fog had incinerated everything on the icefield, the dead and the living. One or two zombie soldiers had avoided the fire and they tried to stop him, but he had crushed them.

We got to the yurt and between us we lifted the cauldron and staggered back to the black hole with it. There was so much chaos and destruction. The ground was black ice where the snow had melted in the firestorm and then frozen hard again mixed with the ash of our enemies. Now, back in the spare room we have the cauldron safe but there are only four of us left, unless the girls can get out of the pot. JudyZ is not happy, she is picking up loads of comms chatter from other satellites, but we can't make sense out of any of it. What happened to the sword you might ask? Best guess is that the shaman managed to throw it through their black hole but whatever happened we have lost it again.

The Nerds locked down the black hole and now we need food and sleep. Everyone is sort of numb. We don't know whether to mourn the girls or not – what happens in the cauldron? Will they come back? And if they do what will they be?...

18 October

Was woken at 4am. I had fallen asleep on the sofa and JudyZ's laptop screen was flashing like crazy and the weird sat nav voice was calling in a sort of *Warning Will Robinson* sort of way. It took me a few seconds to realise that I wasn't still dreaming, and then it dawned on me that the voice was saying that we were under attack. I scrambled over to the screen and it stopped flashing. The image stabilised on a close-up satellite picture, enhanced for night vision, of several armed figures approaching a house – our house.

I bolted up the stairs, The Monkey has been sleeping in the spare room next to the cauldron, he was awake by the time I reached him and as I filled him in, he collected his H&K from the corner of the room and we went to wake the Nerds, taking their weapons with us. It took a lot longer to rouse them and as they pulled on clothes I locked and loaded for them. The Monkey headed up to the loft so that he could get out onto the roof and as I was going back downstairs, I caught a vague silhouette through the glass of the front door. I braced myself on the stairs and aimed from the hip with my AA-12. The door burst in and I saw a figure in black tactical gear about to throw a stun grenade. I opened up with the AA-12 and the blast hit everything in the doorway including the grenade and it exploded just outside the house.

Everything went black and then shortly afterwards cartoon stars started circling around me. Fortunately, the Nerds were still on the landing and the concussion from the blast missed them. They dragged me back up the stairs then I heard Kev's AA-12 thumping away as he fired on the open doorway. Then there was a series of explosions around the house and quite a bit of screaming. I scrambled back down the stairs and dived through the living room door and grabbed the laptop from the table and dropped behind the sofa. I shouted for Tony to check the back of the house and I heard him clatter past, banging into walls as he went. There were single shots outside, but I was surprised nothing was coming into the house. I looked at Judy's screen and the image now showed scattered bodies around the house and a lone figure running towards the trees over the road. It still took me a moment to work out what had happened but then I laughed as I realised The Monkey had set off the IEDs he had planted around the house months ago. I had forgotten all about them.

As I watched the image on the laptop, I saw a small figure drop from the roof and head through the front garden and across the road towards the trees. The Monkey was following the fleeing attacker. I got up to join him and shouted to the Nerds to check for survivors and to secure the house. I reached the trees and stopped to listen. Silence, and then a muffled curse and the sound of branches breaking followed by a groan. I made my way to the location of the sounds and found The Monkey sitting on the back of an unconscious black clad figure. We dragged him back to the house and threw him into the living room and then bound his hands and feet with gaffa tape.

We went outside and scoured the garden. It's amazing what you can get used to. We picked up the bodies and the bits of bodies and carried them up to the spare room, then we threw them through the black hole and closed it up again.

The Nerds set about boarding up the front door with left over lengths of decking and while they did that me and The Monkey went to have a word with our captive. We rolled him onto his back and ripped off his helmet and tactical hood. It was Johno. We looked at each other and then back at Johno. The Monkey slapped him across the face to wake him up, but his mouth dropped open and a whitish froth dribbled out. The Monkey knelt down next to him and sniffed the froth then he sat back on his heels and said 'FUCK!' It was cyanide, a poison capsule. We searched the body and then dragged it upstairs and just as we were about to send it through the black hole The Monkey gave me an evil grin and pushed him into the cauldron.

The tragedy continues – we have run out of Jack...

19 October

Johno crawled out of the cauldron around mid-day. He doesn't look that much different – a bit greyer, a lot less cocky, but not that different. The Monkey began asking him questions and we got some grunted answers in response. Not a great conversationalist but it seems that our latest attackers weren't Illuminati but a merc contract team employed by a mysterious group from the Far East – the breakaways from the Green and Red Society?! Zombie Johno couldn't tell us much more other than he had been contracted to lead the team in and secure the black hole and if possible, capture The Monkey. Johno should have known better, those vampires in town must have sucked whatever sense he had left out of him. The Monkey has sent him outside to guard the house – I hope it fucking rains on him.

Still no sign of the girls. Obviously, it doesn't work on a first in-first out basis. We will just have to wait…

We have been expecting police, army, girl guides, who knows what to turn up after the gunfight and explosions – nothing. Don't know if that's more worrying than an armed police unit rocking up and surrounding the house. We have JudyZ scanning the security comms links to see if we can get a heads up on what the fuck is happening…

20 October

JudyZ has intercepted coded communications regarding a state of national emergency. It seems that the powers that be believe we are in the early stages of a potential zombie apocalypse. Apparently, some of the walking dead soldiers from our Scotland adventure have been found wandering around the highlands – they must have been the trial ones. Also there have been more arrests in the East Midlands related to grave robbing and the eating of the dead. It would appear that the goth party ghouls have been biting other people. The upshot is that we are on the verge of the government declaring martial law as word spreads and panic sets in.

When we were having our little gunfight it all kicked off on the outskirts of Plymouth as some of the locals thought that some of the other locals had become the living dead – probably a dodgy batch of crystal meth. Shooting, petrol bombs, and looting ensued which kept the police fully occupied and when The Monkey asked next door's dog if he knew why the neighbours hadn't reported our little *event* he shrugged and said that we just seemed to be a weird dream as far as the locals were concerned. This could be the Monster Highs' voodoo or possibly the long-term side effects of living in close proximity to the black hole.

The black hole is still pointing at Iceland. Do we have to go back through? Is there still unfinished business there? Don't know and still waiting for the Green and Red to get back to us with some possible answers.

It rained big time on Johno – get in…

She who is death

21 October

Everything is collapsing. The Green and Red Society has imploded, there have been assassinations. There is confusion as to whether it has anything to do with the Illuminati or just a change of management in the form of a Yakuza takeover, but whatever it is has fucked them up big time. They reckon it's not the first time this sort of thing has happened throughout the centuries but this one seems to be different – coordinated. I can't get in touch with our main Mao Shan sorcerer to see if his suspicions have been confirmed so I think that for the moment we are on our own – The Monkey says that's fine by him.

It's still raining on Johno – hope he rots. We have managed to get a couple of bottles of Jack so it's not as hellish as it could be…

23 October

The girls are back but none of us expected THAT...

They are no longer two – they have fused together somehow to become some sort of Ray Harryhausen multi-limbed goddess. Two heads, four arms, two legs – still strangely erotic in a scary as fuck way. They haven't said anything yet – they just sort of look at you and it's like staring into the gaps between stars... JudyZ asked for some pictures and when we sent them, she said that they look like Kali, or at least the statues of the goddess that her family had around and that she used to see in temple.

25 October

We are thinking that Johno's backers were definitely the new power behind the Green and Red Society. We are thinking we are caught between a rock and a hard place...

JudyZ has picked up more comms that are a bit worrying. Military bases are springing up around London and the Home Counties. As troops are brought back from the Middle East and Afghanistan they are being relocated to these bases and effectively the capital is becoming covertly militarised. No more zombies have appeared in Scotland, but it is obvious that fear of an undead apocalypse is beginning to take hold. The ghoul problem seems to have spread – a couple have been located in Coventry and there have been more grave robbing incidents as far west as Hereford.

Obviously, we know it's not a zombie plague and the ghouls aren't really a problem but this could be exactly what the powers that be want in order to promote their own agenda and impose draconian control...

The girls are still silent, but I did find them wrapped around me this morning in bed. I didn't know what to do, I had to extricate myself to go for a piss and when I got back, they were sitting up looking at me with a strange smile on their two sets of blood red lips. This afternoon we gave them Johno to eat – seemed only right...

27 October

The storm is coming...

We apologise in advance for any structural damage that may be caused but we are riding the back of it for our own purposes and that can only make it worse in the short term (hopefully the short term). Anyway, you had better batten down the hatches mutha fuckers because, as The Monkey says, things are about to go ape shit...

Count to thirty, no peeking!

28 October

Using the energy of the storm the girls channelled massive amounts of force through the black hole and caused an insane icestorm on the other side. The Nerds reckon that the temperature must have gone down to minus thirty out on the icefield. Even our satellite feed can't see through the mayhem – there were a couple of choppers on the ground at the north east edge of the icefield and they have totally disappeared. We are going to let it play out and freeze the fuck out of everything left out there. They don't have the cauldron anymore so there can't be many more new undead soldiers, so we will deal with them if they turn up, and with the shaman dead we are pretty certain they won't have a clue what to do with their black hole.

29 October

Everything was frozen. There was a thin coating of ice over everything. Even the snow was frozen.

Twisted shapes lay where they had fallen like Iceland Frozen Foods recreating the last days of Pompeii. The vehicles that lay dotted about had an ice glaze over them and there was no way they were going to work. That was fine because we weren't going far, we just needed to get to the remains of the yurt and the other black hole that was somewhere on the far side of it. We were fully tooled up and fully on edge – anything that moved was going to get fucked up big time. But nothing moved, it was all flash frozen – Birds Eye petits pois the lot of them...

The Monkey seemed huge and he took point with the girls and they swept across the icefield like death incarnate. Me and the Nerds followed behind guns ready, but we made it to the yurt without incident. I asked JudyZ for an update via the sat phone and confirmed that nothing was moving except us and there were definitely no choppers in the air. With nothing to distract us we circled around it and the conjoined Monster Highs quickly identified the position of our enemy's doorway.

We had one last weapon check while the girls set up their fog again in case there was anyone observing on the other side. I readied the spear and watched as The Monkey swung his war hammer in a few practice arcs. No one spoke. We had decided a plan of action before we passed through our black hole and now there was nothing left to say. When the fog was dense enough, we stood before the vortex – The Monkey and the girls would go through first and then we would follow after a 30 count.

And through they went, and we began the count...

30 October

...30...

In we went and split left and right as we had practiced. We were in the middle of a large room, sort of like a warehouse, and over to one side were a couple of tables with computers and monitors. Two bodies lay in ruin on the grey concrete floor and The Monkey was gazing behind us while the girls had gone over to secure the door. We turned round to see what The Monkey was looking at and saw the walls, floor and roof were covered in writhing glyphs and runes, some drawn in black paint and the others drawn in what could only have been blood. It was oddly like the stuff The Monkey had scrawled on the wall of the spare room when he had created our black hole except he had used a Sharpie and his contained a lot more stick figures having sex...

We stripped out of our cold weather gear and left it in a pile against the back wall which had large observation windows with a table and chairs in the room on the other side but was otherwise empty. The girls signalled us over to the door and we slipped through into the corridor beyond. We could hear sounds coming from behind large double doors at the end of the corridor and as we advanced towards them three uniformed guards came out of a side passage. They stood there with mouths gaping in surprise but to their credit it only lasted a second and then their sidearms were taking aim. Tony opened up first with his XM8 and the spray arced across the corridor and caught two of them across the legs as the third dived back into cover. I threw the spear and it tore into the bodies and then disappeared around the corner as Kev's AA-12 blew the remains to a pink mist. There was a gurgled scream that was cut short and then the burning, gore covered spear hurtled back into my hand.

The jig was up, no more stealth after that. The double doors burst open and bullets ripped past us as we sprinted to the side passage and skidded in the guts of the eviscerated guard. The girls rapidly summoned the fog and it began to swirl thickly in the corridor as The Monkey pulled a white phosphorus grenade off his tactical vest and threw it around the corner. We ducked back and the flash lit up the walls and fog with searing white heat. Screams and sporadic firing and then The Monkey threw a second grenade, and after it went bang, we charged out through the fog towards the doors.

I felt a hot sting as a bullet creased my cheek, but the last guard fell quickly and then we were across the threshold and into a vast room of lunacy. Mad scientists ran amongst glass tanks filled with bluish fluid and sickening hybrid figures. A few human looking forms, all of which had oddly familiar, smooth featured faces, floated in what looked like giant test tubes along the side wall. The central floor space was taken up by operating tables on which were strapped convulsing creatures. And there above everything, hands white knuckled on the railing of the observation floor, stood Arno Whitaker that fucking grin plastered on his dead face as his eyes stared straight down at us with a hatred that was physical. Someone behind him shouted something unintelligible and then a siren sounded throughout the building – now it was going to get busy. I pulled back my arm to throw the spear at Whitaker but was forced to change it into a stab as one of the scientist types in a respirator and leather apron, looking like something from a butcher's nightmare wet dream, came at me with an electric saw. I thrust it through his mask and the spear gave a groan and shiver of pleasure as it took another soul. I looked back at the observation floor and Whitaker was still there but now he was flanked by two huge black clad muthas and the one on the left was carrying the sword...

*

The Monkey quickly climbed one of the frames surrounding a tank full of mutant horror and leapt across the gap separating it from observation floor. He crouched on the handrail and blue flames burst in a nimbus around his body and at that moment he looked like a god.

I ran for the metal stairs that descended beneath the observation floor and the guards that were coming down them. The spear shrieked with glee as I scythed it back and forth through the useless layers of bulletproof vests and tactical kit through to the soft flesh beneath. Guns were raised but they were packed too tightly to aim, and they fell over each other as they tried to flee from the spear. I glanced back at the main floor and saw the Nerds shooting down the mad scientists with desperate determination painted on their faces. I had a moment of intense pride and then the bloodlust of the spear took me, and I roared with joy as I cut my way up the stairs.

When I reached the top, I was greeted by the sight of the conjoined Monster Highs crouching over the body of one of the huge guards like a giant spider and tearing it to pieces. The girls were sporting several bullet wounds but seemed totally oblivious to any pain. Beyond them The Monkey waged war against the other giant and the sword. Arcs of plasma cut through the air around them and the air crackled. Everything smelled of blood and iron and a sort of electrical battery smell that mingled with the gun smoke.

The giant wouldn't have been a match for The Monkey but like the shaman he was lent power by the sword, and this bastard could fight. I took aim on the big fucker with the spear, but the girls raised their twin heads and screamed 'NO!' I stared at them, this was the first word they had uttered since their return and my lack of comprehension mixed with surprise must have been obvious because then they simply said, 'The spear and sword must not touch – it would be the end.' I was still going to throw but there was a certainty in their eyes that stopped me. So, I turned my attention on Arno Whitaker...

...Just in time to see his shiny shoes disappearing through a door behind some more incoming guards. Side by side with the girls, and careful not to get the spear head near them, we charged the door and hit the fresh meat. A grenade exploded and knocked me through the doorway and onto my ass. The girls followed but with a lot more style. Whitaker was rapidly approaching a turn at the end of the passage and I scrambled to my feet with the girls' help and started after him. Suddenly the large glass windows along the observation floor side of the passage burst in and The Monkey and sword wielding giant smashed through in a tangle of limbs and flailing weapons. They blocked the passage completely like some sort of demon threshing machine. I looked at the girls and they motioned towards the windows indicating that we could bypass them by getting back onto the observation floor. Through the smashed glass we went, and I could feel the slices from the jagged edges. On the floor we could hear shouted commands from below and looking over the railing we saw that reinforcements were streaming though the double doors and the Nerds had fought themselves into a corner. 'Go!' said the girls and without another glance leapt over the edge. I turned and ran further along the floor until I was past the war going on in the passage and then shot out another window with my pistol before diving through and running for my life from the battle royal that was raging in that confined space.

Then I sprinted after the grinning scumbag...

*

Something strange happened as I skidded round the corner. It was suddenly as if I was running in slow motion and for a moment the walls seemed to stretch and blur. Then it all snapped back and I bounced off the wall and kept going. A door with what I took to be a retinal scanner stood at the end. I jammed the spear into the scanner glass, and it sparked and flared. I guess I had expected the door to open but it didn't. Shit. I stood back gasping for breath. I decided to just trust to the spear and so I threw it. It didn't hit the door, instead it smashed into the wall below the scanner and there was a massive flash and the door slid open.

The spear came back to me as I ran to the door. Bullets smashed into the wall around the opening and I ducked down and threw the spear again. It was shrieking bloodlust as it tore through the guards and I rolled across the threshold and grabbed a dropped MP5 and blasted away. When the spear returned I scrambled up and looked around.

At the far end of this new room was a group of people. Arno Whitaker was in the centre and around him... the Mao Shan sorcerers...

*

It brought me up short. What the fuck was going on?

The sorcerers spread out in a line and Whitaker disappeared behind them. Dark robes fluttered as arms were raised and a chanting began. I felt the air thicken around me and it was as if I was being held by invisible hands – not enough to stop me but enough to slow me down. Then the air began to bite as if it had grown barbs and I could feel myself being squeezed. I slashed around with the spear as best I could, but it made no difference. In the end I pointed the spear and let it go. There was a grinding, tearing sound and the spear halted in mid-air and hung there pushing against nothing, screaming in frustration. The squeezing turned into a crushing, like being dragged down to the bottom of the ocean, and I began to black out...

*

Something grabbed me by the shoulder, and I felt a rush of energy that pulled me back from the darkness. I looked up and there was The Monkey, the blue fire spilling over from him to me as he still fought against the sword wielding giant. The giant had a large wound in his side and was staggering as he fought but the sword kept him going and he flailed it down onto The Monkey's blocking war hammer time and time again.

I rolled across the floor to give him some room and pulled myself up against the wall. The spell was broken and the spear that had hung in the air went for the sorcerers like an unleashed attack dog. How the bastards scrambled to get out of the way! I don't care what mumbo jumbo you can spout, when a possessed, self-propelling spear comes hunting for you, you get the fuck out of the way. But not quickly enough. The spear made kebabs out of the first couple and tore itself free to go after the rest. I recognised some of the black robed Orientals from when we were in Cambodia and I looked for the sorcerer who had been our contact and supposed friend, but he was not there. It had been him who had told us of the rift in the Green and Red Society so maybe these other sorcerers had gone over as well, the supposed last bastions of an ancient dream. Anyway – they were dying now, violently...

Getting to my feet I pulled my Glock and fired into the thrashing mass of bodies. That was when I saw Whitaker's head bobbing down way behind the others. I glanced quickly across at The Monkey and could see he was wearing down the giant who was losing blood at a shocking rate so I ran past the slaughter, kicking one sorcerer in the head for good measure, and went for Whitaker. I could see his grinning face leering at me from floor level and for a moment I thought he had been decapitated but then I realised he was disappearing down through a hatch in the floor. No! I wasn't going to let him get away again. I shot at the head as I ran towards it but that sort of thing only works in John Woo movies and the bullets pinged off the metal grating way wide of the mark. I dived and threw out my arm in an attempt to grab his hair and missed that as well, so I scrambled to the edge of the hatch and looked down. There was Whitaker part way down a service ladder. I wondered why he had stopped and then I realised that below him the many armed goddess which is the Monster Highs was climbing up towards him. He looked from them to me and the twisted grin made strange writhing motions as fear gripped his fucked-up face.

That was when the giant landed on top of me and I fell though the hatch...

*

I could see Whitaker's startled face getting closer as I slipped downwards. I thrashed out and grabbed the ladder with my left hand, but the giant was tangled around me and I thought that my arm would dislocate as his weight pulled down on me. The sword waved around, and I realised that the giant was dead but that made the blade no less dangerous. Out of the corner of my eye I saw The Monkey dropping over the edge of the hatch and then from over his shoulder the spear came roaring, looking for me.

My grip gave on the ladder and I fell with the giant's body now beneath me. We hit Whitaker and the sword chopped into his shoulder and he gave out a long howl as it began to split him open. Then the spear was with me and before I could stop it, it plunged into Whitaker and touched the sword. A vortex began to form where they met and as I fell towards it I saw Whitaker more or less turn inside out as he was drawn into it like water being sucked down the plug hole. The giant followed and I knew I was fucked but The Monkey grabbed the back of my tactical vest and swung me back onto the ladder.

The vortex began to drag in everything around it and The Monkey looked at me with an expression that said – 'Hey, we've had a good run!' I clung to the ladder and pulled my feet up away from the sucking void, but it was only going to be a temporary reprieve. Then something came from behind the vortex, something that enveloped the blackness and closed around it. And there were the girls, their multiple arms encompassing the void and dragging it into themselves. We saw the look in their eyes and The Monkey shouted out, 'No! Fuck no!' But it was too late. They gave us a smile from their beautiful twin heads and then they sort of imploded in golden fire...

*

There was no time to mourn. Shots still rang out below and the startled faces of the Nerds glanced up at us as they fired back at whoever was shooting at them. I could see the shock and loss in their faces, and they screamed out their sorrow and anger as they emptied the clips in their automatics and reloaded.

The Monkey swung past me and jumped to the next unwarped section of ladder below. I followed him, with a lot less panache. We hit the floor next to the Nerds and joined in the shooting. Our enemy was advancing relentlessly from the double doors and the corridor beyond. The floor was swimming in chemicals from the shattered tanks and mutant things flopped around on the floor as black uniformed security splashed towards us. 'Come on!' shouted The Monkey and we began to retreat towards the back of the room and a wide shutter door. At The Monkey's direction Kev put his last two AA-12 shells into the door and blew a massive fucking hole in it and we ran to the gaping rent and dived through.

Cold air greeted us, and we looked out over a darkened industrial estate and in the distance a 24-hour Tesco's...

*

As I turned back towards the shutter, I spotted the name above it, Connect Biomedical. We threw our last grenades back through the wrecked door and then legged it into the night as the doorway lit up behind us, the sign crashing down onto the concrete. It took us a minute to find a vehicle that we could hot wire and then we drove it through the chain link fence gates and out into the black industrial estate.

The Nerds kept asking where we were and what the fuck was going on. Neither of us had an answer so we told them to just keep the guns low but be ready to fuck up anything that decided to follow us. It wasn't until we got level with the Tesco's that The Monkey pointed out the road signs. For a couple of seconds we stared blankly at them and then Kev said, 'It's Welsh, we're in Wales!' Yep, Wales...

We hit the M4 out of Cardiff heading East. Nothing was following us and our *borrowed* Land Cruiser had a full tank of fuel so we didn't have to make any stops before we reached the M5 South of Taunton – not that we really wanted to stop while we were covered in drying blood and gore – but sometimes you just have to. The car park of Taunton Services was dark enough at its far side that we could park up without any undue attention. The Monkey stripped out of his tactical vest and then helped us to get out of the kit we were wearing and the black boiler suits over our other clothes. We went en masse to the toilets and cleaned up as best we could. I grabbed some coffees and bottles of water along with as many Yorkie bars as I could carry and then we climbed back in the Cruiser and just sort of sat there for a bit as the caffeine and sugar did its magic...

31 October

I tried to get JudyZ on the sat phone but there was nothing but static. Tony and Kev both thought it quite possible that my proximity to the tear in space had cooked the phone, so we finished our coffee and got back on the road. I asked why it would be different to the black holes we had travelled through and they said that it seemed to be like matter and anti-matter colliding when the spear and sword touched. Then we all went quiet for quite some time and after a while I heard Tony sobbing...

When we drove up the road towards the house, The Monkey suddenly leaned over and switched off the lights while telling me to kill the engine. I did so and let the Land Cruiser drift over to the side of the road. He pointed up to the house and we could see what was obviously torchlight on the walls of the front bedroom. I looked around at the Nerds and they looked totally beaten, so with a nod from The Monkey I told them that we would take care of it. We slipped out of the vehicle and made our way around to the passageway at the back of the houses, then we climbed the fence and crouched amongst the shrubs at the back of the garden. The Monkey opened the shed quietly and after a few minutes came back with two silencers and a box of ammo. We screwed on the silencers and loaded up our weapons plus a couple of extra clips each. He had also brought the night vision goggles.

The back doors had been forced so it was easy enough to follow that route. In the living room one dark figure knelt by the window keeping watch. The Monkey put a bullet through the base of his skull. We started up the stairs, The Monkey bounded silently ahead and pulled himself up over the banister to keep me covered. I crossed the landing and we scanned the open doorways. There was movement in the darkness and a hissed question from one of the figures – we opened up and the question died with him, as did his companion. There was a noise in the spare room, and we opened the door a crack to find half a dozen men securing a line through the black hole. More men began to come through and The Monkey looked at me with resignation and whispered that we should grab what we could and get out of it. He gently closed the door and then wedged the blade of his knife into the locking mechanism we had installed to prevent them getting out without blowing the door.

We took it in turns to keep watch while the other grabbed what they needed and then we went back downstairs and took the laptop from the table and headed out to the back garden again. The Monkey ran back to the shed and came out with the can of two stroke for the brush cutter and our last claymore mines, then he signalled me to stay put and sneaked back into the house. He was back quickly, and we ran along the passageway and back to the Cruiser. We quickly filled the Nerds in and told them that if they wanted anything from their rented house, they had better go get it. They scurried off quickly and we watched the front of the house in anticipation. As the Nerds got back with a couple of large zip up bags we heard two loud bangs from the house, the sort of sound a shot gun makes when it is being used to blow the hinges off a door. I started the engine and we watched in sick fascination as the top floor blew out in a ball of flame. There was a second and third explosion and then the whole house seemed to implode.

We headed back through the woods and The Monkey opened his bag and produced first his battered teddy and then a bottle of Jack. We are passing it between us as we drive into the darkness...

1 November

We are back at Falmouth docks and in the care of our Russian friends. They are not asking questions but look concerned as they feed us, patch wounds and open more vodka...

2 November

We couldn't find JudyZ in the laptop and it wasn't until the Nerds were able to do some proper searching that we found out that she had made a jump and is actually inhabiting one of the satellites she had worked her way into. She is very sad about the Monster Highs but seems happy to be free of the laptop and says she can use the cameras on the satellite more or less like eyes. There is a strange euphoria about her that is slightly unnerving...

I looked up Connect Biomedical and they are a subsidiary company of Brightstorm. A fire has apparently gutted their UK *distribution* facility but there was no reported loss of life and only some old stock was destroyed – yeah right.

3 November

The Russians are getting us out of the country. They are heading across the channel anyway, so it seems as good a place as any to start.

Back to the Beginning...

4 November

They have docked in Amsterdam for a little R&R, or should that be T&A, and we have decided to join them but it all just seems so fucked up and we ended up getting into several drunken fights. I miss the girls like there has been part of me carved off and thrown away, and I will never, ever get it back. I didn't get to ask them how they had known us before, well I asked but they were always evasive and kept saying that they would tell us everything one day – well that one day is well and truly fucked. Is this PTSD or maybe the onset of it? I don't know whether to laugh, cry, jump in the canal or sit in the corner rocking and hugging my gun...

5 November

Bonfire Night back in the UK. Last year The Monkey taped together a bunch of roman candles and rockets and then fired them across the back gardens, and we watched as they went through the shed window of a house in the next road. There was a massive, multi colour explosion and then the usual flammables that people store in their sheds caught fire and there was a further explosion as the remaining bits of the shed burnt down. Ah, simpler, happier times...

The Russians are sailing in four days but we have decided not to go with them. Now we are sitting in a small Moroccan looking coffee shop on a bridge over a canal and playing backgammon while the weed and the Jack numbs the pain. I seem to recall that the last time I was here a dying man lost a game of Othello and my life changed forever...

6 November

It had all been very quiet – well quiet for us – until last night. There was a knock on the apartment door we are renting and when I opened it (Glock held ready) I was faced with a rather battered looking Shaw Brothers reject sorcerer. My first impulse was to shoot the fucker in the face, but he held up his hands and I realised that he was a victim of what had happened as well. So, I invited him in and he came and sat in the living room while we sat around him – Kev wouldn't lower his gun – and over a mug of tea he told us what had happened...

When the takeover began it had been swift and brutal. The leaders of the Japanese Yakuza, predominantly the Green Dragon Society, had made a secret pact with the Illuminati and drawn in further elements from within the Green and Red Society until the ever-pragmatic Mao Shan had jumped ship as well – all except our friend sitting on the stool it seems. The Monkey said that he had read something about the Green Dragon dickheads in relation to the Nazi/Tibet link and thought that it wasn't a massive stretch to imagine that they had been biding their time in order to get back in with the latest incarnation of the New World Order. Anyway, our friend on the stool – what was his excuse for not joining in with the rest? He had seen the bigger picture and knew that the future was never fixed, never a done deal. It had meant that he had avoided the massacre when I had thrown Lugh's spear into the sorcerers inside the complex but he had been captured early on in the coup and been magically sealed inside a giant bell which his captors rang every hour until he thought he would go insane. When the sorcerers died the spell was broken and he had staggered out of the bell and wreaked bloody vengeance on his tormentors. Then he had come looking for us.

There are still many who support the aims of the old Green and Red Society, and he found safe passage with them across the Middle East and then through Europe until he reached the UK. That was when he had discovered what was left of my house in Cornwall and the cordoned off hole in the ground that the authorities are claiming was mining subsidence. The reports say that the hole is bottomless, or near as damn it, but The Monkey still has the pendant and the eyes have stopped glowing so we know that the black hole is once more spinning into oblivion. Shaw Brothers did a bit of divination and headed east again to Holland and eventually, following the trail of general nonsense we seem to leave behind us, he came to our door.

So? So, he has a little proposition. He wants us to go to South America and find a second monkey temple while he and some Triad henchmen go on a little jaunt to Tibet. He believes he knows the location of the mountain in which there is an entrance to Shambhala, and the location of the glass prison in which the old monkey god was trapped, and he thinks there might be some heavy-duty juju there that we can use to fuck up the Illuminati and their Green Dragon allies, but he needs us to open the vortex in this new monkey temple before he will be able to gain access. There is also the question of Arno Whitaker. Turned fucking inside out, was my response. Well, maybe not, someone looking remarkably like the grinning freak and calling himself Arno Whitaker has been giving a keynote speech at a tech conference in Vegas. Tony grabbed the laptop and after some frantic keytapping he turned the screen towards us with a groan and there, grinning as he paced the stage, was Arno Snakebite fucking Whitaker evangelising about the advances in bioengineering that his company Brightstorm had made. At one point I could have sworn he looked directly into the camera and that sickening grin seemed to get bigger.

Will we go? Be rude not to, especially now we know that Whitaker is still somehow alive. There is a lot of payback outstanding. The Monkey quoted a bit of poetry from the Viking stuff that had been translated by the Prof's team:

> Fearlessness is better than a faint-heart
> for any man who puts his nose out of doors.
> The length of my life and the day of my death
> were fated long ago.

I had better be oiling my gun then...

Andy Darby

would-be Viking, and lover of the bizarre. Mission – infest the world with his strange creations. He is the author of *Me and The Monkey*.

Son of a WW2 Commando, growing up in 1970s Birmingham, as a teenager Andy became a fan of heavy metal, fronting several metal bands over the years. His passion for martial arts also began in the 70s and has continued to the present. Competing as a bodybuilder and playing American Football for the Birmingham Bulls took up much of his 20s.

Following a mixed career involving working in a jewellery factory, spraying cars, and office work, he finally managed to follow his other passion, art, and began a career as a designer. A marketing department honed his skills, and he became aware of the world of designing for live events, joining a small production company, and eventually becoming creative director of their larger parent company. Moving to Cornwall he decided it was time to go freelance setting up his own business focusing on motion graphic design.

In the late 1990s he began to get the urge to write and his laptop drive is littered with the unformed creations that have popped into his head. *Me and The Monkey* is his first novel, coming to life as an experiment in having the discipline to write something every day during a period when he was travelling extensively for work. The story was written during train journeys, flights, backstage at events, 2am in hotel rooms, even during stops at motorway service stations, and was often written on his phone or iPad.

Andy lives on the north coast of Cornwall with his artist wife, teenage daughter, cat, two ponies, and constantly growing library. He still secretly thinks he could be a big wave surfer regardless of what reality tells him.

The Paddington Incident, a prequel to The Monkey's story...

Come on Chapman! Stop punching that anarchist bastard.
We are missing valuable drinking time, and I need a brandy
to take the edge off the opium...

Available at www.amazon.co.uk (or receive it free when you sign up for the ongoing Monkey God Chronicles at www.meandthemonkey.co.uk)

Wear The Monkey on your back... go to
www.meandthemonket.co.uk/merch

Just when you thought it was safe
to go back in the bookstore...
www.badpress.ink

BAD PRESS iNK,

publishers of niche, alternative and cult fiction

Visit

www.BADPRESS.iNK

for details of all our books, and sign up to

be notified of future releases and offers

YOUR INDEPENDENT BOOKSHOP MEEDS YOU!

Help us support local independent bookshops, visit:

www.BADPRESS.iNK/bookshops

to find your local bookshop.

Lightning Source UK Ltd.
Milton Keynes UK
UKHW050812150721
387160UK00002B/64